Babe Parilli

KENTUCKY BABE

BY

DICK BURDETTE

ISBN: 1463703473
ISBN-13: 9781463703479
LCCN: 2011912000

INTRODUCTION

On Oct. 2, 2004, when the Kentucky Wildcats played Ohio University at Commonwealth Stadium in Lexington, a photograph of Vito "Babe" Parilli appeared on all of the 61,514 souvenir ticket stubs. Each ticket holder also received a miniature, plastic-wrapped lapel-pin replica of a blue jersey with 'Parilli" and number 10 inscribed with white lettering.

For some, old enough, fortunate enough, to have seen the Babe in action, it was a heartwarming reminder of those golden 1949, 1950 and 1951 seasons when Parilli, a two-time, first- team All-American quarterback, led Bear Bryant's Cats to 27 wins, including a dramatic 13-7 Sugar Bowl victory over undefeated, top-ranked, defending national champion Oklahoma and the following year, a 20-7 win over Texas Christian in the 1952 Cotton Bowl.

They knew, because they saw it first hand, that *Memphis Commercial Appeal* reporter David Bloom had not been exaggerating when he wrote:

"With T quarterbacking, the fakes are the thing. Parilli carries this past credibility. Just where and how he hides the ball is mystery enough, but to baffle people further, he's always doing something with his hands well after the ball has been disposed of. As a consequence, the opposition mills around in utter confusion."

Neither his image nor his accomplishments, detailed on the back of a card also inserted inside each little packet, had the same impact on the majority too young to have seen him play. After all, that had all happened more than half a century ago.

But even those old enough to recall the dazzling, now-you-see-it, now-you don't wizardry of the man Bear Bryant said was so deceptive he "could hide a six-room house in a vacant lot'; the player about whom Tennessee coach Gen. Bob Neyland said, "We regard Parilli as the best passer in the country"; the one legendary Ole Miss coach Johnny Vaught called "The best quarterback in the business, bar none, including the pros"; the one University of Cincinnati coach Sid Gillman described as "one of the finest quarterbacks in the history of the college game" knew far more about his heroics between the goal posts than the reality of his life before, during and after his playing days at UK.

Off the field, as well as on, what was Babe Parilli really like? What about his childhood? His high school days? What of his relationship with The Bear? With Paul Brown and Vince Lombardi, two other Hall of Fame coaches for whom he also played? With other professional football stars, including Paul Hornung? Bart Starr? Joe Namath? What did he think, hear, see, feel before, during and after that dramatic New Year's day when he and his teammates knocked off Oklahoma? That historic 1969 Super Bowl when Namath, the young quarterback he tutored, and the New York Jets upset the heavily favored Baltimore Colts? That play he called as a member of the Pittsburgh Steelers' coaching staff that resulted in running back Franco Harris catching a deflected pass that became forever known as the "Immaculate Reception"?

His was a story that remained untold.

Until now.

From his boyhood days in Rochester, Pa., a grimy, gritty little industrial town near Pittsburgh, to collegiate stardom at Kentucky, through 16 seasons of professional football at Green Bay, Cleveland, Oakland, Ottawa, Boston and finally New York, this is the way he remembers it.

This is the way it was.

PROLOGUE

Every summer, the backyard garden behind the old gray two-story house at 315 Henon Avenue was as lush as it was large. Radishes, peppers, tomatoes, lettuce, squash, carrots – all flourished in the hazy, humid, dog days of the muggy western Pennsylvania heat.

So did a gnarled grape vine, its thick branches drooping under the weight of dark, dusty purple bunches larger than a man's hand.

Looming above them all was a young fig tree, laden with fruit all the sweeter because of the precarious nature of its unlikely existence. Each fall, after its leaves had fluttered to the ground, the boy and his father dug a narrow trench, then tied a rope around the trunk made flexible by its soft wood, its veins filled with milky latex, and bent it like a drooping, wilting flower and buried it deep beneath the surface.

Come spring when they resurrected it, no matter how harsh the winter, how cold the temperature, how deep the snow, the fig tree always sprang back to life, stronger, healthier, more productive than ever.

CHAPTER 1

I don't want to be greatest coach in the world
I just want to walk off the field a winner

—Bear Bryant

_____

Nothing that comes easy is worth a damn

—Woody Hayes

_____

To be alive at all is to have scars
—from John Steinbeck's *The Winter of Our Discontent*

_____

Struggle is progress

—source unknown

_____

Don't worry about Babe. He will find his way

—Christina Parilli

* * * *

Dick Burdette

ROCHESTER, PA.
1938

Suddenly, the floor seemed to disappear beneath the boy's feet. He lost his balance and stumbled forward against the back of one of the seats. A few minutes before, as he had done numerous times before, he had climbed aboard a Pennsylvania Road passenger train idling in front of the depot and wandered through the cars hawking this day's edition of *The Pittsburgh Press* and the local paper, *The Valley Times*. The price for each was three cents. For each copy of the *Press* he sold, he received a commission of three fourths of a cent; for each *Times*, half a cent. He gave all the money he made to his mother. Except for a nickel. He always kept a nickel so he could treat himself to his one and only luxury: a bowl of bean soup, at the rectangular little restaurant that stood along the railroad tracks like a weathered, forlorn boxcar without wheels.

Always before, he had gotten off before the train pulled away.

This time, without warning, it started to move. As he lurched from one side of the aisle to the other, the broad strap of the faded canvas bag chafed his shoulder; the newspapers stuffed inside it banged against his leg. He could barely remain standing, let alone walk. As he held on to the back of the seat, the train began to pick up speed.

Someone tapped him on the shoulder.

He thought it was a customer.

It wasn't.

It was the conductor.

"What's your name, kid?"

"I, uh, it's. . . . it's . . .. Babe," the boy said.

"Gabe?"

"No, sir. Babe."

"*Babe?* Babe who?"

"Babe Parilli."

"How *old* are you?"

2

"Uh, nine."

Babe volunteered to hop off the train as it eased past town.

No, the conductor replied, he could not let him do that. Too dangerous. He would have to stay aboard until it reached New Brighton, the next town several miles north. Then he turned and walked away.

Behind him, as the conductor opened the coach car door, Babe could feel the sudden rush of gusting wind, hear the thunderous clatter of the churning steel wheels, the bellow of the coal-eating steam locomotive. Then the door slammed shut and the deafening noise subsided and he was standing there alone. Alone with the realization that he was indeed alone and that with each revolution of the wheels he was going farther and farther from home to a town where he knew nobody; farther from home than he had ever been.

He reached into his pocket, fingers searching for money that he knew was not there. Having sold only a couple of papers, he did not have the 10-cent fare to get back home.

Now what was he going to do?

* * * *

Later, when his sister Martha, three years older, heard that much of the story she still had no idea how Babe had gotten back to Rochester. But she knew what her brother had done in the meantime.

Remained calm. Thoughtful. Stayed positive.

That was his nature. That's what he would have done.

Babe was a bright, cheerful, thoughtful boy. Quiet, modest, although not shy. He never said much, but when he did, he had something to say because he always gave whatever he decided to say plenty of thought before he said it.

Perhaps most important of all, he never seemed to become discouraged or surrender to doubt or fear.

Things always work out for the best, he said.

He got that from his mother, Christina. That was what she always said when something went wrong or looked like they soon would.

* * * *

A few minutes before the train pulled into New Brighton, the door opened again and the wind and deafening noise rushed into the coach car. Then it closed and here came the conductor.

He walked up to Babe and reached into the pocket of his worn-shiny dark uniform pants.

And smiled.

And handed Babe a dime.

* * * *

After his adventure on the train, Babe went back to selling his papers at the depot and along the streets in Rochester. He also resumed selling vegetables door to door from his father's backyard garden.

August Parilli, Babe's, father, was a first-generation Italian immigrant who worked as a grinder at the Phoenix Glass Company factory in Monaca, Pa. a mile away on the opposite, south side of the Ohio River. Like Rochester, Monaca was a small, smoky industrial town a few miles northwest of Pittsburgh. In his spare time, August Parilli, short, stocky, possessed of thick workingman's hands, a quick, curious mind, an iron will, a lively sense of humor and strong, non-nonsense, old- country beliefs, also was a cobbler, carving new soles and replacing run-down heels to make a little extra money.

At the age of 16, August Parilli had immigrated to the United States from Sparanise, a small farming village near Naples, Italy. Two years later, he was drafted into the army and found himself aboard a troop ship headed back to Europe to fight in World War I. In the Argonne Forest, he was hit by shrapnel from a hand grenade, suffered a broken arm and spent an extended stay in the hospital before being shipped back to the states. He still knew little English, but after recuperating and finding a job, went to school after work to learn. He never completely lost his pronounced Italian accent, but he had a keen mind. He studied history, politics.

Yes, for August Parilli, life was good. Hard, perhaps, but good. He was a happy man. Especially after he returned to Italy at the age of 28 and visited his relatives. There, he met a shy, beautiful 16-year-old girl whose name was Christina Feola.

Christina, who worked long, exhausting hours on her father's farm, had attended school only through the third grade. Her father thought it was a waste of time. Christina, he declared, would marry young and have children and going to school would serve no purpose. He was right about the first part. When August Parilli returned to America, he brought his new child bride with him.

* * * *

Perhaps it was merely the affordable price that led August Parilli to buy the old, weathered, two-story house at 315 Henon Avenue near the south end of town. Maybe when he gazed for the first time at the big back yard he saw not what it was but what it could be: a thriving, bountiful garden filled with rows and rows of vegetables and fruit trees bordered with colorful flowers. He certainly didn't buy it because the street teemed with other Italian families who had emigrated from the old country. All of the other Italian families in town lived in the north end. Other than August and his family and his cousin who lived a few doors away, everyone else who lived nearby was German.

No matter.

Largely, perhaps, because of the Parillis' backyard garden and their generosity with all that they raised in it, they quickly became not only a part of the neighborhood but their home a community center of sorts. For it was raising that backyard garden that was August Parilli's greatest talent, his fondest pleasure.

The whole neighborhood enjoyed it too because August Parilli never sold vegetables to his neighbors. He gave them away. Tomatoes, for example, to Mrs. Newell who lived next door and used them to make catsup in her back yard, then gave some of it to the Parillis. All up and down the street, people were always sharing things, especially food. Come meal time, there was never a vacant chair at the Parillis' kitchen table. The house was never empty. Somebody was always dropping in, returning something, or asking to borrow something, a cake pan perhaps or a cup of sugar or a sauce pan or bringing something to give them, a fresh-baked pie or a plate of cookies maybe or catfish caught in the Ohio River or fresh eggs right out of the coop.

Sometimes, when Babe or Martha walked into the kitchen, they would see someone they had never seen before, and would never see again, sitting self-consciously, eyes averted, at the table.

"They just stopped in to say hello," their mother would say. "I asked them to stay for dinner."

Babe knew what that meant.

They were hungry and had knocked on the back door and said so and their mother would rather go hungry herself than turn someone away who needed help.

"House of Plenty."

That's what Martha always called it.

Plenty of food. Plenty of friends. Plenty of neighbors. Plenty of warmth and love and affection. Plenty of laughter.

It was a great time, a great place, to grow up.

* * * *

Like Christina, August was kind. Gentle. He wasn't shy though. He loved to laugh and talk to people. But he expected his children to be polite. Respectful. Trustworthy. Honest. Just like he had been taught in the old country. And when it came to behaving the way

6

their father expected them to, Babe and Martha, four years older, and brother Frank, three years older, knew he meant business. All he had to do was slowly strip off his belt. When Babe saw it begin to slither through the loops, he knew that the only smart thing to do was run as fast as he could, as far as he could.

August Parilli never had to whip Babe. Not once.

* * * *

Once a month, one place Babe had run, at a far more leisurely pace, was to a government office a mile or so away and pick up what during the Great Depression was called "commodities"— free five-pound bags of corn meal. Flour. Sugar. Cheese. Powdered milk. For parents with three children to feed, even with their father working full time, commodities were a necessity. Even with them, an evening snack rarely consisted of anything more ostentatious than a bowl of Quaker oats. Being Catholics, they had fish every Friday night. But the highlight of Babe's week, any week, was when his mother heated the oven and baked potatoes and chicken.

* * * *

Martha had a monthly errand to run too. When her father left $7.53 on the kitchen table—always the same amount, right down to the last penny—she knew what she was supposed to do with it. She took the money down to the bank to apply toward their home mortgage.

By the time Babe went to college, the balance was still $500. And later, when Babe, because of football, was able to give his father the $500 to pay off the mortgage, his father beamed like someone had just given him the moon.

* * * *

Like all the other houses along Henon Avenue that stood so close together you could spread your arms and touch both of them, the Parillis' two-story, four-bedroom home did not have indoor plumbing or running water. An outhouse, equipped with Sears & Roebuck catalogues for reading as well as other more practical purposes, stood at the back of the back yard. Their water came from a well. They pumped their drinking water out of a cistern.

Like their neighbors, they heated with coal. But unlike many of the others, they had a coal furnace rather than a coal stove. Each winter morning, Babe's father arose at 5:30 and shoveled coal into the furnace. Babe was inclined to continue reclining somewhat longer, snug and warm beneath the covers. Say, until nearly the moment school was about to begin. After all, it didn't take any time at all to get there. The public school he attended, Rochester Township No. 4, stood right behind the house. But even when he was tempted to turn over and go back to sleep, or toyed with the idea of skipping school entirely, he knew he wouldn't.

Because he couldn't.

Mr. Anthony, the school janitor, always made sure of that. If Babe had not darkened the schoolhouse doorway by the time Mr. Anthony thought he should, here he came, huffing and puffing his way across the back yard, into the kitchen without knocking and there he stood, at the foot of the stairs, bellowing:

"Hey! Babe! Get up! You gotta get ta school!"

* * * *

Mr. Anthony wasn't the only one from the school who dropped in regularly. So did some of the teachers. When lunch hour rolled around, they headed over to Christina's kitchen.

They were always welcome.

* * * *

When the weather was good and dusk settled over the neighborhood, one of life's finest pleasures was sitting on the front porch watching the world go by.

Not much of the world went past 315 Henon Avenue. Mr. Parilli did not own a car—never drove one in his entire life—and neither did anyone else along the pitted, unpaved street that sometimes was oiled to suppress the powdery dust.

But occasionally, someone would stroll past savoring an ice cream cone and when that happened, the whole family knew something far better than sitting on the porch was about to take place.

Seeing as how he made $5.30 a day —- 53 cents an hour for a 10-hour day—Mr. Parilli figured he could splurge now and then. And so he sent Babe down the store to buy an 18-cent pint of ice cream. One pint for five people didn't go very far, but ice cream was still ice cream, even if only a little bit.

As for how much money he made or had, Mr. Parilli never talked about such things. But the summer after he finished the eighth grade, Babe found out first hand. He got a job at the glass factory too working as a grinder, right beside his father.

He made 53 cents an hour too.

* * * *

Babe never had a bicycle. But then he never expected to have one. Nor did he have store-bought toys. In Rochester, Pa., as in lots of places across the country in the late 1930s and early '40s, the kid who had no money possessed something every bit as valuable though.

Imagination.

Find a wooden spool, a couple of match stems and a rubber band or two and –presto!

You had yourself a windup toy car.

A reasonably straight tree limb made a good pretend rifle; your finger, a shoot-em-up pistol to chase off the bad guys or pick them off as they hid behind a garbage can.

* * * *

The Parilli family never bought a Christmas tree.

August and his sons went out into the woods along the Ohio River and cut one.

One for the school too.

Come Christmas morning, there was no expectation of toys under the tree either.

Two shirts.

That's all Babe ever expected.

And all he ever got.

CHAPTER 2

He could do without a bicycle. Store-bought toys and Christmas presents too. Without great expectations there are no great disappointments. Besides, Babe and the rest of the kids along Henon Avenue now—finally— had the one thing they wanted more than anything else.

A football.

One day, one of the kids who lived down the street had appeared, big as you please, with one in his hand. How he got it, or where he got it, no one bothered to ask. What mattered was that he had it. So what if it was scuffed and scarred and there was a knot in the black rubber bladder sticking up around the frayed laces like a baby goiter. A football was a football, the same way ice cream was ice cream, even if it wasn't much of a football the same way an 18-cent pint of ice cream split five ways wasn't much ice cream.

Imagine that.

A real football.

Before then, they had used a battered hat, tossing it into the air and who ever caught it took off running, everybody else hot in pursuit trying to tackle him. Among its other limitations, you couldn't throw a hat very far. Certainly not to those two electric poles way down the street there. At first they seemed like they were a mile away. Try though he might, Babe couldn't keep the ball airborne even half way. But the more, the harder he threw, the longer the ball sailed. Sooner or later, he vowed to himself, it would fly past those poles. All he had to do was keep working at it.

* * * *

In the 1940s, major league baseball was the National Pastime. Every kid everywhere seemed to know not only the name of every player on every one of the eight teams in the National League and eight in the American, but their batting average, how many home runs they had hit and how many runs they had batted in as well as how many games every pitcher had won and lost and how many batters he had struck out. But on Henon Avenue, as all over Rochester, as throughout the Beaver Valley, as all across western Pennsylvania, nothing, absolutely nothing, not even major league baseball, was as important as football. Especially in small steel mill and factory towns where there wasn't much else to do for enter- tainment and even less money to do it with.

In Rochester, Friday night high school football was more than just a game. It was a unifier. An equalizer. A universal source of pride. It awakened, intensified, a sense of community. Of place.

The rest of the week, the rest of the year, as the first slanting light of dawn glittered against storefront and factory windows, as whistles wailed summoning workers back to their shovels and tools and benches and machines for another grueling 10-hour work day, as freshly washed clothes drooping on sagging backyard clothes lines turned gray from the coal soot that spewed like black snow from passing freights, as delivery trucks rumbled down the town's main street, as cash registers dinged, *cha-ching*, as children played in the streets and in vacant lots, as the few prosperous enough to own one drove their automobiles along quiet, shaded streets through neighborhoods sprinkled with spacious brick homes sep- arated by deep, well landscaped lawns, as sleek, silver passenger trains clattered through town, as party-line telephones jangled, as dogs ran free, as long, low-riding, tug-powered coal barges sent gentle waves lapping against the muddy shore on both sides of the

Ohio River, as the evening newspaper skittered across the front porch, as merchants lowered their front window shades and locked their doors and reversed the sign in the front window from **Open** to **Closed,** as weary men wearing drab, worn, soiled clothes and blank expressions and carrying empty lunch buckets trudged home, as the smell of wood smoke, of cabbage cooking and fish frying permeated the air, as the sun slowly set, Rochester, like many Pennsylvania coal and steel towns, was fragmented, divided, an ethnic patchwork of those of means and those without. Those who spoke English and those who didn't.

Although the few better off families, the doctors, the lawyers, the teachers, the merchants, were mostly Anglo-Saxon, Rochester also was home to Italians and Croatians, Poles and Irish, all of whom called themselves "immigrants' although they were not un-mindful that others looked down on them and referred to them, in whispers behind the hand, as Wops and Dagos, Polacks and Micks. At the same time, the smug, pejorative name callers remained un-aware that many of those of foreign origin, recently arrived, called them all "Madigons"—the closest they could come, in their halting, broken attempts at English, to say Americans.

But come fall, come Friday night, none of that mattered.

The Rochester High Rams were about to take the field again.

And no matter what language you spoke or which side of the tracks you lived on or where you worked or how much money you had or didn't have, that's all that did matter.

* * * *

Now that Babe and his friends had a football, the next question was where were they going to play and how soon. After all, if they were going to be ready to try out for the high school team in a few months, they had to start practicing. They had no experience play-ing on a team, as a team. None whatsoever. Like the other elemen-tary schools in town, Rochester No. 4 did not have an organized team. Or even a disorganized one for that matter. In Rochester, the first time a kid had an opportunity to play on a football team was when he entered the ninth grade.

Eager, stressed, one eye on the calendar, knowing full well how fully unprepared they were, the Henon Avenue boys decided to begin practicing in an uneven, weed infested, hard-clay field near the school. They also got permission from the principal to leave school half an hour early each day so they could.

A battered ball, a grassless field and precious little time. It was a start.

But not much of one.

And so each school day afternoon, as the late spring wind became a little stronger, the temperature a little higher, the cloying humidity a little stickier, Babe's parents, like those of his friends, did not have to wonder where their sons were or what they were doing.

And yet, for some of their mothers and fathers, there was an aching sadness about their sons' naïve enthusiasm, their unbridled high hopes and dreams of glory.

Football.

What good was it anyhow?

Where did it lead?

Nowhere, that's where.

All too soon they would grow up and like their fathers, with their fathers, awaken each morning before dawn and head out the door, lunch bucket in hand and spend another long, hard, monotonous 10-hour day with no prospects of things getting any better and when they neared the end of their lives, have pitifully little or next to nothing to show for it.

* * * *

Rochester High, enrollment 496, was the smallest Class AA football school in western Pennsylvania. Had it included only those who lived within the town limits, its student body would have been even smaller. But because it bordered Rochester Township and a few others, it drew students from the surrounding area as well.

As a result, it drew football players too.

Good rough, tough football players.

Italian and Croatian and Polish and Irish football players.

For Coach Mike Sebastian, a former running back at the University of Pittsburgh, depth was never an issue.

There wasn't any.

He began each practice, as well as each game, with only 22 to 25 players and two crossed fingers. Heaven forbid that anyone got hurt—a persistent possibility considering that they were required to play defense as well as offense.

Nor did it help that "The Valley" – the Beaver County League— was considered one of the hottest, perhaps *the* hottest, of all the hotbeds of high school football anywhere in the entire state. Unlike neighboring Ohio, which crowned a big-school champion each year based on a statewide Associated Press poll and decades later, a playoff system, Pennsylvania had neither. But just as no one disputed the fact that year in and year out, almost all of the best football teams in Ohio were concentrated in the northeast quadrant of the state, neither did anyone doubt that the state's very best high school football was played in Western Pa.

Aliquippa, Beaver Falls, Ambridge, Farrell—all produced consistently strong teams. Further proof of their superiority: the numerous players they produced who excelled not only at the college level, but in the National Football League. Among them who already had, or soon would: Aliquippa's Mike Ditka, who starred for the Pitt Panthers; Ambridge end Jim Mutscheller, an All-American end at Notre Dame; Beaver Falls quarterback Lou D'Achille, a left-hander who starred at Indiana and engineered a rare and convincing 32-10 victory over Ohio State in 1951; and Beaver Falls quarterback Joe Namath who set all kinds of passing records for Bear Bryant's Alabama Crimson Tide.

Notre Dame end and Heisman Trophy winner Leon Hart, Johnny Unitas, Jim Kelly, George Blanda, Joe Montana—they too played their high school football in western Pa.

Yet, tiny Rochester with its tiny roster, was a force too and as early as his sophomore season, everyone in The Valley could see that another star was emerging, this one from Rochester. He too, they said, was destined to play big-time college football and in the NFL.

His name wasn't Babe Parilli.

* * * *

If Dick "Skippy" Doyle wasn't an All-American boy as well as in all likelihood a future All-American football player, he sure looked like one. Handsome, popular, happy-go-lucky, Skippy Doyle was a fast, strong 6-foot 1, 180-pound running back who soon had college scouts running to Rochester to see him in action.

Skippy Doyle, whose father was a factory foreman, did not live in town. The Doyle residence, a large, brick house well apart from their neighbors, sat two miles or so from the old, drab facing frame houses that lined unpaved, dusty, sometimes muddy Henon Avenue.

The Doyles' house cost considerably more than the Parillis'. But then the Parillis' house on Henon Street cost considerably more than the one in which teammate Vincent "Sonny" Bagley lived. In fact, so did every other house in Rochester and neighboring Rochester Township.—maybe in the entire state of Pennsylvania.

One day, when Lou Pagley, Sonny's father, was headed down the road, he saw a man standing out in front of a vacant house. He stopped to talk. What he was about to do, the man said, was demolish the old house.

"Don't do that," Lou Bagley said. "I'll buy it from you."

"Nah, I won't sell it, but I'll give it to you."

Lou Bagley looked as shocked as if he'd just found a raccoon in his lunch bucket.

"*Give* it to me? I can't letcha do that. I'd like to have it but I'd wanna give you something."

"All right," the man replied. "How about $50?"

And that was how Lou Bagley and his family moved into and fixed up a not bad, mortgage-free house.

* * * *

When he was a senior, Skippy Doyle had scholarship offers galore. Penn State, Pittsburgh, Notre Dame, Ohio State, Villanova, North Carolina, Kentucky—Skippy received, and accepted, invitations to visit them all. Sometimes, Babe tagged along, including to Cleveland's Municipal Stadium to see Kentucky play in the first, last and only Great Lakes Bowl game against Villanova.

As Kentucky's guest, Skippy got to sit on the Wildcats' bench and roam along the sideline. So did Babe, seeing as how he was a friend of Skippy's and all. Nearby, stood a metal cart filled with more footballs than Babe had ever seen in one place at one time. He picked one up and felt the laces and gripped it like he was squeezing an orange and twirled it like a swirling globe.

When the game ended, Babe was still holding the ball. Still had it in his hands when he and Skippy filed out of the stadium and climbed into Skippy's father's shiny new Buick and headed back to Rochester.

The next day, he heard his father say:

"They musta liked Babe up there. They gave him a football."

* * * *

College coaches weren't the only ones drooling over Skippy Doyle. So were some of the best-looking girls in the school—and perhaps many more swooning secret admirers who weren't girls any more. And after having seen Skippy Doyle play his sophomore and junior seasons, those who raved about how good he was and how much better he was likely to become were not disappointed.

* * * *

Babe inspired no such wholesale adulation. As a freshman, sophomore and junior, he was not even a starter. Backup fullback. That was his only claim to fame. A second teamer on a team that barely had enough players to have two teams. He spent so much time on the bench he might as well have been sitting in the stands.

And, his future appeared to offer no future. At least, as had been the case for his older brother Frank, no future playing football. Frank, who had played at Rochester earlier, hadn't been bad, but he hadn't been big enough to merit a college scholarship. As his senior season approached, Babe's prospects appeared no brighter.

Of course maybe he could enroll and play football at Geneva College, up at Beaver Falls, or at one of the numerous other small colleges scattered all over the state. Could, that is, if he had the money. He didn't though and he knew he couldn't hope to get a scholarship to Geneva or any of the rest because none of them offered any.

And yet, despite non-existent success and only one season remaining, he still was determined to aim higher. Still wanted to play major college football.

But how?

Where?

It was not an aspiration he discussed with his parents. Nor did they, or could they, offer any advice. They knew nothing about football; even less about what it meant, or took, to go to college. His father had dropped out after the sixth grade; his mother, the third. Understandably, their little world, transplanted when they were teenagers from a poor, dusty village in Italy, extended no farther from Henon Avenue than the Catholic church, the grocery, the glass factory across the river in Monaca, and the Rochester–Rochester Township line.

Time was running out. If he was ever to have an opportunity, it had better start knocking soon.

* * * *

ROCHESTER, PA.
Fall, 1947

At last, Babe was a starter. He was still a fullback, but a fullback with duties and responsibilities few fullbacks ever shouldered. He was a passing fullback who called the plays; who sometimes lined up under center in T formation and became a dropback passer or a decoy after handing the ball off to a halfback. Other times, shifting from the T formation to single wing, he was a dual threat, a tailback capable of passing or a bruising, full-head-of-steam runner. Because of his large, strong, yet soft hands, he also was the holder on extra point attempts.

But Rochester's most potent weapon was Skippy Doyle. Skippy Doyle left, Skippy Doyle right, Skippy Doyle up the middle. Skippy Doyle off tackle. Skippy Doyle at large. Skippy Doyle also was the Rams' extra point kicker.

Although either Babe or Coach Mike Sebastian usually decided who ran where and how often, Babe, unbeknown to his coach, had two other factors to consider as well when it came to calling plays.

Their names were Barbara and Eleanor.

Babe had a crush on Barbara.

Eleanor too.

But Barbara and Eleanor both were wild about Skippy Doyle.

And for some reason Babe never figured out and never asked, it all boiled down to this: On any given Friday night, if Skippy Doyle wanted a date after the game with Barbara and Eleanor—not just Barbara *or* Eleanor but *both* at the same time—he had to score no fewer than three touchdowns.

Sometimes, depending upon the opposition, he was able to do it without saying a word. Other times, he had no choice but to plead his case.

"C'mon, Babe, let me take it in. I gotta score one more or I can't take Barbara and Eleanor out tonight."

So Babe would call Skippy's number and off he would go, galloping toward the end zone. And after the game, after Babe showered and came out of the locker, there they were, Barbara and Eleanor, the two girls that made his heart flutter. And off they walked with Skippy Doyle in the middle hugging both of them.

And all Babe could do was stand there, crushed.

* * * *

Germantown Township, Midland, Elwood City, New Brighton, Aliquippa , Beaver Falls — six games into the 1947 season, the Rochester Rams were still undefeated. Now came the big one. Their opponent: Ambridge. At Ambridge, a city of 20,000. The Rams' stadium seated 2,500. The Ambridge stadium held 16,000.

It was sure to be a sellout—and then some.

And, sure to be an Ambridge victory, their fans confidently crowed.

To their dismay, however, Rochester took a 14-0 lead. Then the momentum shifted big time. Ambridge reeled off 19 straight points and with less than two minutes to play, held a 19-14 lead. Things looked even rosier when, on third down, Sammy Bambiana, Ambridge's shifty, speedy scatback, broke into the clear and appeared to be about to haul in a pass that would give his team a first down and a chance to run out the clock.

Then, seemingly out of nowhere, came a Rochester defender who separated Bambiana from his senses as well as the ball. It was a clean hit. A fair hit. But it was a blow delivered with such fierce intensity that Ambrige fans were outraged. A huge roar reverberated across the jam-packed stadium.

The tackler was Babe Parilli.

Despite the angry outcry, the officials ruled the pass incomplete.

After Ambridge was forced to punt, Babe drove his team to the Ambridge four yard line and with 1:20 left to play, he stood in the huddle and surveyed the faces of his teammates.

Four yards away.

Fourth down.

This was it.

The obvious choice was to hand the ball off to Skippy Doyle. Skippy Doyle, a touchdown or two short, had already lost his double date with Barbara and Eleanor. But none of that mattered now. The problem with doing the obvious, handing off to Skippy Doyle, was that it was obviously too obvious.

Babe turned his gaze toward his tight end, Vincent "Sonny" Pagley.

"If I throw it to you, can you catch it?"

Pagley said he would.

Babe took the snap, faked a dive into the middle and threw a jump pass to the wide open Pagley.

Touchdown.

Final score: Rochester 21; Ambridge, 19.

Enraged Ambridge fans poured onto the field. They began assaulting the referees. One suffered several broken ribs. He was hospitalized for months.

Meanwhile, after all the shrieking and swearing and wholesale chaos had subsided and the stadium lights dimmed, Babe's Uncle Frank was calmly walking across the parking lot one hand over his heart like he was pledging allegiance to the flag. Except what he was really doing was cradling the bulge under his shirt to make sure he wasn't dreaming; that what he thought had happened really had happened.

Before the game began, Uncle Frank had arrived with $600 in his pockets, then proceeded to wander through the stands loudly proclaiming that he would bet anybody—*C'mon, c'mon— put your money where your mouth is*— that Rochester would beat Ambridge. By the time the game started, he had wagered every dime of that $600 and when it was over, had doubled his money. His pockets were so full, he felt like a bumbling shoplifter who had swiped too much too fast and now was attempting to stroll, nonchalantly, out of a fancy Pittsburgh department store.

Imagine. Twelve hundred dollars.

That was more than his brother, August, made in nine months at the glass factory.

* * * *

A week later, the Rams beat Beaver. If they could beat Farrell in their final game, they would finish with a perfect season. Once again, as they had against Ambridge, the Rams scored a touchdown with time running out. The score was tied, 20-20.

One point was all they needed. One point.

As they stood in the huddle, Babe looked at Skippy Doyle. What he sensed was not encouraging. Skippy looked pale. Nervous.

"Do you want me to kick it?" Babe said. He was trying to minimize the pressure.

"No," Doyle replied. "I can do it."

The snap was perfect. So was Babe's hold. The kick was high enough. Long enough.

The ball veered wide of the goal post.

Later, a panel of sportswriters agreed that's the 1947 Rochester Rams were the best team ever in the history of Beaver County. They also declared that the Rochester-Ambridge game was one of the all-time 10 best.

* * * *

For Skippy, Babe and their teammates, the season was over. But for a tall, gruff, gravel-voiced coach 400 miles southwest of Beaver Valley, football season never ended.

In the spring of 1946, after serving one season as head coach at the University of Maryland, Paul "Bear" Bryant had resigned to become the head football coach at the University of Kentucky.

His record at Maryland, six wins and only two losses, had been more than satisfactory. The Bear couldn't say the same thing about his relationship with Maryland president Harry Clifton "Curley"

Byrd, though. After suspending one of his players for violating a team rule, The Bear had gone on a brief vacation. While he was gone, Byrd, who had served as Maryland's football coach from 1912 until 1934, had reinstated the player.

No one messed with Bear Bryant's football team, not even a university president.

The Bear abruptly resigned and accepted an offer to coach at Kentucky.

* * * *

Over the three-year period prior to his arrival, the Wildcats had not exactly anointed themselves with glory. In 1943, because of the war, UK did not even field a team. Some of their more cynical, outspoken critics brayed that they didn't field a team the next two seasons either. In 1944, UK, coached by A. D. Kirwan, finished 3-6, including a weird 2-0 loss to Michigan State. In 1945, under coach Bernie Shively they lost eight of 10.

Bear Bryant immediately turned the program around—as well as upside down. In large part because of George Blanda, a talented quarterback of Croatian descent from Youngwood, Pa., a small coal town southeast of Pittsburgh, his first Kentucky team finished 7-3; in 1947, at 8-3.

And now, in the spring of 1948, The Bear once again was out hunting the best talent he could find. The Pittsburgh area not only seemed like, but indeed was, an ideal place to go hunting. One of the players he had already zeroed in on was Skippy Doyle, Rochester's highly ballyhooed running back. Another was Beaver Falls end Jim Mutscheller. Bryant invited both of them to visit the University of Kentucky.

They accepted.

* * * *

That morning, when the train pulled out of the Pennsylvania Railroad depot in Rochester, Skippy Doyle and Jim Mutscheller weren't traveling alone. Vincent Bagley, who had caught the game-winning pass in the Ambridge game, went along, as did Vic Weiss, a friend of Mutscheller's whose father owned a dry cleaning business in Beaver Falls. Vic Weiss idolized Skippy Doyle. Babe Parilli had decided to tag along too. If he had any hope of playing major college football, he had to begin somewhere and going along for the ride seemed like a good way to start. Besides, what did he have to lose except the $15 he had managed to scrape together to pay for his train ticket?

As the train clattered through the greening countryside bathed in bright sunlight, Skippy Doyle, always good for a laugh, always the source as well as the subject of an abundance of stories, was holding court. Sooner or later, he was certain to razz Jim Mutscheller about not only the time Rochester had beaten Beaver Falls 19-0, but what had happened when Mutscheller had demanded a rematch.

Later, as the train approached Steubenville, Ohio, Skippy did bring it up. Babe got up and walked back to the men's room. Like most of Skippy Doyle's stories, he had heard it before. In this case, he had been the one who had taken to call from Mutscheller. And when Mutscheller insisted that they play again, Babe had replied, "Okay, come on down Sunday. We'll climb over the fence."

And so, they had played again. This time without uniforms. Without pads. Without referees. Without spectators.

And when all the snarling, the grunting, the groaning, the swearing, the hitting, the gasping for breath were over, Rochester had won again.

As he stepped out of the restroom, Babe Parilli decided to take a little walk. He opened the door, strolled through a couple of other coach cars and then found himself walking into a baggage car. Sitting in a battered wooden chair was the conductor. After exchanging a few pleasantries, Babe asked if it would be okay if he sat down.

The conductor looked around and laughed.

"Sure, if you don't mind sitting on a casket."

Babe grinned.

"No, I don't mind."

And so they sat and talked. About everything and nothing, even though Babe never had been much of talker. Especially in school when everyone in the class had to memorize the Gettysburg Address or a poem or something and then stand up in front of everybody and recite it. Memorizing was never a problem, but getting up there in front of everybody, well, he just couldn't do it. And so when his name was called, he always mumbled that he forgot to do it or didn't know it and as a result, got a bad grade. He considered a bad grade a mighty small price to pay though for escaping the paralyzing stage fright he knew he could not overcome.

Before he knew it, the train had passed through Columbus and was nearing Cincinnati. Soon they would be in Lexington.

He was already beginning to feel a little apprehensive.

What would he say to the Kentucky coach?

What would the coach say to him?

Tomorrow, he would find out.

What was the coach's name anyhow?

He couldn't remember.

* * * *

They spent the night in what the assistant coach who escorted them there called a "football house." It was one of three on Washington Street near the UK campus used to accommodate visiting recruits. Old, dingy, sparsely furnished, inside and out it looked more like a bleak railroad boarding house.

The next morning, the football office didn't look much better. It was located in the basement below the basketball gym. Dingy, musty, dimly lit, it looked more like a cellar than a basement. Through one open doorway, they could see frayed wrestling mats scattered across the floor. The door to Bear Bryant's office nearby was closed. They waited in eerie silence, saying nothing, hearing nothing.

Then the door opened and an assistant coach stepped out, closing the door behind him.

"Which one of you is Skippy Doyle?"

"I am," Skippy replied.

The assistant nodded his head, motioning for Skippy to follow him.

They disappeared into Bear's office. The door once again closed.

After what seemed like an interminable wait, the door opened again.

"Jim Mutscheller?"

Skippy Doyle grinning, returned to his seat.

"Jim Mutscheller?"

Mutscheller and the assistant coach disappeared into Bryant's office.

The whole experience seemed as cold, as impersonal as sitting in the waiting room at a doctor's office.

Another endless wait.

And when Mutscheller returned, the visit to Bear Bryant's office was over. Not only did Babe not have an opportunity to talk with Bear Bryant, he didn't even have a chance to meet him.

"Skippy," Babe said as they walked back to the football house, "I don't know how I'm going to get home. I don't have any money to buy a train ticket."

"Go see the athletic director. He'll give you the money."

The athletic director gave him the $15.

That afternoon, as they rode back to Rochester, Babe was more quiet than usual. If there had ever been even a remote chance of playing football at Kentucky, there sure wasn't now. Babe considered his options. There weren't many to consider.

The previous October, a Beaver County businessman, a Purdue graduate, had driven him to West Lafayette, Ind. to see the Purdue-Illinois game. But neither Purdue coach Stu Holcomb or anyone on his staff had expressed any interest in him. When he attended an Indiana game in Bloomington, Hoosier coach Clyde Smith had though.

He hadn't heard anything from Pittsburgh though. Or Penn State. Skippy Doyle—he was the one everybody wanted. Babe knew that Skippy was planning trips later that spring to North Carolina and Villanova. Perhaps Babe could accompany him on both.

Notre Dame? Hah. He knew Notre Dame didn't want him. Jim Mutscheller, yes. But not him.

It was a long, long ride home.

* * * *

After graduation, Babe took a job as supervisor of Rochester's playground. He was in charge of maintaining the grounds and equipment, scheduling games and coordinating other activities, including inviting an occasional guest speaker.

One who had accepted his invitation was none other than the "Flying Dutchman," Honus Wagner, the legendary shortstop for the Pittsburgh Pirates. Wagner, one of the first five men inducted into baseball's Hall of Fame in Cooperstown, N.Y., was in his 70's by then. He had retired in 1936. Some, if not nearly all of the kids, probably had no idea who he was.

But Babe did and that was thrill enough. It sure would be tough to top that one.

Then one day, as he and Harry Tallon, a black receiver and teammate on Rochester's 1947 football team, were sitting under a shade tree at the park, a tall, muscular man approached. His gaze was penetrating, unwavering; his voice a deep growl.

His name, he said, was Paul Bryant. He was, he said, the head football coach at the University of Kentucky.

What he wanted, he said, was for Babe to come visit UK.

"I've already been there," Babe replied.

"When?"

"With Skippy Doyle and Jim Mutscheller. I didn't have a chance to meet you."

"Well, you've met me now. We want you and your daddy to fly down to Lexington."

"My Dad doesn't fly," Babe replied.

"Then we want you to fly down."

Babe turned and looked at Harry.

"I'll come to Kentucky if Harry can come with me."

After a pause, The Bear replied: "We don't allow coloreds to play at Kentucky."

Later, after Bryant had left, Harry told Babe:

"You go on and go, Babe. That's just the way it is."

* * * *

Harry Tallon received a scholarship to play football at Indiana University.

He later became a police officer in Rochester, Pa.

CHAPTER 3

LEXINGTON, KY.
Late spring, 1948

By the time Babe arrived in Lexington, most of the abundance of white and pink and lavender dogwood and redbud blossoms that adorned the city's downtown and neighborhood streets and parks had disappeared. Spring was nearly over. But not spring football practice. Once again, Bear Bryant was utilizing every minute, every opportunity to prepare his team for the upcoming season. Because freshman recruits had not yet arrived on campus, only varsity players were participating in the drills. They wore no pads. There was no contact. That would all come later. Now, the emphasis was on conditioning. Ball handling. Footwork. Passing. Receiving.

The Bear was not present. He was off and gone once again on a far more significant mission.

He needed to find a quarterback.

Not just any quarterback. The right quarterback. Someone who could provide and maintain the continuity that had made the Wildcats so successful the previous two seasons when they had won 15 of their 21 games with George Blanda under center. Someone with the potential to become as good, as steady, as skilled a passer, as strong a leader, as intense a competitor as Blanda.

Come fall, Blanda would be playing his final season.

Then what?

Because freshman were not eligible to play varsity sports, The Bear had one year to tutor, to polish, to groom Blanda's successor.

First he had to find one.

* * * *

As Babe worked out with the varsity, The Bear's assistants evaluated his speed, his coordination, his ball handling, his field vision, his footwork. Most of all his arm strength, his accuracy, how quickly, how far he could throw.

Babe had never thought about becoming a quarterback. At Rochester, sophomore Pete Chambers, although listed in the programs as a quarterback, was used exclusively as a blocker. Babe, the fullback, had called the plays and done all the passing.

As a kid, the only football players he had ever idolized and pretended he was were runners: Felix "Doc" Blanchard and Glenn Davis, Mr. Inside and Mr. Outside, the stars of Army's powerhouse at West Point, and Phil Collea, a swift, elusive halfback at Rochester High who later played at Notre Dame. He sure wished he could juke like Phil.

Nor had he ever even dreamed of becoming a professional football player, regardless of position. In his senior yearbook, under a heading called Future Ambitions, he wrote: "Professional baseball player."

Becoming one certainly wasn't beyond the realm of possibility. As a senior shortstop he had been selected to play on an All Western Pennsylvania All Star team which had traveled to Philadelphia to play the Eastern All Stars. The game was played in Shibe Park, home of the American League Philadelphia Athletics, later renamed Connie Mack Stadium.

After The Bear returned and the workouts were over he told Babe:

"We want you to come here to play."

Play what, he did not say.

Nor did Babe ask.

But he accepted the offer.

How in the world did The Bear found out about me anyhow?

Later, Babe found out.

Mo Rubenstein, the football coach at Ambridge, had called Bryant.

"You don't want Skippy Doyle," Rubenstein told him. "You want Babe Parilli."

* * * *

In addition to his round-trip airplane ticket, Babe received $15 in expense money for his visit. At the Cincinnati airport, he spent $4 of it to buy a fuzzy toy dog.

He wanted to impress his girlfriend, Frieda.

* * * *

When he arrived back in Rochester, Babe went back to work as the town's playground supervisor. Somehow, it all did not seem real. Especially to his parents. They were overwhelmed by the sudden change in their lives. Although he no longer was the baby of the family--a younger brother, August, born 15 years after Babe, was going on four now—he still was their "Babe." And now, for the first time his life, he was going away from home.

And although no one talked about it, they all knew what that meant.

Except for an occasional visit, he was going away for good.

* * * *

A few weeks later, a car pulled up in front of 315 Henon Avenue. Behind the wheel sat UK assistant coach Carney Leslie. The Bear had sent Leslie to Rochester to transport Babe and John Netoskie, a guard, who lived in nearby New Kensington, to Lexington to enroll.

Like Babe, Carney Leslie wasn't much of a talker.

Not much of a driver either, Babe soon discovered. Leslie never exceeded 35 miles an hour. Counting rest and meal stops here and there, the trip took 17 hours.

* * * *

It didn't take long for Babe to learn that being a freshman football player at the University of Kentucky that fall was about as exclusive as riding on a standing-room-only passenger train.

The Bear had signed 109 new recruits.

Babe also learned that whoever won the starting quarterback job as a sophomore sure was going to have to earn it.

Among the 109 newcomers were nine candidates.

Including himself.

Only 12 would remain at UK for four years.

* * * *

In the beginning, Babe's freshman season at UK seemed uneventful. But as it progressed, he understood more and more that while playing little—the freshman team schedule included only three games—he was doing something far more important.

He was being taught *how* to play.

His mentor was Ermal Allen. As a player, Allen had apprenticed under one of the best. He had served one season as backup quarterback to the Cleveland Browns star Otto Graham.

Allen taught him that successful passing did not begin with throwing the ball. It started with a clean exchange between center and quarterback. Because the snap was where the process began, that was the first thing Babe and the other freshman quarterbacks rehearsed, over and over and over and over. It was a repetitive ritual, a daily requirement that never ended because its importance never diminished.

Even today, one of the greatest vulnerabilities a football team can face is an injury to its starting quarterback or center. When a substitute at either position enters the game, the biggest concern is, especially on the next play, will the new quarterback or new center, unaccustomed to playing together regularly, make the exchange without fumbling?

Bear Bryant and Ermal Allen had that one covered too. All of the quarterbacks and all of the centers rotated and worked together, over and over and over and over.

Throughout his career at Kentucky, Babe Parilli and the center, no matter who he was, never bungled a snap.

Sometimes, Ermal Allen even let some of the air out of the ball so that Babe had to maintain the correct grip under adverse conditions.

It was a simple matter, a monotonous exercise, but as Babe would learn too, it was a manifestation of The Bear's all-encompassing philosophy:

You play the way you practice.

* * * *

As a freshman, Babe also recognized another of The Bear's most important and universally applied coaching techniques:

The way to become stronger is to focus on your weaknesses.

Sheer speed could not be taught. But by developing proper footwork, quickness could be learned. A quick pivot, a sudden stop and start, a planting of the feet in the proper position, could mean the difference between gaining and losing yardage; between having a second or two more time or hurrying before deciding to run or throw; between a completion and an interception.

There was much to learn. And with each passing day, Babe was determined to learn it.

* * * *

There were a few humbling things to learn scrimmaging against the varsity too. The freshman "Orange Team," so named because they wore orange jerseys, served as what later became known as the scout team. The Orange Team took on the role of the Wildcats' next opponent, running their plays, employing their defensive schemes, emphasizing their known tendencies under given game-condition circumstances.

On both offense and defense, the cannon-fodder freshmen also absorbed ample samples of the punishment the varsity intended to dish out come game day. In those days, the quarterback did not wear a red shirt as a reminder not to pound him during scrimmages because there was too much risk of injury.

But any varsity player who ran at less than full speed or threw half-hearted blocks was a candidate to end up flat on his back with a mouthful of sod. If there was one thing, more than an abundance of others, The Bear could not stand it was a lack of effort. More than once, Babe saw The Bear, a fierce defensive end at Alabama and still in his mid thirties, charge out on to the field and level a loafer with a jarring cross-body block.

"Get your ass back in the huddle!" The Bear bellowed.

He also let them know they were about to go on a diet.

"If you don't shape up," The Bear snarled, "I'll break your Goddamn plate."

They all knew what that meant.

No food when they arrived for the evening meal.

* * * *

Because Rochester coach Mike Sebastian had incorporated both the T formation and the single wing into his offense, Babe was well versed in both.

As a high school senior, he had both passed and run after taking a direct snap under center and five yards deep as a runner-passer fullback. As an Orange Team scout quarterback, that gave him an advantage over his rivals who had never played single wing football.

Being a sideline spectator had its benefits too. It gave him a golden opportunity to observe how two-year starter George Blanda, an experienced and talented quarterback, operated as a drop-back passer.

Before long, Babe was beginning to emerge as the best of the nine freshman quarterbacks, although The Bear never told him he was.

The Bear wasn't big on praise.

Improvement. Striving for perfection, even though you knew he knew you would never achieve it. That's what he was after.

* * * *

On Sept. 18, in Lexington, the UK freshman beat Tennessee 7-0 in what the Associated Press called a "football thriller" watched by "8,000 shirt-sleeved fans."

"The Kittens," the AP reported, "dominated play throughout most of the game, but had to call on their expert young passer, Vito "Babe" Parilli, from Rochester, Pa., to register the score.

"Parilli passed 15 yards to John Netoskie, a fellow Pennsylvanian from New Kensington who ran another 16 yards without protection.

"Kentucky's victory came as a mild surprise because the baby Vols had been freely touted in Knoxville as one of the best freshman squads in Tennessee football history.

". . . Parilli's punting was almost as impressive as his passing. One of his boots went out of bounds at the six yard line."

He averaged 45 yards per punt.

After the win over Tennessee—and largely because it was a rare football win of any kind over Tennessee—both Babe and the freshman team received little mention in the press the rest of the season.

The following weekend, the varsity would play its season opener.

* * * *

On Sept. 25, riding a wave of exuberant optimism, the Kentucky Wildcats opened their 1948 season with a 48-7 victory over Xavier.

The tide went out in a hurry.

The following week, at home, they lost to Ole Miss 20-7.

The week after, in Athens, the Georgia Bulldogs thrashed them 35-12.

On Oct. 16, visiting Vanderbilt won 26-7.

After four games, UK not only had lost three of them, but in those 12 quarters, been outscored 81-26.

The Bear was furious. Even the managers, water boys and the freshmen who seldom if ever got a chance to scrimmage against the varsity looked or headed the other way when they saw-- or even heard-- him approaching.

Among the things Babe learned that edgy October was that the only thing more menacing than an irritable, growling Bear was an enraged Bear. Practices became longer, tougher, more brutal; his criticism, his outbursts, more intense, more frequent. His players were mad too. Mad at him. Mad at themselves. Mad at each other.

Like an early, unexpected winter storm, gloom had settled over the city.

Things had to change.

* * * *

Meanwhile, for Babe, life as a freshman off the football field remained as routine, as uneventful as it did on. Adjusting to one was about as unsettling as it was to the other.

For him and his roommate, John Netoskie, living in a dorm was pleasant enough, although sometimes the halls were as noisy as a Greyhound bus depot; at other times, deathly quiet as a funeral home. Their only form of entertainment was to go see a movie at the Ben Ali Theater and the other downtown theater whose name he could never remember. Seeing as how they had little money except for the $15 laundry allowance they received each month, the only reason they could go to the movies whenever they chose was because Bob Cox, who operated both theaters, let them in free.

They did not join a fraternity. None of the football players they knew did. One reason was that The Bear was opposed to them. They were too selective, he said. Too exclusive, too restricted to those with connections and means. Besides, his football team formed its own fraternity. They lived together, took their meals together, celebrated their triumphs together, endured their disappointments together as well.

The house at 147 Washington Street. That was where the freshman aspired to live. That, along with other "football houses" at 121 and 123 Washington, were where the varsity starters lived.

Nearby, on South Limestone, across from the UK campus, was their social center: Jack Cook's Texaco station. That was where they assembled to hang out; to shoot the breeze; to watch the world go by.

* * * *

On Oct. 23, the visiting Wildcats took out their pent-up frustration on Marquette, 25-0.

The following week, they traveled to Cincinnati and beat the Bearcats 28-7.

Now they were even at 3-3. That's the way their next game, against Villanova ended too.

Even.

They tied, 13-13.

On November 13, UK beat Florida 34-15.

Now came the big one: at Tennessee. If ever there was a surefire prescription for redemption, it was beating the Volunteers.

The Wildcats came close, but not close enough. The game ended in a scoreless tie.

So now they had one last chance to finish with a winning record. On Nov. 25, the Wildcats traveled to Miami and beat the Hurricanes 25-5 to finish 5-3-2. Those predisposed to see the bright side pointed out that after losing three of their first four games, the Wildcats had not lost again all season.

Others saw a dark cloud within the silver lining. If Kentucky, led by three-year starter George Blanda, a sure-fire NFL draftee, could win only five of 10 games, how were they going to do better, or even as well, without him and without an experienced quarterback to take his place?

Although he wasn't saying publicly, Bear Bryant must have been thinking the same thing.

For many UK sports fans, there was more than ample reason to look at the bright side, however. The previous spring, Adolph Rupp's basketball team, led by guard Ralph Beard, 6-4 forward Wah Wah Jones and 6-7 center Alex Groza, had won the national championship. All three were back, along with a deep, experienced supporting cast. Come spring, there was every reason to believe they would do it again.

Which, in fact, they did.

* * * *

When spring practice began, seven candidates were on hand to replace George Blanda: Babe; Bob Buzek of Ambridge, Pa.; Edward Vanek, Whiting, Ind.; Jim Horn, Wellsburg, W.Va.; Paul Varley, Alliance, Ohio; Charles Porter, Prestonsburg, Ky.; and Ken Knight, Russellville, Ky.

Perhaps it was merely coincidental that Babe's name was first on the bold-face list published in a Lexington newspaper. Perhaps not if some of the subsequent stories were any indication.

One said:

". . . Babe Parilli, the much heralded Pennsylvania quarterback, spent most of the afternoon calling signals for the first team, and from the way things looked, he'll be handling that chore a great deal of the time next fall.

"Parilli seemed cool and poised under the fire of a tough, hard-charging defensive team. Observers were pleased to note that he was very adept at broken-field running, especially when he appeared to be trapped behind the line. His passes were finding their mark consistently.

"It is doubtful whether Parilli can match the graduated George Blanda's kicking ability, but it seems quite possible that he will be able to fill Blanda's passing shoes. Parilli is already a capable runner, something that Blanda was weakest."

The next to last paragraph stated something, the significance of which, Babe already realized had he read it:

"Kentucky is carrying more seniors on this coming year's team than ever before since Bryant came to Kentucky three seasons ago. A check of the records reveals than 13 Wildcats will be playing their final year of football next year season. The list includes eight linemen and five backs.

"The only way an inexperienced, first-year quarterback can succeed is if he has a strong supporting cast, particularly linemen."

* * * *

A story published in *The Ashland Independent* said:

"One of the brightest new lights in the University of Kentucky grid picture in recent years may be exposed by Coach Paul Bryant, the Wildcats' T formation chief, during the forthcoming 1949 football campaign.

"By name, the top-flight prospect is Vito (Babe) Parilli, 20-year-old Rochester, Pa. All-State selection and star quarterback on the successful Kentucky freshman team last season.

"Whether the six-foot-one inch, 185 pound sophomore develops the poise and form predicted for him may depend on the Wildcats' grid fortunes for 1949. A superior field general possibly is the most important item in the modern football machine and Kentucky this season is faced with the necessity of developing one from a field of four sophomore and one junior candidates (none of them lettermen) to replace the graduation loss of George Blanda.

"On the basis of his performance in directing the field play of the Kentucky yearling gridders last year, Parilli is being groomed as the leading candidate for the T quarterback post on the 1949 varsity. In spring exhibition games played by the 'Cats this year in various parts of the state the Rochester ace displayed brilliant flashes of form and comparatively consistent generalship that brought smiles to victory-hungry fans and an optimistic look on the faces of his coaches.

"Especially adept as a passer, Parilli excels in getting back from the line in a hurry, picking out the open receiver and getting the ball away with speed and accuracy. When the intended receiver is covered, the versatile speed merchant pulls another trick out of his triple-threat bag and runs with the ball with all the polish and speed of a halfback. Often, he will leap into the air with a twisting motion while on the dead run to shoot the pigskin downfield to an uncovered receiver.

"While it may be the least developed of his triple threat abilities, the Rochester ace can punt with better than average power and accuracy. And even this ability may be improved before the season opens because Babe is often the last one off the practice field of taking advantage of free time to practice his kicking.

"With such determination to make good plus natural ability he has highly impressed Coach Bryant and the Kentucky coaching staff. To them and to other qualified observers generally, he seems destined to become a great performer, if he proves to have the 'heart' and stamina necessary to stand up under extremely tough Southeastern Conference competition."

* * * *

In his widely read column, *It Says Here*, Ed Ashford reported:

". . . Coach Paul Bryant feels reasonably certain that (Parilli), the sophomore from Rochester, Pa. will have little trouble filling the shoes of George Blanda despite the great showing Blanda is making in professional football this year.

"At a grid gabfest the boys were discussing Parilli and Blanda. The general consensus was that Blanda could kick farther than

Parilli but that Parilli's higher punts would give Kentucky ends more time to get down the field and as a result the opposition's punt returns would be cut down more than enough to make up for the added distance Blanda got.

"It also was pointed out that Parilli is as good, and perhaps better, than Blanda when it comes to pass throwing, but the biggest edge Parilli holds over the ex-Wildcat is in his running ability. Blanda can kick and pass with the best of them. But when he had to carry the ball he seldom reached the line of scrimmage, one observer noted.

"Parilli, if unable to find a pass receiver, can take off on his own–and in a hurry. The opposition always looked for a pass or a punt whenever Blanda got the ball. When Parilli gets it, they won't know what to expect."

* * * *

In a 1949 pre-season article published in *Look* magazine, legendary sportswriter Grantland Rice also spoke highly of Babe. It was Grantland Rice who wrote the most famous lines in sports journalism history while covering the 1924 Army–Notre Dame football game:

Outlined against a blue-gray October sky, the Four Horsemen rode again. In dramatic folklore they are known as Famine, Pestilence, Destruction and Death. These are only aliases. Their real names are Stuhldreher, Miller, Crowley and Layden.

Rice called Parilli one of the most promising sophomore newcomers in the entire country.

* * * *

That spring, Babe discovered that although the road to success was sure to be difficult, it couldn't be any worse than the road to Columbus, Ohio.

Following the annual Kentucky Blue-White spring game, Babe and teammate Cliff Lawson decided to visit Skippy Doyle at Ohio State. After hitchhiking to Maysville, they decided that instead of following U.S. 52 to Portsmouth and then U.S. 23 to Columbus, they would save time by continuing north on U.S. 68 through Adams County to Hillsboro, then take U.S. 62 northeast through Washington Court House northeast to Columbus.

Unfortunately, they did not know that thru-traffic through sparsely populated Adams County was all but non-existent.

The trip took 25 hours. Between long waits for cars and trucks that never came, they cat-napped along the shoulder of the road. Once, when Babe was suddenly startled awake, he found a cat walking across his chest.

* * * *

Following World War II, collegiate teams were allowed to conduct spring practice far longer than they can now. But even The Bear could work his team only so long without breaking the rules.

It was not illegal, however, to go fishing.

And on this occasion, when The Bear went fishing, he didn't go alone. With him were three dozen or so burly young men who looked remarkably like football players. At the end of their weekend stay in a broad grassy meadow that just happened to be about as long and wide as a football field, at some remote location bordered by a small stream, The Bear dropped a net into the water.

There.

So much for fishing.

And when he glanced up and saw a man walking down the hill toward their camp, he dispatched two of his biggest fellow fishermen to go intercept him.

"If he gets any closer," The Bear growled, "get him the hell out of here."

CHAPTER 4

LEXINGTON, KY.
September 17, 1949

It was time. Time for Babe to demonstrate that all that pre-season hype, all that praise, all those predictions about him that had appeared on the pages of *Look* magazine as well as in the *Lexington Herald* and other area newspapers were not misguided.

Even if he were as gifted as advertised, how would he handle the pressure not only of playing in his first major college game, but throughout the season against what was sure to be far tougher Southeastern Conference competition than Kentucky's first opponent, Mississippi Southern?

Cautiously optimistic UK fans took comfort in knowing that in order for the Wildcats to succeed, Babe did not have to be sensational. If he was merely adequate, the Wildcats stood a good chance of surpassing last season's somewhat disappointing 5-3-2 record.

One big reason was experience, despite Babe's total lack of it. There were 13 seniors, eight linemen and five backs—more than The Bear had ever had in his first three seasons at UK.

For all the speculation, all the analysis, no one expected what was about to happen. Trounced, destroyed, massacred, annihilated, humiliated, flattened, bludgeoned, bombarded—the game was so one-sided, sportswriters covering it had to rummage through their frayed bag of threadbare clichés to search for a word that would describe it.

None seemed adequate.

Kentucky won 71-7.

Wiseacres giggled that the game was not as close as the score indicated.

"The Cats tallied the first two times they had the ball," the *Herald* reported. "And that was enough to show that Babe Parilli is a passer of considerable merit. His passing accounted for the first touchdown and played a prominent part in other markers.

"At the half, someone asked an Ole Miss scout how Parilli stacked up with Chuckin' Charlie Conerly, the ex-Rebel passing great who owns almost every passing mark.

"'By the time Parilli is a senior, he'll be greater,' said the Old Miss representative without batting an eye."

Southeastern Conference Commissioner Bernie Moore, watching from the press box, said "I've seen most of our teams and I'll say Kentucky has to be figured in the picture this year. These fellows have got speed, and plenty of it. They've got a brilliant young passer in Babe Parilli, too. The boy not only is a good passer, but a workhorse with lots of sense, it seems to me."

Next up: LSU, in Baton Rouge.

* * * *

What was troubling LSU coach Gaynell "Gloomy Gus" Tinsley wasn't just how well Babe had played in his first collegiate game but how utterly unpredictably he had played. The previous three seasons, when UK quarterback George Blanda had dropped back to pass, Gloomy Gus didn't have to worry. Blanda was too slow afoot to do anything but pass.

But Babe . . .

There was no telling what he might do when he had the ball--or for that matter, *if* he had it, what with all that razzle-dazzle ball faking.

"Gloomy Gus Tinsley, who runs the football show at Louisiana State, can't decide whether to worry more about Babe Parilli's feet than about his hands," the Associated Press reported.

"'All along, we've been hearing about what a great runner he is. Then he passes rings around Mississippi Southern. He carried the ball once. Lost a yard.'

"'I don't see how we can keep Parilli from passing,' Tinsley says. 'He had invulnerable pass protection. All we can do is concentrate on covering the receivers because we can't stop him from throwing.'

"And then Tinsley shrugs his shoulders.

"'That's when I guess he'll cut loose and run.'"

* * * *

Two minutes and 13 seconds into the game, after LSU fumbled at its own 33 yard line, Babe rifled a pass to Dopey Phelps at the 10 and Phelps loped into the end zone.

With 43 seconds remaining in the first half, "Gloomy Gus" had another reason to shake his head. LSU fumbled again, this time at its own 30. Two running plays moved the ball to the 16 and a first down. Then, Babe took the snap and pitched the ball to halfback Dopey Phelps for what appeared to be an end sweep.

Appeared to be.

Then Dopey did something Gloomy Gus thought only Babe would do. He stopped in his tracks and lofted the ball to Jimmy Howe standing all alone in the end zone.

In the early minutes of the final quarter, Phelps returned a punt to the LSU 36. Then Babe drilled a clothesline pass straight through the middle of the Tiger defense for a first down at the 12. On the next play, halfback Clayton Webb took a pitchout from Babe and raced into the end zone.

LSU drove to the UK three, but the Wildcat line, outweighed 10 pounds per man, thwarted three straight attempts to score.

Kentucky 19; LSU 0.

* * * *

LEXINGTON, KY.
Oct. 1, 1949

Back home after two weeks on the road, the Wildcats beat Mississippi 47-0. Babe threw for one touchdown, ran for a second, and set up a third with his running and passing.

But once again, it was the defense that did much of the work and received little of the praise in the newspapers.

In the second half, Kentucky's defense became its best offense.

Late in the third quarter, Wilbur Jamerson picked off a pass at the Kentucky 29 and raced all the way to the Ole Miss nine yard line. That led to a score.

In the final quarter, after Jamerson ran 47 yards for a touchdown, Ole Miss attempted a lateral. Don Frampton intercepted it and ran 82 yards to score.

A few plays later, Kentucky's James McKenzie intercepted another Ole Miss pass and ran 77 yards for the final touchdown.

In three games, Kentucky had scored 137 points.

And given up seven.

* * * *

LEXINGTON, KY.
Oct. 8, 1949

The day before Kentucky's homecoming game with Georgia, a story in *The Lexington Herald* began this way:

"Not since the days of turtleneck sweaters and the flying wedge has Kentucky faced a more important football game than tomorrow night.

"The fast-rising Wildcats encounter brawny Georgia, defending champions of the Southeastern Conference, here at 8 p.m. It's a collision of possible football greats, one which many observers believe will be the most important for Kentucky in its modern football history.

"Apparently, most Wildcat followers feel the same way. Some 35,000 are expected to jam Stoll Field to capacity for the homecoming battle and to compose the biggest crowd ever to see a football game in the state.

"Aside from the attendance record, the surprising Wildcats will be gunning for an additional mark. They'll be trying to whip a third S.E.C. foe in a row. The Wildcats have never done that.

"The battle, glutted with emotional overtones, could be the vital step toward the first conference championship for the Wildcats. They have never finished better than sixth, back in 1935.

"And finally, this clash with a beefy, highly aggressive Georgia forward wall will provide still another stern test for Vito "Babe" Parilli. The sophomore quarterback, who has already put in a bid for football greatness, can rise still another niche in the estimation of fans and observers if he can outwit, outrun and outmaneuver the Bulldogs. He isn't expected to have much time to stand back and rifle his demoralizing passes."

The *Herald* also noted that Georgia would outweigh Kentucky both in the line and backfield. What no one in the press box or the stands anticipated was that a pair of Kentucky boys, Don (Dopey) Phelps and scatback Emery Clark, would offset Georgia's strength with speed.

In the second quarter, Clark, whom Bear Bryant had told three times that he was too light to play major college football before relenting and giving him a scholarship, broke a scoreless deadlock by returning a punt 61 yards, giving Kentucky a 6-0 lead.

Then early in the second quarter when Georgia punted, the ball sailed clear to the goal line where Phelps gathered it in. When he reached the 30-yard line, Phelps put on a burst of speed and weaving, spinning, reversing direction, suddenly broke into the clear. Only one man, the kicker, stood between him and the end zone. The kicker upended Phelps on the nine yard line. Two plays later, Bill Leskovar plunged across for the score.

In the third quarter, Dom Fucci scored on a 24-yard run and later, caught a Babe pass and scored again.

Kentucky had beaten the vaunted SEC champs, 25-0.

* * * *

LEXINGTON, KY.
October 15, 1949

Kentucky was expected to beat The Citadel Bulldogs easily.
And did.

Their fans expected to see more of the exciting plays they had witnessed against Georgia the week before.

They didn't.

A headline in *The Lexington Herald* read:

RAGGED KENTUCKY FLATTENS THE CITADEL 44 TO 0

The lead paragraphs said:

"A ragged University of Kentucky football team, intent upon taking things easy, rolled to a 44-0 victory over The Citadel before a crowd of 25,000 last night at Stoll Field.

"It was the fifth straight win of the season for Coach Paul Bryant's undefeated Wildcats, who showed none of the polish, speed and finesse which enabled them to wallop three tough Southeastern Conference foes in succession but nevertheless turned in a workmanlike job in snowing under the scrappy Bulldogs from the Southern Conference.

"Scoring in the first 23 seconds of play when a Citadel lateral went awry and resulted in a safety, the Kentuckians were in the driver's seat throughout but the crowd went home disappointed because it failed to see any sensational runs such as the ones that turned back Georgia a week before."

If The Bear or any of his players read the *Herald's* account of the game, they probably were more amused than offended.

A *Bear Bryant* team?

Intent upon taking things *easy?*

If The Bear's players had a dollar for every time they had seen The Bear take things easy, or allowed them to, they would all still have nothing in their pockets except lint and perhaps a few cookie crumbs.

Both the reporter and those who left the stadium disappointed had no idea that what they thought they saw was not what was happening at all. What they perceived as a methodical, lackluster performance, was instead a matter of focusing on what they believed would work and then staying with it because it did. Namely, running rather than passing.

The man who dictated the tone and pace of what was widely perceived as a boring, uninspiring game was the one who called all the plays.

Babe.

Unbeknown to press and public alike, The Bear had begun grooming his quarterback for the task before the season had even begun. Every day, during the lunch hour, Babe went to The Bear's office. There, they played a simulated football board game, a game The Bear had designed himself.

"Second down, the ball's on your own 37 yard line, three minutes to play—what play do you call?"

Babe told The Bear what he had decided.

"You gained three yards. *Now* what are you going to do?"

Babe tried again.

Failed again.

Learned again.

Returned again the next day for another lunch-hour grilling.

As the weeks went by, as the spot on the field, the down, the score, the quarter, the time remaining changed, as he continued to have only a few seconds to make a decision, Babe became better and better at knowing exactly what this coach wanted in a given set of circumstances, what The Bear himself would do if he were the quarterback.

No longer did The Bear have to send in plays. He already had during those lunch hour, simulated football games each day in his office. It was a daily ritual, an intense, one-on-one football education that would continue the rest of Babe's career, even after he had become a first-team All-American as a junior and was on his way to being named to the first team again as a senior.

And so, early in the Citadel game, Babe had observed that UK could move, and continue to move, the ball down the field and score by rushing and in the process, control the tempo and depend upon the defense, led by All-American tackle Bob Gain to protect a mounting lead.

Babe had managed the game exactly as he knew The Bear would do if he were the quarterback.

"Babe Parilli," The Bear would say later, "is a coach's dream."

* * * *

DALLAS, TEX.
Oct. 22, 1949

For the benefit of those prone to place a bet or two, a headline in a Dallas newspaper declared:
MUSTANGS IN UNDERDOG ROLE
FOR FIRST TIME SINCE 1947

Professional odds makers, the story said, picked visiting Kentucky, unbeaten and ranked seventh in the country, as a three-point favorite. A quick check of the records showed why it was big news when Southern Methodist was not expected to win.

In 1947, SMU had finished 9-0-2 and the following season, 9-1-1, their only loss in 22 games at Missouri. Two big reasons for the Mustangs' considerable success were Doak Walker and Kyle Rote, two of the biggest names, the most versatile stars, in all of college football. Walker had won the Heisman Trophy in 1948.

The odds makers, the Dallas paper reported, were not the only ones who predicted a Kentucky victory. So did Southern Methodist head coach Matty Bell, also known as "Moanin' Matty."

"Coach Matty Bell of Southern Methodist was feeling his oats today," a Dallas newspaper reported. "He figured he had won his spurs as a football prognosticator and that he had wiped away forever his tag of Moanin' Matty.

"It was Bell who last week predicted Rice would beat his team by one or two touchdowns. Quoth the SMU coach: 'If I was a sportswriter, I would pick it like that.'

"Today, he had a slight sneer for sportswriters, practically all of whom selected Southern Methodist to win.

"The score was 41-27 in favor of Rice.

"Bell also predicted-- before the season began—that Southern Methodist would lose four games this year. So it's one down and three to go.

"Matty says the second one will come Saturday when his Methodists play undefeated, untied Kentucky. He said mournfully:

"'We have been executed once and we will be executed again. Look at the record. Kentucky beat Louisiana State 19-0, Louisiana State beat Rice 14-0 and Rice beat us badly.'

"He declared that while Tobin Rote of Rice is a great passer and beat SMU with his throws, Kentucky has an even better one.

"'This Vito Parilli is a much better passer than Rote. Kentucky also has a big, fast line and one of the greatest running halfbacks in the country in Donald Phelps.'"

In a separate interview conducted at his office, Bell said:

"Parilli (Babe Parilli, Kentucky's great passer), is a fine boy and a fine passer," Matty said. "I know, for I used Parilli in demonstrating football techniques at a grid clinic in connection with Kentucky's spring drills," he said.

While some dismissed Bell's prediction as nothing more than a combination of reverse psychology to fire up his team and to blunt criticism if his team did indeed lose, there were two overriding reasons to believe that he might be right.

One was that Kyle Rote had suffered a broken blood vessel the week before and his leg was heavily taped during practice. The other: Doak Walker, perhaps the best all-around football player in the country, was suffering from the flu, had been admitted to a Dallas hospital and definitely would not play.

Would the Mustangs, stung by the loss to Rice, perhaps even more so by their own coach's public prediction that they would lose again, as well as severely weakened by Kyle Rote's injury and Doak Walker's unavailability, be even more fired up, or emotionally deflated when they faced the Wildcats?

Everyone, including Kentucky, would find out when the two teams squared off in that cavernous Texas stadium known as the Cotton Bowl.

* * * *

Moanin' Matty's prediction came true. Southern Methodist did lose to four teams during the 1949 season.

Kentucky wasn't one of them though.

Despite the absence of Doak Walker, the Mustangs won 20-7 before a crowd of 48,000.

Three minutes into the game the Wildcats saw their best play of the day turn into their worst disappointment. Halfback Emery Clark, who had returned a punt 61 yards for a touchdown against Georgia two weeks earlier, broke loose on a 68-yard run for what appeared to be a touchdown. But the play was flagged back for offsides, a call the Kentucky team, coaching staff and bench considered the football equivalent of Texas-flavored unarmed robbery.

Near the end of the first quarter, Southern Methodist began a drive on its own 36 yard line. Thirty-two seconds into the second, they scored to take a 6-0 lead.

It didn't last long. UK halfback Emery Clark ran the ensuing short kickoff back to the Kentucky 40. Dopey Phelps slithered down to the SMU 48. After Bill Leskovar broke loose on an 18 yard run to the 30, Babe dropped back and fired a strike to Dominick Fucci in the end zone.

Kentucky, 7-6.

But in the opening minutes of the third quarter, SMU, beginning on its own 12 yard line, marched 88 yards in 14 plays to take a 13-7 lead.

Emery Clark's first-quarter, 68 yard touchdown run nullified by a disputed offsides call, loomed larger and larger.

Late in the fourth quarter, SMU had the ball on its own 35 yard line. Fourth down. Four inches to go.

Moanin' Matty elected to go for it.

First down, Southern Methodist.

Shortly after that, sophomore quarterback Fred Benners dropped back to the SMU 40 and lofted a pass that sailed nearly to the goal line where a Mustang receiver hauled it in and scored to give Southern Methodist a 20-7 lead.

At last, someone had shredded Kentucky's celebrated defense, rated among the best in the nation, and because of that and numerous other reasons—penalties, fumbles, an interception seven yards shy of the goal line—the Wildcats had lost their first game of the season.

* * * *

LEXINGTON, KY.
October 29, 1949

A *Lexington Herald* reporter began his game story this way:

"The skies were dull in Lexington yesterday afternoon and with the exception of a few flashes of brilliance, so was the performance turned in by the University of Kentucky Wildcats as they sputtered to a 14-7 gridiron victory over a steamed-up University of Cincinnati Bearcat eleven at Stoll Field. It was Kentucky's sixth win in seven starts this year.

"A crowd of 27,000 football fans was present at the Dad's Day game, expecting to see Coach Paul Bryant's touted Kentuckians blast the underdog Bearcats off the field but instead they saw Coach Sid Gilman's warriors outplay and outfight the Wildcats during most of the contest.

"The Bearcats threw up a tough defense which stopped the Cats in every period but the second when the Bryantmen struck quickly for two touchdowns and a 14-0 lead."

Babe did the striking.

First, he threw a pass to Jim Howe who ran to the Cincinnati 15 yard line. After two running plays that moved the ball to the six, followed by a Babe completion to the three, Clayton Webb plunged into the end zone.

On UK's next possession, Babe completed a third-down pass to the Cincinnati 35. He then connected with end Nick Odlivak at the five and Odlivak scored to give the Wildcats a 14-0 lead.

Thereafter, following its uncharacteristically porous performance against Southern Methodist, it was Kentucky's defense that saved the day.

* * * *

Having won six of their first seven games, the Cats prepared to meet the Xavier Musketeers. On paper, Xavier, like Cincinnati, did not appear to be a major threat.

True, Xavier was undefeated (7-0) but none of the Musketeers' opponents--West Virginia Wesleyan, Dayton, Quantico Marines, Miami of Ohio, John Carroll, Louisville and Dayton again—

seemed likely to appear in the Associated Press Top 10 poll anytime soon.

Then there were the three previous meetings since Bear Bryant had become the coach at Kentucky. In 1946, the Cats had won 70-0; the following year, 20-7, and in 1948 by a score of 48-7.

Maybe this time, unlike in the forgettable Cincinnati game, the Wildcats would start playing like themselves again.

* * * *

CINCINNATI, OHIO
October 29, 1949

Once again, the Wildcats focused on running the ball, finishing with 206 yards rushing.

Once again though, several time-consuming drives did not lead to touchdowns.

Once again, as it had in every game except against Southern Methodist, the Kentucky defense was all but impenetrable. The Musketeers netted only nine rushing yards.

Babe completed five of 15 passes for 83 yards. Three were intercepted. Xavier quarterback Bob McQuade completed only one.

Kentucky 21; Xavier 7.

Next up: the Florida Gators.

* * * *

Since the Bear arrived at Kentucky in 1946, the two teams had played only once. During Babe's freshman a season, the Wildcats had beaten the Gators 34-15. But things seemed to be looking up for the Florida program. Considering what had happened during the 1946 season, up was the only way they could look though. Florida had lost all nine games and in the process, been outscored 264 to 104.

But in 1947, its record had improved to 4-5-1 and to 5-5 in 1948. This season, the Gators had won four, lost two and tied one. Both teams had beaten defending SEC champion Georgia; Kentucky by 25-0; the Gators, 28-7.

"Kentucky completely outclassed the Florida Gators last night," *The Tampa Tribune* reported. "Rolling up a 35-0 score and never permitting the Gators to advance beyond the Wildcat 30 yard line.

"The estimated 21,000 fans which overflowed Florida Field saw the toughest line in the Southeastern Conference completely throttle the Gators' offense.

"It was the Wildcats' fourth straight win in the conference, and their fourth shutout. It also marked the first time in history that Kentucky has won as many as four league games in a single season.

"Florida never had the slightest chance, and the score could have gone to astronomical proportions had the Wildcats decided to pour it on in the second half.

"As it was, Kentucky scored in all but the third quarter, racking up one score in the first period, two in the second and two more in the fourth.

"The Kentucky line opened gaping holes through which Dopey Phelps, Ralph Genito and Emery Clark poured for long gains.

"In the air, the Wildcats were potent only when Babe Parilli was in the game in the first half. The star passer saw no action in the second half.

"Most disheartening factor was the completeness with which Kentucky stopped Chuck Hunsinger, the Gator All-Southeastern Conference back who ran Georgia off the field at Jacksonville last week.

"Hunsinger carried the ball 10 times for 22 yards, his total for the first half as minus one, and he picked up only 22 in the second.

"Bob Gain, Kentucky's candidate for All-American tackle, was the top lineman and probably the best player on the field last night. He stopped about a third of all the Gators' plays himself.

"Kentucky gained 411 yards to 138 for the Gators."

* * * *

As sportswriters in both states eagerly awaited the beginning of the annual border war between Kentucky and Tennessee the following week, they had no trouble finding plenty of material to document how important the game would be, especially for Kentucky.

For the Volunteers, a victory, more than anything else, would mean extending a domination over the Wildcats that had continued uninterrupted since 1926, the year General Bob Neyland had become the Tennessee head coach. The only time Kentucky had beaten Tennessee was in 1935 when Neyland had been serving in the military in Panama. Otherwise, the best the Wildcats had been able to muster against his teams had been a couple of ties.

For Kentucky, ending the Tennessee jinx would be only one of the benefits. A victory over Tennessee followed by one the following week at Miami would enable them to:

1. Finish undefeated in Southeastern Conference play with a 5-0 record and win the SEC title.
2. Win nine games in a single season, the first time that had happened since 1909.
3. Perhaps qualify for an appearance in the Orange, Sugar or Cotton game on New Year's Day.

The oddsmakers favored Kentucky by 13 points.

But four hours before kickoff, Bear Bryant painted a totally different picture when he stood before a gathering of reporters. Although he did not say so, he was well aware of all the reasons Kentucky was the favorite.

Yes, Kentucky was No. 1 in the nation in total defense, allowing only 153.6 yards per game.

Yes, UK had not given up a single touchdown in four SEC games.

Yes, whereas Kentucky had scored 283 points and allowed only 41, Tennessee had scored 182 points and given up 91.

Yes, the game was to be played in Lexington, in front of 38,000 fans, the largest crowd ever to watch a sporting event in the state except the Kentucky Derby.

And, yes, the Wildcats had Babe Parilli, the finest quarterback in the conference-- and perhaps in the entire country.

But "Tennessee," The Bear said, "will be the toughest defense Kentucky has been up against this season.

"If we win, we will have to win with straight football. A team can't pull any of that Fancy Dan stuff against one of Neyland's teams and win.

"If we can gain through their line—and it's a tough one—we'll have a chance. Their pass defense is rugged. Maybe we can complete some and maybe we can't.

"Their overall kicking game is much better than ours. They have better punting and better coverage on punts. Their kicking game could keep us in a hole."

In its game story, *The Lexington Herald-Leader* reported:

"The way the game was played showed that Bryant knew whereof he spoke. It was Tennessee's defense and kicking game that kept the Wildcats deep in their own territory most of the contest.

"Statistically, everything favored Kentucky before the game. The Cats ranked above the Vols in every phase except punting and pass defense.

"But victories aren't won on paper, it's what happens on the playing field that counts, as the Wildcats learned to their sorrow. And the statistics yesterday afternoon were all in the Vols' favor.

"Tennessee racked up 14 first downs to a meager four for the Cats and outgained Kentucky more than two to one on the ground, 134 yards to 63. In passing, the Cats held a scant 33-26 edge, but the Vols threw only six times to Kentucky's 12.

"After the visitors put across their touchdown late in the first quarter with the aid of a pass interception and an extremely painful penalty against UK, the Wildcats couldn't even register a first down, to add to their earlier trio, until the game was less than five minutes from the death knell."

The following Friday, November 25, the Cats headed for the Orange Bowl—the stadium, not the New Year's Day game—to play Miami.

* * * *

That Babe threw only nine passes and completed five for 65 yards hardly mattered. From start to finish, the Cats once again focused almost exclusively on rushing and defense. UK wound up with 274 yards on the ground while Miami gained only 62 and threw 26 passes with 10 completions but for only 63 yards. Kentucky had 25 first downs; Miami, 9.

That night, the Orange Bowl committee announced it would meet the following day to decide who would meet Santa Clara in the Orange Bowl game on New Year's Day.

And when the news was announced, the Wildcats learned that they would once again being playing in the Orange Bowl—this time, despite the demoralizing loss to Tennessee, on New Year's Day.

CHAPTER 5

Despite all of the pageantry, the parties, the receptions, the dinners, the beauty queens, the parades, the sightseeing tours and all of the other exciting activities leading up to the New Year's Day Orange Bowl game, the Wildcats might as well have been back in Bourbon County on the practice field behind tiny, somber, spartan Millersburg Military Institute. When they boarded a bus to their hotel, they were nowhere near Miami.

They were in Cocoa Beach, 200 miles away.

And for all practical purposes, after leaving their luggage in their rooms, they *were* at MMI. The Bear led them straight to the nearest high school field to scrimmage.

All week long, they were right back in pre-season boot camp. As at MMI, their morning began with a shot of orange juice and a jolt of what the Bear called his "eye opener" drill. As they had at Millersburg Military Institute back in July, they formed two lines, one player pretending he was the ball carrier, the other from the other line, not pretending, smashing him to the ground like an armored car plowing over a stop sign. Each morning and after-noon, broiling beneath the relentless Florida sun, they ran, they blocked, they tackled, they ran and blocked and tackled some more and when night came, they plopped into bed, exhausted. When the Bear wasn't pushing them to the limit, they were bored. Their only form of amusement was standing on the beach catching

Blowfish, no real challenge because there were so many of them so close to shore.

Even arriving in Miami and then at the Orange Bowl was no big deal. After all, on Nov. 25, they had played there, beating the Miami Hurricanes 21-6.

If the Bear's intent had been to make them surly, mission accomplished.

* * * *

As he trotted out onto the field and gazed about the jam-packed stadium, Babe could not help but think back to Kentucky's first-ever bowl game two years before; back when he and Skippy Doyle, his high school teammate, had gone to Cleveland in Skippy's father's new Buick to see the first-ever—and as it turned out, last-ever—Great Lakes Bowl pitting the Kentucky Wildcats against the Villanova Wildcats. He had been a raw high school kid back then. A kid shivering in the bitter winter wind that whistled in off Lake Erie . A kid who wanted his very own football so much, and had for so long, that he had removed one from a UK sideline cart full of footballs and taken it home.

It still pained him to remember his father saying, in broken English :

"They musta liked Babe up there. They gave him a football,"

And now, here he was, on New Year's Day, in 74-degree weather, in front of nearly 65,000 fans, Kentucky's starting quarterback, about to play in the Orange Bowl.

* * * *

The Santa Clara Broncos (4-2-1) were an unknown quantity. Not so the quality of the two teams who had beaten them. On Sept. 17, Santa Clara had lost to California 21-14, and on Nov. 19, to Oklahoma, 28-21. Along with Notre Dame and Army, the Golden

Bears and Sooners were the only major college teams to finish the regular season unbeaten and untied. Oklahoma was ranked No. 2; California, No.4 behind Notre Dame.

The Broncos were not a high scoring team, having averaged only 19.2 points per game, but then they did not allow many either (10.7).

Kentucky entered the game averaging 27.6 and allowing 4.8.

But this day, the Cats scored a little less than half as many as usual and gave up far more than usual. A banner headline across the front page of *The Miami Herald* read:

Santa Clara Humbles Kentucky 21-13

The lead story writer by sports editor Jimmy Burns said:

"Tougher than the wiry, bucking ponies from which they borrowed their nickname, Santa Clara's football Broncos Monday stunned Kentucky and a record Orange Bowl of 64,816 fans.

"Flattened by a touchdown in the second quarter, the Broncos bucked and galloped through an explosive last half rally to trample the Wildcats, 21-13 in Miami's 16th annual gridiron classic.

"Cowhands will tell you that breaking a Bronco is a tough assignment. The Wildcats will contend that tackling and blocking human Broncos is even tougher.

"They couldn't rope, brand nor halt their hard running foes who will make a triumphant return to the Far West with their perfect bowl record, three victories, intact.

"With them will go the plaudits of the 64,816 fans who saw the end of the game shift like 20 mph winds which whistled through the packed stadium. There were only a few scattered drops of rain—no wetter than the tears of Kentucky supporters who saw their Wildcats upset.

"Only Kentucky's first touchdown enlivened the opening half, with the two teams feeling each other out as cautiously as boxers the initial quarter almost became boring. But there were no complaints about those last two sizzling quarters when the tempo of action was fast and furious.

"The Broncos' victory was a great advertisement for train transportation. The Santa Clara squad was only three days removed from a four-day transcontinental trip.

"Santa Clara's chief advantage was a stout-hearted , durable line which wouldn't yield to the heavier Wildcats. Another asset was the great punting of Hall Haywood, whose kicks became an offensive weapon as Santa Clara gained yardage in kicking exchanges. They profited from Abe Dung's fleet return of punts; Benny Vogel's hard smashing and John Pasco's skillful direction of the team.

"The Wildcats were not slashing and cutting. Neither were they rocking, or socking. These expressions are used by Coach Bear Bryant to describe hard blocking, and deadly tackling. He had no need for those phrases Monday. Time again the Wildcats could have turned drives into offensive infernos if the blocking had been more devastating.

"They also had the satisfaction of exploding the most thrilling single play—the 52-yard pass which netted the Wildcats' second touchdown.

"Kentucky had Bill Leskovar, a ripping, plunging fullback, as its more heroic offensive figure. It had Bob Gain and Lee Truman as its leading defenders. For some reason, the Wildcats did not have the fire of regular season play.

"The Wildcats clawed a dent in the Broncos' hide in the second quarter. Pasco fumbled and John Netoskie pounced on the ball at the Kentucky 49. The Wildcats hurried 51 yards to a touchdown in 14 plays, including two passes for 13 yards.

"Wilbur Jamerson climaxed the attack with a two-yard smash through right guard. Bobby Brooks kicked the extra point (it was his 25th conversion in 33 tries) and Kentucky was ahead 7-0. That was no more than the crowd had expected because the Wildcats were favored by six points.

"Leskovar and Babe Parilli, who completed six out of 11 passes for 128 yards, almost clicked on a perfect play near the end of the half. Leskovar turned the pass into a 45-yard gain, being knocked out of bounds at Santa Clara's three by Dung.

"Leskovar and Dopey Phelps failed in their attempts to smash over before time ran out. The ball was resting within inches of pay dirt when the intermission came. There are those who will argue that if the Wildcats had left leading by two touchdowns, instead of one, it might have been a different tale.

"It was then that fate indicated it was frowning on a team which was not playing up to its regular season form. The Wildcats were expected to come back snarling and clawing, but the Broncos started kicking the dope and the Wildcats all over the field. They were writing another happy chapter into the Santa Clara football story.

"A nine-yard punt by Phelps earlier in the third quarter could be termed the turning point. It resulted from a poor snap from center and gave the Broncos the ball at their 46. The drive sparked by a 25-yard pass from Pasco to Larry Williams rushed the Broncos to Kentucky's 12.

An exchange of fumbles then set the stage for the tying touch-down. Gene DeFilippi fumbled at the Wildcats' nine, where James Bentley recovered. Two plays later Leskovar fumbled and the alert Dung recovered. The Broncos fought to a first down at the one and on third down Pasco wormed through on a quarterback sneak. Joe Vargas kicked accurately and the score was tied 7-7.

"This should have set the Wildcats to clawing. Instead Dung returned a punt nine yards and the Broncos started kicking from Kentucky's 42. They retained the ball despite a 15-yard holding penalty.They'd reached the one-yard marker when that happened.

"Then pass interference was ruled on Pasco's throw to Williams, who failed to make the catch in the end zone. Santa Clara was given the ball at Kentucky's four and on the second try Haynes went over. Vargas kicked accurately again. Santa Clara was ahead 14-7.

"Kentucky showed old-time class in a 79-yard drive, climaxed by a 52-yard pass play from Parilli to Bobby Clark, who had eluded Bronco defenders. He was 10 yards past them and sped into scor-ing territory. Brooks missed the kick. Santa Clara still led, 14-13, but Kentucky hopes were revived.

"They were extinguished like a brush fire by a downpour as the Broncos showed new life. Their four-day train trip was supposed to have sapped their strength, and slowed their timing. They must have got their second wind because they finished stronger than their rivals.

"Dung whizzed back 35 yards with a punt, but the Broncos had to kick. They gained on the exchange, starting their next attack from Kentucky's 39. The drive was climaxed when Vogel exploded through the line for 16 yards, churning his legs like a real Bronco kicking and bucking. Vargas converted again and it was Santa Clara 21, Kentucky 13.

"It was that way at the finish, a few seconds later after a Kentucky pass interception turned another Bronco threat into a dud."

* * * *

The United Press reported that Santa Clara coach Len Casanova and the Bear had different opinions about why Santa Clara won and Kentucky didn't.

"We out conditioned them," Casanova said. "I had a hunch that I shouldn't work my team too hard in practice in this climate and it paid off."

"Downcast Coach Paul Bryant of Kentucky said the reason the Broncos rolled over its team in its initial bowl appearance was 'because they wanted to win worse than we did.'"

* * * *

In a sidebar story, the *Herald* reported:

"Bryant chain-smoked throughout the game and was up and down from his seat with the start and end of every play.

"Casanova was a cool customer on the sidelines. When things got tense, he merely sucked on an orange—California, at that."

* * * *

Babe blamed himself for the defeat.

It was his fault, he believed, that the Wildcats had not scored to go ahead 14-0 in the waning seconds of the first half with the ball only inches from the goal.

As they broke from the huddle, one of the tackles had asked:

"Do you want me to shift over to the other side?"

Meaning, create an unbalanced line to provide an extra blocker.

No, Babe had replied. He was sure Dopey Phelps would plow across.

But Phelps didn't and there was no way to stop the clock.

And when time ran out, Babe saw the Bear barreling down the field toward him.

Babe raced to the locker room.

"I wanted to give him a little time to cool off."

CHAPTER 6

Will they be even greater this year?

As the 1950 college football season approached, that was the question posed in a headline in a national magazine.

It could have been referring to Notre Dame or Oklahoma. The defending national champion Irish were riding a 37-game winning streak; the Sooners, 21 in a row.

Instead, the story was about four sophomores who, above all others, had become nationally known stars in their first season of collegiate football. One was Harry Agganis, Boston University's left-handed quarterback, billed as the greatest all-around player in college football. The second: Illinois running back Johnny Karras, described as "the Modern Red Grange." The third: Hugh McElhenny, Washington's 205-pound fullback about whom UCLA coach Red Sanders said: "He's the darndest animal you've ever seen on a football field. He runs around you, through you, and if the situation demands it, right over you."

The fourth was Babe.

* * * *

A headline above an accompanying article raised a second question:

Best Quarterback: Williams or Parilli?

Williams was Bob, who had followed in the successive and highly successful footsteps of Notre Dame stars Johnny Lujack, George Ratterman and Frank Tripucka and in 1949 had led the Irish to yet another undefeated season as well as to a national title. In doing so, Williams had completed 83 of 147 passes for 1,374 yards and 16 touchdowns. Along with two teammates, Heisman Trophy winning end Leon Hart and fullback Emil Sitko, Williams had been named to the All-American team.

As a sophomore, Babe had completed 87 of 160 passes for 1,206 yards and nine touchdowns. What comparative statistics did not show, however, were his clever, game-managing play calling, how many running touchdowns he had set up with his passing, his sleight-of-hand faking that had given defenses fits and his running backs plenty of opportunities to pick up extra yardage.

"Parilli," one football writer declared, "handles the leather with the baffling skill of a transatlantic card shark and dots a receiver's eyes, left or right, at 50 yards."

Those who favored Parilli, the article said, pointed out that if he had the supporting cast that Williams had, most notably Notre Dame's offensive line, there was no telling how great Babe would be.

Those who favored Williams, it added, countered that Parilli did not have to deal with the enormous expectations and pressure that Williams did.

"Every time Bobby walks out on the field, he's thinking of four years without a defeat and the idea of directing the game that ends the streak isn't pleasant."

* * * *

A third article, previewing the Southeastern Conference, included a poll conducted among a panel of southern sportswriters. They picked Tennessee to finish first; Kentucky, which had come within a touchdown and extra point of going undefeated in five SEC games and winning the league championship, was favored to finish second.

Not mentioned was that SEC coaches had voted Kentucky No.1.

Kentucky tackle Bob Gain was voted the SEC's best lineman and Babe its best quarterback.

* * * *

On Sept 17, the Kentucky Wildcats, ranked sixth the Associated Press pre-season poll, opened their season with a 25-0 victory over North Texas State. Fans filed out of Stoll Field satisfied, if not ecstatic.

As his players were quietly aware throughout the game, Bear Bryant was neither. In The Bear's opinion, the only one that really mattered, they had played a #$%^&* game filled with too #$%^&* mistakes. What the @#$%^&* had they been thinking? He was so @#$%^*& mad he couldn't even think of the right @#$%^&* words to express how #$%^&* angry he was.

So, after the stadium emptied, he had his players line up at the goal line and begin running dozens of 100-yard sprints. Babe tried to keep up, but the pain was so agonizing, he felt like he was going to faint.

The previous season, The Bear had been reluctant to let Babe run the ball. He was too valuable to risk injury. Besides, they had Dopey Phelps, Clark Emery, Bill Leskovar--plenty of experienced runners.

But before the 1950 season began, The Bear had hinted that he might turn Babe loose. Combined with his passing and baffling ball faking, his ability as a runner might add a whole new dimension to the Wildcats' offense.

And so, in the waning minutes against North Texas State, Babe had carried the ball. Not very often, but as in turned out, once too often.

Babe had been kicked—hard—in the groin.

When they got to the locker room, Babe, barely able to walk, limped up to his coach.

"There's something wrong with me," he told The Bear.

"Take down your pants. Let's take a look."

The Bear was horrified.

Babe's badly bruised testicles were the size of oranges.

No better after spending the night in the infirmary, he was rushed to the hospital. As soon as Dr. Ralph Angelucci and another physician arrived they proceeded to operate. Afterwards, they all went out for a hamburger.

A day or so later, The Bear walked into Babe's room in the infirmary and tossed a sheath of papers onto the bed.

"LSU. Ranked seventh in the country. Saturday night," he said. "Be ready to go."

Babe stared at The Bear.

This man is crazy, he thought to himself. I can't even *walk*.

The Bear came to visit again. This time he took Babe to his home to spend a couple of days. After The Bear came home from practice, he got out the simulated football game they had played every lunch hour during the 1949 season and continued to use.

He's really serious, Babe thought. *He really believes I'm going to be ready to play . . .*

Babe was fitted with a belted, leather-covered steel protective cup.

And, a game plan no one, most of all LSU, expected.

* * * *

Later, in an interview distributed by the Associated Press, The Bear talked about his relationship with his star quarterback.

"The biggest trouble I've ever had with Parilli was getting him to talk to me. You know, he's the shyest kid in the world.

"When I'd walk into a room, he'd walk out. But one day he got injured in practice and instead of sending him to the hospital, I took him home with me for a couple of days.

"He stayed a while and we got to know each other. He's a coach's dream."

Since then, the AP reported, "Bryant and Parilli have become inseparable. When the Babe is not in classes or practicing, he's in Bryant's office.

"But he finds time to make better than average grades, which is in itself remarkable. Bryant admits he called a few plays from the bench when Parilli was a sophomore. But as the year wore on, Parilli gained confidence and became the field general.

"Now Bryant unhesitatingly admits:

"'Babe has called better plays than I have. I just let him take over. Yes, sir, he's sure a coach's dream.'"

* * * *

Louisville Courier-Journal writer Larry Boeck reported the LSU game this way:

"LEXINGTON, Ky. Sept 24- A hard-charging Kentucky line, a super-charged fullback and a quarterback who generated skill and courage combined here tonight to completely conquer a powerful Louisiana State 14-0.

"Both the inspired bullish Kentucky offensive and defensive lines simply battered a heavier LSU wall into crumbling submission. Bill Leskovar, 195 pounds of speed and sheer force, set up both Kentucky touchdowns, one on a breathtaking 54-yard gallop. And quarterback Babe Parilli, badly injured last week, came out of the infirmary with virtually no practice to brilliantly engineer the Wildcats to victory.

"It was a most convincing performance by the whole hopped-up band of Wildcats whom Southeastern Conference coaches picked as the No. 1 team in the loop.

"The first conference decision for the Wildcats was a weird sort of thing to begin with as Kentucky abandoned the T formation and had Parilli passing off the single wing.

"This, however, only served to set the scene for the first UK touchdown in the second quarter. Leskovar set it up on his 54-yard gallop to the one foot line, from where he later scored on a buck.

"In the third quarter, Kentucky spectacularly repulsed two Tiger thrusts—one to the one-foot line. And then the Wildcats –hammering away in the line and striking with equal determination in the backfield—scored the clincher in the fourth quarter.

"But before adding this insurance touchdown on a quarterback sneak by the indomitable Parilli, they twice were thwarted by the heavy, fighting LSU wall.

"They would have scored one touchdown on a buck from the one had not Ed Hamilton, who helped set it up with two nice runs, not fumbled into the end zone."

"Just before the game yesterday, the team physician told Coach Paul Bryant that Parilli had made a satisfactory recovery from his groin injury.

"'He can play, I'm satisfied, without danger of aggravating his injury,' he said. 'The thing now is how can take it physically – how he can take the pain of moving around.'

"Parilli played the complete ball game except for two of three plays in the waning minutes.

"And guard Pat James gave the tipoff to the spirit of the Wildcats two days before the game.

"While Parilli was in the locker room after the Cats came in for a practice, one of his line mates, Bill Wannamaker, said to him: 'Babe, if you can get in there and anybody roughs you, let me know.'

"'And if Bill isn't in there, let me know,' another mate added.

"'You won't have to worry about any of that stuff,' said guard James, 'because there ain't gonna be anybody getting near you.'

"And what protection Parilli got in that first quarter.

"Since Parilli couldn't run the ball because of his injury, Bryant had early this week changed his offense—for almost the entire first quarter, Kentucky, surprisingly, operated off the single wing.

"On the first 18 plays, Parilli, unhurried and aided by his protecting mates, threw 16 passes. Only three were completed, but butter-fingered Kentucky receivers dropped four of these aerials.

"Kentucky baffled LSU with this passing assault. It was, it seemed, a stratagem to set up what was to follow.

"The Wildcats went into the T formation.

"During the second half, the Wildcats played possession football, passed only three times, and stuck to straight football."

When the game statistic were handed out, they showed that Kentucky had piled up 323 yards rushing; the Tigers, 83.

* * * *

The following week, as they prepared to play Ole Miss in Lexington, the Wildcats moved up to 5th in the AP poll.

Meanwhile, a newspaper reported that Babe had received high praise from an unlikely source:

A referee.

"There's one backfield player in America the referee has to keep a safe distance from, and he is Vito Parilli of UK," says Fred Koster, top SEC referee from Louisville.

"Parilli ducks and weaves and darts about so quickly in avoiding would-be pass blockers that he would run right over you if you were too close. I give him plenty of room."

* * * *

Since Johnny Vaught had become head football coach at Ole Miss, in 1947, his teams had been held scoreless only once: 47-0, at home, by Kentucky, in 1949.

On Sept. 30, in Lexington, it happened again.

"LEXINGTON, Ky. (AP)-- Quarterback Vito Parilli struck damaging blows to the Mississippi defense with his bulls-eye passes here tonight to lead Kentucky to a 27-0 victory in a rough and tumble Southeastern Conference football game.

"The classy junior passing ace delighted the partisan Kentucky crowd of 32,000 by passing for one touchdown and by striking vital blows in the other scoring drives.

"Kentucky tallied with a 64-yard drive immediately after the opening kickoff; added another six pointer in the first frame and scored once each in the second and third rounds.

"Ole Miss, building its offense around long-striding John Dottley, the nation's rushing champion last fall, got only to the Kentucky 25."

Another AP story said:

"Mississippi Coach Johnny Vaught rates Babe Parilli, Kentucky star, as the best quarterback in football. Vaught praised the Kentucky junior in an interview as his team headed back for Mississippi after a 27-0 loss to Kentucky. Parilli led the attack.

"'He handles that football as if it were an acorn,' Vaught said. 'He is great as a passer and he's an extra football weapon—a coach on the field in his selection of plays.'"

* * * *

The Wildcats had yet to give up a point. They didn't against Dayton either.

"LEXINGTON, Ky. Oct. 7--The Flyers of Dayton could not evade the fire of Babe Parilli here tonight," *Louisville Courier-Journal* reporter Larry Boeck wrote, "and were sent plunging into a 40-0 defeat by the Kentucky Wildcats.

"Coach Paul Bryant cleared the bench in this glorified scrimmage before 20,000 fans. Only fullback Bill Leskovar and center Doug Moseley did not play and this was only because they have been injured.

"Both teams passed freely. Kentucky, of course, got much the better out of its aerial attack with quarterback Babe Parilli and end Al Bruno again teaming up brilliantly.

"The passing perfectionist tossed four touchdown aerials, and two were to Bruno. He also scored himself with a 38-yard romp. His efforts could have been even more impressive had he not been withheld most of the second half."

* * * *

That same day, in South Bend, Ind., after opening the season with a 14-7 victory over North Carolina, Notre Dame and quarterback Bob Williams ran head on into that unpleasant experience Williams had dreaded so often for so long.

Purdue beat the Fighting Irish 28-14 to end their 37-game unbeaten streak.

* * * *

Prior to the UK-Cincinnati game on Oct. 14, a headline in a Cincinnati newspaper said:

UC 'NOT GOING DOWN TO LOSE'

When the two teams trotted off the field at halftime, there was ample reason to believe that they wouldn't. Late in the first quarter, after stalling at the Wildcat 11 yard line, the Bearcats, who had lost to Kentucky only 14-7 the year before, launched another drive, this time scoring to take a 7-0 lead.

During the first 13:10 minutes. Kentucky had had possession of the ball for only four plays. At the half, the score was tied, 7-7. Kentucky's lone score coming on a pass from Babe to end Al Bruno.

But with less than two minutes gone in the third quarter, some back in Cincinnati listening on the radio must have wondered:

If the Bearcats had not gone to Lexington to lose, what the heck had they gone there for?

First came another Parilli TD pass, again to Bruno. Forty seconds later, after Kentucky recovered a Cincinnati fumble, Babe struck again to give the Wildcats a 21-7 lead. The rout was on.

By game's end Babe had completed 18 passes in 29 attempts for 383 yards and five touchdowns and narrowly missed a sixth when the ball was spotted at the one yard line.

Kentucky won 41-7.

* * * *

Following the game, there was no shortage of praise for Parilli:

Xavier head coach Ed Kluska: "The Kentucky passing attack is wonderful. This Parilli, the way he throws the ball is wonderful. A really fine football player. Parilli took personal charge of the game, making the calls and following through with them. He is likely as not to make any good team look bad."

Detroit News sportswriter George Knebbel, a longtime observer of Big 10 football: "He's the best I've seen since Benny Friedman was pitching for Michigan (*1924-1926*). He's great. What makes him so good is he throws several different types of passes. He can toss a long one, a sharp short one or lob one into a receiver's arms. He knows how to lead his man, just right."

* * * *

PHILADELPHIA
Oct. 20, 1950

The Villanova Wildcats, eastern species, were not perceived as posing much of a threat to Kentucky. Pre-game perceptions proved to be true.

Quickly.

Kentucky rang up 20 points in the first seven minutes.

A Philadelphia newspaper reported:

"Vito "Babe" Parilli, a sharpshooting passer who can fake and twist his way out of almost any situation, led Kentucky's unbeaten football forces to a 34-7 victory over Villanova today.

"Parilli's passes, some of them completed after he seemed hopelessly trapped, were directly responsible for four of the five Kentucky touchdowns although actually only one was scored on an aerial play."

Another newspaper account said: "Parilli, passing and quarterbacking with the skill of an All-American, was the talk of virtually everyone in the huge stadium and press box with his brilliant performance spearheading all of the touchdown drives."

* * * *

ATLANTA
Oct. 28, 1950

From *The Atlanta Journal:*

"Vito (Babe) Parilli, Kentucky's T magician, lashed Georgia Tech by air and feinted them off balance with bewildering sleight-of-hand to lead the Wildcats to a 28-14 win at Grant Field Saturday that left 35,000 people wondering how any other quarterback could carry Babe's helmet.

"Parilli popped passes to his stooges as a man cracks a black-snake whip. Twelve of his 18 passes found receivers for a total of 102 yards. Parilli made the ball disappear and come to light in the arms of hard-running backs for 262 yards on the ground.

"Tech's team was smartly prepared and gave a peak performance. They forced Parilli to exploit an astonishing variety of plays before yielding the game.

"No more versatile, better armed football team has appeared in the South since the war than Kentucky was Saturday. In Parilli and Gain, they offered players of All-American caliber. Their line offered exceptional performers in Doug Moseley, Pat James, Walt Yowarsky, Bill Wannamaker and Gene Donaldson."

* * * *

The AP wrote:

"Babe Parilli, a ball-handling Houdini, scattered Georgia Tech with short, flashing passes, then ordered Kentucky's line-breaking brigade into the breach as Kentucky won today 28-14.

"What Parilli was to the offense, big Bob Gain was to the defense. On approximately three of five Tech plays, All-America candidate Gain charged far into Tech's secondary and often ended the rush with a hard, low tackle. Gain's performance was one of the great games for a tackle ever played on Tech's Grant Field."

* * * *

Jack Cook, proprietor of the little Texaco station where Babe and other members of the UK football team hung out when they weren't in class or practicing or playing football, said he had a little problem.

"What's that, Jack?" Babe asked.

"I ain't got no tickets to the game Saturday."

Meaning, against Florida.

"No problem," Babe said. "I can get you one."

"Don't need one," Jack replied. "Need four."

Babe and a teammate glanced around. Through a dirt-streaked window, they saw an old car sitting behind the station.

"Tell you what," Babe said. "We'll trade you four tickets for that ol' car back there."

Jack knew a good deal when heard one. The car was a bucket of junk.

"Okay, deal," he said

The next day, Babe and his teammate delivered the tickets. Jack handed them the key to the car.

The old car sputtered and groaned, and finally started. When they started down Limestone, the smoke was so thick Babe couldn't see his teammate sitting in the passenger's seat.

The Monday after the game, they took the car back.

"We've changed our minds," Babe said. "That car is too far gone."

Jack Cook rubbed his chin as he stared at the floor.

"Well. . ." he said. "Okay."

Then he gave them back the four tickets.

"I forgot to go to the game," he said.

They decided to keep the car and let Jack keep the tickets.

* * * *

The Gators no doubt wished they had forgotten to go to the game too.

First, there was the weather, so cold they insulated themselves with long underwear.

Then there was the rain and snow. An hour before the game, groundskeepers scorched the field by burning 1,000 gallons of gasoline to dry it off. Had the rain and snow stopped then, the footing would have been a lot better. They didn't. By opening kick-off, the field had become a black, slippery quagmire.

And then, for the shivering, mud-covered Gators, things got even worse.

By halftime, their hopes of winning were as empty as half the stadium. With Kentucky leading 26-6, many of the 38,000 fans attending Homecoming headed for the exits. But not before witnessing one of the season's most memorable, not to mention bizarre, plays.

In the second quarter, UK fullback Bill Leskovar, mud in his eyes, ran the wrong way.

"Parilli," The *Herald-Leader* reported, "fortunately tackled him before he had a chance to contribute what might have been Florida's longest gain of the day."

It would have been. Florida finished with minus-eight yards rushing.

"After three plays netted a loss of 35 yards," the *Herald-Leader said*, "one Florida fan yelled, 'Hey, we're going this' a way!'"

Kentucky gained 340 yards on the ground.

Babe, who entered the game with 13 touchdown passes, threw two more to put him within three of tying the all-time SEC record set by Mississippi's Charley Conerly. He did not play beyond the middle of the third quarter.

* * * *

On Nov. 11, Babe threw his 16th, 17th and 18th touchdown passes to tie Chuck Conerly's all-time, single season record as the Cats swamped Mississippi State 48-21.

The United Press report began this way:

"STARKVILLE, Miss. (UP)—Babe Parilli threw three touchdown passes and palmed the ball like a riverboat gambler today to lead Kentucky to a resounding 48-21 victory over Mississippi State before 28,000 fans.

"Kentucky rolled on unbeaten and untied in its greatest season of the century over a team that until today was rated the best offensively in the nation despite a mediocre won-lost record."

The Associated Press account noted:

"Parilli's rifle passes held the balance of power as the Wildcat quarterback tossed three times for touchdowns. In addition, the Rochester, Pa. youth set up two other scoring plays.

"The victory moved Kentucky closer to a possible Sugar Bowl invitation on New Year's Day. Only North Dakota State and Tennessee stand astride their path to a perfect season."

Bob Steber, covering the game for *The Nashville Tennessean*:

"Deftly, like a great artist, Vito (Babe) Parilli tinted a brilliant touchdown scene before 28,000 disappointed Mississippi State fans here yesterday afternoon, sending his Kentucky Wildcats catapulting to a 48 to 21 Southern Conference victory.

"Kentucky looked like the top team in the nation, let alone the SEC yesterday, as it smashed for four second-quarter touchdowns in just a little more than three minutes and coasted to a brilliant victory over the game battlers of Coach Arthur (Slick) Morton.

"Parilli was an All-American yesterday, just as he has been all season—but a little more so.

"Headed by burly Bob Gain, who turned in another All-American performance, the Kentucky line limited State to 31 yards aground, meanwhile grinding out 159."

* * * *

Louisville Courier-Journal reporter Larry Boeck recounted this anecdote.

At halftime, Zip Newman, sports editor of *The Birmingham News*, spotted UK Athletic Director Bernie Shively in the press box.

"Bernie," Newman asked. "Do you really think Parilli is a great quarterback?"

"Why, I certainly do," Shively replied.

"How do you know?" Newman asked.

"Well, I just know. It's hard to explain, but, well, I know he is."

"It gets me how you can even know he's good, let alone great," Newman said, "when you can't even see what he is doing."

To which another sportswriter cracked:

"Over 28,000 people in this stadium watching the game and nobody knows where the ball is but Parilli."

* * * *

Nobody, including Bear Bryant, knew much about North Dakota State, the Wildcats' next opponent. The Bear told Babe that the reason the Bisons were on the UK schedule was because, like Tennessee, they ran a single-wing offense and therefore would provide the Wildcat defense game with experience playing against it the week before Kentucky met the Volunteers in Knoxville.

By the end of the first quarter, however, everyone in the stadium, including The Bear, knew more than they needed to know about NDSU. Kentucky led 21-0, scored 35 in the second quarter and buried the Bisons 83-0.

Before leaving the game midway through the second quarter, Babe had passed for five touchdowns, giving him 23 for the season and a setting a new all-time collegiate record previously held by Stan Heath of Nevada who had thrown 22 in 1948. He also had increased his total passing yardage to 1,477 yards, eclipsing the record Frank Sinkwich of Georgia had set in 1942 with 1,392 yards.

And, that same day, because Alabama had beaten Georgia Tech, the Wildcats cinched the SEC title.

So now it all came down to one game.

Tennessee.

In Knoxville.

* * * *

"KNOXVILLE, Tenn., Nov. 20 (AP) – One of college football's foremost questions will be answered here Saturday when Kentucky tangles with Tennessee.

"The puzzle is: Can Kentucky's Vito (Babe) Parilli , one of the nation's best passers, connect against Tennessee, the country's top team on pass defense.

"The question is a $100,000 one, for the winner is a virtual certainty to receive a bid to the New Year's Day Sugar Bowl game at New Orleans

"Parilli has smashed passing records with reckless abandon this year. In directing the Wildcats to 10 consecutive triumphs, he has netted 1,477 yards on 100 completions for 23 touchdowns.

"The 23 touchdowns shattered the previous collegiate mark of 22 set by Nevada's Stan Heath of Nevada in 1948. And the 1,477 yards eclipsed the Southeastern Conference record of 1,392 established by Frank Sinkwich, Georgia's great All-American star, in 1942.

"To cope with Parilli's sensational passing, Tennessee has a pass defense which has permitted nine opponents to average only 55 yards per game.

"The Vols led the nation in pass defense a week ago with an average yield of 61 yards a game. They bettered the figure last Saturday against Mississippi, which they limited to 10 yards on three completions.

"'We're scared to death of Parilli's passes,' Gen. Bob Neyland said today.'We regard him as the best passer in the country.'

"Neyland conceded Tennessee's pass defense record is 'pretty good,' but he added that there is 'nothing unusual about our defensive tactics.'

"'Defending against passes is mostly just luck,' Neyland went on. 'We probably spend more time in practice on pass defense than most teams. That may account for our success.'

"Despite Neyland's claim that pass defense is 'just luck,' the fact remains that Tennessee always comes up with one of the tightest screens against aerials in the country.

"First requisite in Tennessee's defensive pattern is to rush the passer. Ted Daffer, All-America guard candidate, and tackle Bill Pearman are two of the best in the business at this. They made life miserable for Duke's Billy Cox, Alabama's Butch Avinger, North Carolina's Dick Bunting and Mississippi's Rocky Byrd—all better-than-average pitchers.

"Secondly, Tennessee defensive backs are trained mentally to guard against passes. They are trained to think along this line:'That guy can't complete one against me. Just let him throw it out here and I'll show him.'

"Bud Sherrill, defensive left halfback, is a case in point. Last year, Sherrill set a new collegiate record by intercepting 12 passes in 10 games. That was enough to put opposing coaches on guard and this year only two have been thrown into his territory all season.

"Sherrill intercepted three Parilli passes in last year's game, the first one setting up the touchdown which gave the Vols a 6-0 victory."

However, in another pre-game story, the *Courier-Journal's* Larry Boeck noted:

"Tennessee's aerial defenders are faced with the challenge of slowing down the passer who has accomplished this in 10 games:

"Passes thrown—173.

"Completions—100.

"Percentage—57.6 per cent of passes completed. Here Parilli is traveling at a record-breaking clip once again; the record for highest percentage of passes completed in a minimum of 150 attempts is 57.1, owned by Charlie Connerly of Ole Miss.

"Interceptions—Eight.

"Yards—1,477. This averages 147.7 per game compared to Tennessee's holding its opposition to 55.3 yards per tilt.

"Touchdowns –23.

"Parilli, of course, has compiled this record with the aid of excellent receivers ends Al Bruno, Ben Zaranka and Dom Fucci and backs Shorty Jamerson and Clayton Webb."

* * * *

Among those present that day was Charles C. Zatarain, president of the Sugar Bowl. Zatarain had traveled to Knoxville specifically to get a first-hand look at the second-ranked Wildcats—and, if they won, invite them to the Sugar Bowl.

What he saw first was weather not likely to bring out the best in either team. The temperature was eight degrees. Four inches of snow blanketed the ground. The field was slippery. Many of the grandstand bleachers were glazed with ice and some rows clogged with head-high snowdrifts.

"It was so bad," Zatarain recalled, "that at the half, I could see the special train just getting fans in. They marched downhill like a troop. It was a miserable day."

But when wire service reports of the game were transmitted nationwide, they contained little or no details of how bitterly cold and how utterly bad playing conditions had been.

The United Press covered the game this way:

"KNOXVILLE, Tenn. Nov. 25 (UP)—Tennessee's bonechilling Volunteers put a polar bear hug on Babe Parilli today and knocked

Kentucky from its unbeaten perch, 7-0, with one perfect pass in the second period.

"Only a valiant stand on its one-yard line in the fourth period saved Kentucky from a worse upset as Gen. Bob Neyland's Vols proved to the loud satisfaction of 45,000 fans their right to the Cotton Bowl invitation they already had accepted.

"The defeat spoiled what would have been Kentucky's first perfect season of the century. The Wildcats had hoped to beat Tennessee and go on to the Sugar Bowl and may still go despite the setback. They had previously clinched the Southeastern Conference title.

"For the graying Neyland it was a soul-satisfying revenge for three ties plastered against his Vol teams by Kentucky in the 1930 era when Tennessee otherwise had perfect records. Kentucky has never beaten Neyland teams.

"The alert Vols who concentrated on jarring the ball loose from Kentucky carriers and then pouncing on it, turned a fumble into their lone score near the end of the first half.

"They recovered a bobbled punt on the Kentucky 34 and Hank Lauricella piloted his team to the 18-yard line. Thrown back to the 27 by a mad Kentucky defense, Lauricella caught wingback Bert Rechlchar at the corner of the field with a fourth-down touchdown pass. Given a second try a Kentucky offside, Pat Shires kicked the seventh point.

"Parilli, holder of a new national record for touchdown passes thrown, ran into a series of frustrations in the first half when four completions were called back, three of them because an ineligible receiver took the ball.

"Then, in the second half, when the thawed-out Babe began finding his mark, Tennessee forwards led by guard Ted Daffer, seeped through to throw him for huge losses which nullified his gains. Kentucky penetrated beyond midfield only once in the first half.

"Thrice, the angry Kentuckians pounded within the Tennessee 30 in the second half as the game turned into a wild battle of fumbles and recoveries. But Tennessee always came up with a vital recovery or interception.

"Tennessee almost scored again in the dwindling minutes after Jimmy Hall intercepted a Parilli pass on the Kentucky 40 and ran it to the 18. An offside put the wilting Wildcats on the 12 and Lauricella plunged to the eight.

"Hal Payne went to the one, but in two massive pileups Kentucky took over and worked out of danger.

"The crunching Vol line, led by Daffer, sophomore Doug Atkins and tackle Pug Pearman, charged for Parilli on every play and the percentage paid off as he was Kentucky's only hope."

* * * *

Babe, the Associated Press reported, completed 14 of 31 passes for 150 yards. Despite the finger-numbing cold, woefully inadequate pass protection throughout the game and four more completions called back because of penalties, he had compiled nearly three times as much passing yardage as the Vols defense had allowed on average per game (53.6) all season.

* * * *

When The Bear walked into the dressing room, he found his dejected players sitting stoically on benches and on the floor staring into space. They had suffered a devastating defeat and nothing could change that, not even the news he was about to deliver.

"I think we have a chance to play in a bowl game," he said.

It was an announcement that triggered no cheers; lifted no spirits. Silence hung in the air like sweaty, frozen, grass-stained jerseys draped over a blackboard.

"I'll let you think about it," he said as he headed out the door.

The Bear met with Zatarain, UK Athletic Director Bernie Shivley and SEC commissioner Bernie Moore.

"We had a line open to the Sugar Bowl office," Zatarain was quoted as saying later. "I told them Kentucky was a great team and that as far as my vote was concerned, I still wanted them. The committee talked it over, then came back to tell me to ask Bryant if he'd play if he got the invite.

"Bear reached out, took the phone and said, 'If you invite me, I'll beat Oklahoma!'"

* * * *

When he returned to the locker room a little while later, he told his team they had been invited to play in the Sugar Bowl.

If they wanted to go.

They didn't, they said.

Then he was told why.

Memories of their trip to the Orange Bowl the year before were still too fresh; too raw. It wasn't the losing to Santa Clara. It was *why* they thought they had lost. They had practiced too intensely too long. He had driven them so hard, Shorty Jamerson, one of the team captains, had passed out. When game day arrived, they had nothing left, physically or emotionally. No, they did not want to suffer through another ordeal like that again.

There would be no repeat of that Cocoa Beach boot camp, he assured them.

The Bear left again.

Later, co-captains Bob Gain and Shorty Jamerson appeared at his door.

"We'll go if we can play the best team in the country," Gain said.

The Bear grinned.

"We're playing Oklahoma."

And so, they went and they played in one of the greatest, if not the greatest, games in Kentucky football history.

CHAPTER 7

Why Kentucky in the Sugar Bowl? Why not No. 2 Texas? No. 3 Tennessee? No. 4 California? No. 5 Army? No. 6 Michigan?

Why No. 7 Kentucky?

Simple, at least to those who paid close attention to such matters. Second-ranked Texas and No. 3 Tennessee had already accepted bids to face each other in the Cotton Bowl. California, No. 4, for the third straight year, was headed to the Rose Bowl. No, 5 Army, like Notre Dame, never participated in bowl games; and No. 6 Michigan also was headed for the Rose Bowl.

Even knowing all of that, some still strongly opposed the idea of Kentucky playing in the Sugar Bowl. The overriding question wasn't so much whether the Wildcats could score on Oklahoma's so-so defense, but whether the UK defense could stop the Sooners' offense.

Even occasionally.

Only Texas had limited the Sooners to 14 points and Iowa State (20-7) to 20. Otherwise they had run hog wild. beating Boston College (28-0); Texas A.&M., (34-28); Kansas State ,(58-0); Colorado (34-28) ; Kansas (33-13); Missouri (41-7); Nebraska (49-35); and Oklahoma State (41-14).

All of which translated into a hefty 345-135 scoring edge over 10 opponents for an average of 34.5 point per game to 13.5 for the opposition.

It was not an encouraging prospect.

* * * *

When the Wildcats boarded a plane in Lexington, the temperature was 15 degrees.

When they arrived in Baton Rouge, on Dec. 26, the temperature was a balmy 72.The Bear also encountered some not-so-hot information he could have done without.

"'Five teams have trained here for the Sugar Bowl and they all lost,'" a reporter said. "'What do you think of that, Coach?'"

"'A football game is won or lost on the field,'" he said seriously. He looked up and added with a broad smile:

"'This is a helluva time to be telling me. I'd like to have known that before we came.'"

* * * *

Two days before the game, *Louisville Times* reporter Marvin N. Gay, Jr. offered this assessment of the two teams:

"Psychologically, the advantage is all with the Wildcats in the Sugar Bowl football game coming up Monday afternoon.

"Unbeaten Oklahoma, the No. 1 team in the nation, has no new worlds to conquer.

"The pressure is on the Sooners, as never before—and they showed in their workouts in Biloxi, Miss. They were tense and wishing it was all over.

"Coaches Bud Wilkinson of the national champs, winners of 31 games in a row, and Paul Bryant of the Southeastern Conference kingpins, have pronounced their teams as fit as they ever will be, and both are anxiously awaiting the kickoff before an expected 82,000 fans.

"In response to a query as to whether he foresaw a high-scoring game, Wilkinson said, 'It depends on what you mean by that. I think Kentucky will do some scoring, definitely. Our defense hasn't been too good. I doubt out ability to move the ball against Kentucky, I really do.'

"Bryant was plainly worried about his offense. He said, 'Heaven only knows whether we can score on anybody. Our offense at Baton Rouge (training camp) has been far behind what I had hoped.'

"After watching Kentucky in nine games and seeing the Oklahoma boys in several workouts, including one long scrimmage, these are the general impressions.

"The game shapes up as Oklahoma's running attack versus Kentucky's aerial bombardment. The Sooners have faster backs, quicker backs, by that, boys who get off faster. Nobody can quite match Babe Parilli throwing the ball, but it would be a mistake for UK to underestimate Oklahoma's Claude Arnold, who is no slouch himself.

"Oklahoma will do more running than Kentucky, has all season. Kentucky has passed on approximately two of every five offensive plays, averaging 20.9 passes to 45.4 rushes a game, and may up the figure considerably New Year's Day. The Sooners originated 56.2 rushes to only 14.9 passes a game.

"It's doubtful that the Oklahomans, using a split-T offense, have been up against as rugged a line as Kentucky's, and the Wildcats get the nod here though the Sooners have two they're proud of in Jim Weatherall, tackle, and tumultuous end Frank Anderson, end. Anderson made the Associated Press defensive All-America team, and Weatherall was everybody's choice.

"The Sooner linemen don't look as large as the Kentuckians, but have more speed. They would seem to have rugged assignments in trying to move tackles Bob Gain, All-America; Jim McKenzie' guards Pat James, John Ignarski and Bill Wannamaker.

"Used to playing against larger boys, the Sooners have become adept at working the trap, letting the opposing linemen charge through and then knocking them into the end zone seats. Whether than can do this against Kentucky's 'old pros' who've been at Lexington almost as long as Bryant is exceedingly doubtful.

"The Wildcats can't come close to matching the speed of the champs' halfbacks, Billy Vessels and Tom Gray, 10-second men who are likely to go all the way any time, if given even half a chance.

"In the Oklahoma camp, there's a strong undercurrent that Vessels will get the Sugar Bowl's star of stars award. He is a big boy, not just fast, can either cut or run over you. He makes some mistakes, being an 18-year-old sophomore. But he's so fast that often as not he can rectify a mistake whereas a slower man would be out of luck.

"Vessels is a versatile kid. He scored both Oklahoma TD's against Texas, spurted 50 yards for one against Kansas. Kentucky's main reliance in the halfback department is Shorty Jamerson, a plucky, never-say die senior who simply lacks the physical equipment that Vessels possesses.

"You've gotta give Oklahoma the best of it at fullback, too, with Leon Heath, the All-American, in there. But Bryant has a hunch the pull may not be too great, says Bill Leskovar, his 195-pounder, is playing like 'the flat-top of old.' Bill did fine work until injured in the Mississippi game, then was on the shelf much of the time thereafter, and was in only one play during the loss to Tennessee. If he comes through, it would make a tremendous difference to Kentucky's overall attack.

"In all probability, Oklahoma's strategy will be to try and sweep the Kentucky ends, and snub that tough middle of the line.

"When you get to the final analysis, of course, everything hinges on what kind of day Parilli has in the pitching department. It he's connecting, he'll give his season's total of 23 touchdown passes another boost and Oklahoma may suffer the fate of Notre Dame and Army, other erstwhile possessors of the No. 1 rating.

"Otherwise, you can write down a third-in-a-row victory for Oklahoma in the Sugar Bowl."

* * * *

Lexington Herald sports editor Ed Ashford offered a somewhat less glowing, who's-afraid-of *–them* appraisal of the Sooners:

"University of Kentucky fans know that 1950 brought them a fine football team, although no powerhouse and no great team, and those who've studied the thing enough are well convinced that the Wildcats are by no means outclassed by the undefeated Oklahoma outfit they meet here Monday in the Sugar Bowl.

"The current Sooners, although they won all 10 games and piled up a lot of points, are without much doubt somewhat less than the mighty Oklahoma aggregation of 1949. Comparisons of results during the two campaigns makes that quite evident.

"This observer, plumping for both Tennessee and Kentucky to win their bowl engagements, has the feeling that the Sooners likely were overrated when polls slotted them as best in the land this year.

"They compiled a pretty record, yes, but they didn't go around slaying intersectional giants, they didn't win too convincingly over foes of actual top rank, and they didn't actually outdo Kentucky by much, if any, in the matter of scheduling although the Wildcats were faulted freely because of a slate none too robust. The Sooners weren't pitted against any Eskimo teams or any foolishly optimistically ambitious out of North Dakota , but they did face such weak sisters as Kansas State and Boston College and they had other foes which at best were hardly more than mediocre or ordinary.

"The Sooners of '49 had about their toughest game when they were held to a 28-21margin by the same Santa Clara team which toppled Kentucky by one touchdown in the Orange Bowl. The Wildcats of last season had their points but lacked the explosiveness of the current edition, while the Oklahoma of this year generally had much more trouble beating the same opponents that were polished off rather handily by the rampaging '49 aggregation."

* * * *

While neither Gay nor Ashford ventured a prediction as to which would emerge the winner, numerous others did. The day before the game, a newspaper reported:

"The swing is to Kentucky as time for the Sugar Bowl classic draws near. Oklahoma's Sooners are 6 1/6 point favorites with the lads who make their living putting their cash on the line, but among sports writers, coaches and plain, ordinary football fans here, the idea that Kentucky has a big chance to end the Sooners' long streak of grid victories seems to be gathering force.

"One of the latest men of distinction to switch to the Wildcats is Hap Glandi, the personable sports editor of *The New Orleans Item*. Glandi, who succeeded Fred Digby when the latter took over full-time duties with the New Orleans Mid-Winter Sports Association, sponsor of the Sugar Bowl, had been an Oklahoma man all season—up until now. Now he's stringing along with Kentucky, and here's how he explains in his column, "*Looking 'em Over*":

"'Kentucky Babe, the football player, not the lullaby, will be No. 1 in the Sugar Bowl's Hit Parade Jan. 1. I'm selecting Bear Bryant's Kentucky team to defeat the National Champion Oklahoma Sooners and I believe the Babe, Vito Parilli, is the fellow they'll be toasting in song on Monday at dusk.

"'I'm moving in with the Bear and the Babe because I am of the opinion that the Southeastern Conference champion has more depth, is sturdier on defense and possesses a better-balanced team.

"'Oklahoma, I believe, is sharper on offense. Its attack is powered by Leon Heath, the All-American fullback and hero of last year's game; the sensational sophomore, Billy Vessels, and the quarter, Claude Arnold. But Kentucky, blessed with the magic of Parilli's ball handling and sharp passing and the power running of Bill Leskovar , is not too far removed in this respect.'

"Charles Brennan of *The New Orleans States* took a poll of several writers, ex-players and coaches and got the following answers:

"Happy Chandler (baseball's high commissioner) – 'I just can't be rational in my outlook on this game. Being a former governor of Kentucky and graduate of the university, I want Kentucky to win. Oklahoma has a fine team, but I don't think they've met as rugged a defensive team as the Wildcats.'

"Bernie Moore (Southeastern Conference Commissioner)—'I don't want to put Bear Bryant on the spot, but I think Kentucky will win. At least I hope they will. I also think Tennessee should beat Texas in the Cotton Bowl.'

"Lester Lautenschlaeger (former Tulane coach and quarterback)—'I'll say Kentucky. They'll have psychology on their side. The other team has been here before and may not be worked up as much as it. Kentucky, too, is still smarting from that defeat from Tennessee and should want to redeem themselves.'

"Bob Broeg (*St. Louis Post Dispatch*) --'Oklahoma. I'm from Missouri and they've shown me quite often. Seriously, I believe their all-around class and poise tell the story.'

"Ed Danforth (*Atlanta Journal*) – 'Kentucky will win a close game on their defensive superiority, their ability to hold Oklahoma's scoring down, while scoring on their own hook.'

"Monk Simons (former Tulane coach and All-America)— Oklahoma by a touchdown or two. Oklahoma's overall offensive strength and team poise should be the difference.'

"Sterling Slappey (Associated Press)-- 'Kentucky. I'm basing that on Babe Parilli's ability to get those cheap touchdowns.'

"George Leonard (*Nashville Banner*) 'I think Oklahoma will win with their offensive game and running attack the deciding factor.'

"Jim McCafferty (Loyola assistant coach)—'I'm an Oklahoman, you know, and I'll stay with the Sooners. They have the most bowl experience, both the coach and the players.'

"Wilfred Smith (*Chicago Tribune*)—'I haven't seen either team, Oklahoma seems to have lots of enthusiasm and Kentucky Parilli. Take your choice. I believe the game will be good as the other fine Sugar Bowl games I have seen.'

"Bob Busby (*Kansas City Star*)—'The Sooners remind me of the old pros. They have that know-how and the poise to come from behind.'

"Ike Carriere (former coach and LSU quarterback) -- 'Kentucky. On a dry field, I believe Kentucky's passing attack and better defense will offset Oklahoma's running game.'

"Tom Haggerty (Loyola basketball coach) –'Oklahoma's all-around offensive strength should whip Kentucky.'

"Barney Ghio *(Shreveport Times)* -- 'Oklahoma, probably by about two touchdowns. The Sooners seem to have an edge in offensive power.'

"Bud Montet (*Baton Rouge Advocate*) – 'Kentucky. The game will be a case of too much Parilli.'

"Tom Siler (*Knoxville News-Sentinel*) –'Kentucky will win and the difference will be Parilli.'

* * * *

"NEW ORLEANS, Jan. 1 (AP)—Oklahoma, the Goliath of college football and holder of the greatest victory streak in modern times, fell today in the Sugar Bowl before Kentucky, 13-7, on the jet-like passes of Babe Parilli and the vicious line pay of Walt Yowarsky.

"The defeat before 82,000 was Oklahoma's first since the opening game of the 1948 season – 32 games ago. Two of those victories were in the preceding Sugar Bowl games.

"The mighty Sooners, ranked first in the nation in the Associated Press poll, started toward their downfall this chilly, windy day in the first quarter. Yowarsky recovered a fumble by Oklahoma quarterback Claude Arnold on the Oklahoma 25 and on the next play, Parilli passed to Wilbur (Shorty) Jamerson for a touchdown.

"Four other Oklahoma fumbles kept the national champions in trouble and not until late in the fourth quarter could the Sooners zip downfield as they have done so successfully for three seasons.

"Kentucky, however, would not let them. Oklahoma managed one touchdown very late and might have challenged again but the Southeastern Conference champions from the Blue Grass stood stalwart in the final minutes protecting their lead.

"An Oklahoma runner bobbled the ball after a Kentucky punt and Yowarsky covered it for Kentucky. That cut the life out of Oklahoma and gave even greater spirit and dash to Kentucky.

"Parilli, a second-string All-American, passed far less than usual. Apparently, Kentucky was satisfied to play it safe with a 13-0 lead.

However, when Parilli passed, he usually connected. The long pass from Parilli to Al Bruno set up the Wildcats' second touchdown.

"The first half was a clear story of Oklahoma's superior running versus Kentucky's outstanding passing and the passing was by far the more productive.

"On the sixth play of the game, Oklahoma quarterback Arnold fumbled on his 23 and Yowarsky recovered for Kentucky. The ball dumping was expensive.

"On the next play, Parilli, "the Kentucky Babe," was rushed badly on a pass pattern. He jumped to throw on Oklahoma's 23, but couldn't find a catcher. He squirmed around among Oklahoma tacklers until he spotted Jamerson deep in Oklahoma's end zone. Then the Babe jumped again and fired the ball in a hard, horizontal throw. Jamerson was well guarded, but the throw was accurate and Jamerson came down with the ball for a touchdown.

"Kentucky's All-America tackle Bob Gain, another line star, made the conversion and Kentucky had a 7-0 lead after two minutes and 50 seconds. For the next 15 minutes, the game was fruitless of touchdowns.

"Kentucky end Ben Zaranka dropped a pass from Parilli in the end zone to cut away another Kentucky touchdown. Just a few minutes later, however, Kentucky made up for Zaranka's flub.

"The Wildcats got the ball on their 19 and 81 yards down the field they went in seven quick plays. Their second touchdown was set up primarily on another brilliant Parilli pass. The Babe threw down the middle of the field to Bruno who was finally knocked down by Jack Lockett on Oklahoma' one-foot line. Jamerson banged across for his second scoring honor. Gain's kick was no good and Kentucky had 13 points.

"Oklahoma had several good chances to score in the second half, but Kentucky was too much except on one of the thrusts.

"The Sooners, usually a five or six touchdown production outfit, finally managed to get going in the fourth quarter. Gain tried a field goal for Kentucky and missed. Oklahoma took over and blasted 80 yards, mostly on the fine running of Billy Vessels and

Heath. Twice, Heath made first downs on fourth down power smashes.

"Arnold, with nothing like the passing and ball handling wizardry of Parilli, threw a looping pass to Merrill Green for the touchdown. The play covered 17 yards. All-America tackle Jim Weatherall kicked the point.

"Kentucky stood off an Oklahoma thrust in the third quarter which reached the two and a half yard line. Here again, Yowarsky was in the right place at the right time. He tackled Vessels for a vital five-yard loss and on the next play, Arnold threw poorly to All-America Frank Anderson, end, who couldn't get to the ball."

* * * *

Statistics accompanying the AP story published nationwide showed that Oklahoma had more first downs (18) than Kentucky (7) and, as expected, gained more net rushing yards (189 to 84) The Sooners had completed three of eight passes for 38 yards, giving them a combined offensive net total of 227 yards compared to Kentucky's 189. Babe had completed nine of 12 for 105 yards, threw for one touchdown and set up the other.

What the two columns of comparative figures did not show, however, was what did *not* happen—and why.

Beginning with defensive strategy.

The Bear had inserted his four biggest and best tackles into the defensive line, among them, Yowarsky.

The move had had multiple purposes: 1) To pressure OU quarterback Claude Arnold into giving up the ball quicker than he wanted to and in the process, perhaps make mistakes; 2) keep Leon Heath, the Sooners' All-American fullback from exploding up the middle for long gains. 3) Unless Heath was stopped, the UK defense would be forced to congregate in the center and leave its perimeters even more vulnerable than they already were to Oklahoma's superior breakaway speed, especially that of halfback Billy Vessels.

The Bear also devised a variety of constantly changing defensive formations, varying from what sometimes amounted to a nine-man line to oddball shifts into a 6-2-2-1 alignment, or perhaps a 4-4-2-1.

It was all very confusing.

And effective.

Oklahoma fumbled five times and lost all five.

Nor did statistics reveal how the Bear had instructed his line to block when UK was forced to punt.

Don't.

Scramble on downfield to blanket-cover the kick returner, he told them. Stop him from getting started.

Yes, it was risky, leaving Dom Fucci, UK's outstanding punter, back there unprotected with a horde of Sooners barreling down on him, but a blocked kick was less of a risk than Vessels settling under a long, spiraling kick and cutting and weaving, dodging and darting and suddenly bursting free, untouched, for a touchdown.

It worked.

Oklahoma received eight punts and averaged less than half a yard per return.

Meanwhile, The Bear utilized Fucci's booming punts to control field position. Fucci averaged 41.7 yards per kick: Oklahoma, 33.4 on six. Which meant that no matter whether Kentucky could move the ball or had to punt, or Oklahoma couldn't either, the Wildcats gained 8.3 yards on every punt exchange.

Offensively, going into the second half with Kentucky leading 13-0, the Bear ordered Babe to concentrate on managing the clock.

"Babe," he said at halftime, "don't throw the ball. We'll get 'em with defense."

It was a strategy Babe found unsettling. Like everyone else, he was well aware of how quickly, how often, how explosive the Sooner offense could be. A 13-0 lead could evaporate in a flash.

And so, in the second half, as the Sooners continued to do what they were expected to do—run the ball—the Wildcats did not do what they were expected to do: pass. After completing seven of nine in the first half, including UK's first touchdown and setting up the second, Babe passed only three times, completing two.

Oklahoma rushed 59 times; the Wildcats, 40. So what if they gained only 84 yards? Each time a UK ball carrier disappeared into a tangled pile of bodies, they ate up as much time as the clock would allow—and a couple of times, more than it allowed. Twice, they were penalized for delay of game.

No matter. If they failed to make a first down, Fucci merely rocketed another long, spiraling, well covered punt that produced yet another half-yard-or-so return.

Meanwhile, if the Wildcats had to worry about the Sooners breaking loose at any moment, the Sooners had to fret about Babe and his sleight-of-hand faking and disappearing-act handoffs and all the while, fading back, one hand hidden behind his back, like he still had the ball and was about to pass. The more Kentucky continued to run the ball, the more likely it seemed that on the very next play, Babe would throw a bomb and put the game out of reach for good.

It became a war of nerves.

On defense, clog up the middle like the aisle of an overcrowded bus. On offense, pound the ball gradually, methodically, relentlessly down the field like a jackhammer chewing up concrete. All the while, protecting the lead and winding down the clock.

Woody Hayes, ol' Mr. Three Yards and A Cloud of Dust, would have been proud.

CHAPTER 8

In 1946, when Bear Bryant became head football coach at Kentucky, he had cautioned officials and fans not to expect any miracles anytime soon. Building the kind of team they wanted, he said, would take five years.

Five seasons later, UK had finished 10-1, won the Southeastern Conference championship, and snapped undefeated National Champion Oklahoma's 31-game winning streak.

Now what?

All indications pointed toward a rebuilding year.

In a *Courier-Journal* magazine article published prior to the Sugar Bowl, Larry Boeck had assessed the Wildcats' prospects for the 1951 season.

"The drain on experienced manpower for the last seasons has been substantial. After the Orange Bowl contest in 1950, the Wildcats lost a number of men, but they had on hand sufficient sophomores and juniors to fill the gap. Even so, the losses suffered by that Orange Bowl outfit don't compare to the mass exodus slated after the Sugar Bowl.

"For instance, of the first 22 men on this season's squad, which won 10 and lost one game, only eight will remain next season.

"The big loss is in the line. The backfield, with some talented performers expected from the freshman team, is expected to be as strong offensively as it was this season. The defensive backfield, however, will be hurt by the graduation of such stars as Dick Martin, a vicious tackler, a keen pass defender and a player with the ability to dope out an opponent's offense well. Gone, too, will be the all-around whiz and safety man--Dom Fucci. The team also loses linebackers Harold Woddell, one of the most underrated players in the game today, and Bill Schaffnit."

The biggest loss of all: All-American tackle Bob Gain.

* * * *

Considering what happened in their season opener on Sept. 15, it would have been easy to disregard all the talk about 1951 being a rebuilding year.

The Cats pulverized Tennessee Tech 72-13, amassing a team record 31 first downs, 636 net yards passing and running, and recovering eight fumbles.

By halftime, UK led 39-0. Babe had completed 11 of 16 passes for 175 yards and two touchdowns. He did not play in the second half.

Despite the abundance of exciting offensive fireworks—10 different Wildcats scored a touchdown--*Courier-Journal* reporter Larry Boeck offered a few sobering conclusions about UK's performance, including that 1) blocking had to get better; 2) the Cats were more than a week away from being ready to play a team the caliber of Texas; 3) the defense lacked sufficient depth; 4) extra-point kicking was especially poor—the Cats missed five of 11; and 5) punting could be a problem unless Babe took over that job too, although it was difficult to tell because UK kicked only twice.

* * * *

AUSTIN, TEX.
Sept. 22, 1951

The Associated Press called it The Game of the Week.
Kentucky at Texas, before an expected record crowd of 50,000.

Kentucky, attempting to deal the Longhorns their first season-opening home loss since 1893.

Kentucky, the team that had ended defending National Champion Oklahoma's 31-game winning streak; Texas, the team that the previous October had nearly broken the string before losing to the Sooners, 14-13.

Kentucky, because of Babe, conceded a big edge through the air; Texas, stronger on the ground.

The *Austin Statesman* reported:

"The Wildcats were slight favorites at game time with the cooler weather wiping out the Steers' usual September advantage of being more accustomed to the usual heat than visitors from the South and East."

* * * *

Given what he was to encounter this day, Babe might have been better off practicing running backward rather than passing forward. Pass protection fluctuated between inadequate and non-existent.

Larry Shropshire of the *Herald-Leader* recounted the game this way:

"AUSTIN, Tex. Sept 22—The rebuilt grid machines of two powers of the 1950 collegiate football season staged a titanic early-season struggle before 47,000 fans here this afternoon with Texas taking a 7-6 decision over Kentucky for a triumph as hard-earned, and perhaps as lucky, as the local school has achieved in 59 seasons.

"One of the three forward passes completed by the Longhorns gave Texas its first quarter touchdown and an accurate placement boot by Gib Dawson, a junior halfback, added the extra point that gave the verdict to the team that gained the least yardage.

"A falter by 'The Finger' on the conversion attempt following Kentucky's third-quarter market cost the scrappy Wildcats a tie with the Southwest Conference defending champions in the schedule opener for the host team.

"Herb Hunt couldn't get the ball on the kicking tee after it was spiraled back for the boot Harry Jones was waiting to make and Texas adherents, who have never seen the Longhorns beaten in a home opener, probably are ready to build a shrine to the boy's bad moment that saved their orange-clad warriors from being dead-locked.

"The Wildcats, many of them comparative novices in college football, but apparently all of them battling their hearts out against a much more seasoned squad, made only one serious scor-ing threat thereafter, but the Longhorns and their supports were kept in mortal dread right up to the final whistle.

"All-America Babe Parilli, in all his life never given a tougher day while trying to pass, kept firing his bullets into the tough Texas defenses although hurling with little or no protection much of the time, and the partisan crowd gave up a mighty sigh of relief when time finally ran out on the big clock.

"Only then were the Longhorn faithful certain the ace quarter-back wouldn't pitch more points onto the Kentucky scoreboard."

* * * *

On September 29, a week after their heartbreaking loss to Texas, the Wildcats went on the road again, this time to Oxford, Miss.

"You had to see it to believe it."

That was the lead on Larry Boeck's *Courier-Journal* game story.

"Even then," he wrote, "the incredible fashion in which Ken-tucky was upset 21-17 by Ole Miss here this afternoon would have you rubbing your eyes in disbelief.

"The Wildcats handed this wild thriller to battling University of Mississippi, presenting the gift on the fumbling fingers of its ball carriers and pass receivers.

"Twice in the final quarter, ahead by a comfortable 17-7, the Cats fumbled to set up touchdown thrusts for the rebellious Johnny

Rebels. And then, in the last 15 seconds of play, a pass was dropped in the end zone—and that aerial would have meant victory.

"Thus, Kentucky lost the game by virtually the only way it could have blown it. They scorned victory by making the Rebels gifts of the ball twice in the final chapter; and then by failing to score in the waning moments after driving from their 22 to the Old Miss 8-yard line and a first down.

"It was another heartbreaker, the Texas story of last week rewritten with an even more bizarre touch as UK once again won everything but the ball game.

"Kentucky, behind 17-21 with six minutes to go, carried to within the shadow of the Ole Miss goal line on the heroic throwing of Babe Parilli. And the Babe was magnificent this afternoon this balmy afternoon, amazing 20,000 fans with his passing, particularly in the last half.

"Those last six minutes showed Kentucky at its best—and at its worst. Once before the Wildcats had been behind and had come back. That was after losing a 3-0 lead on Harry Jones field goal, and a later first-quarter touchdown by the Rebs.

"Kentucky went into halftime with a 10-3 lead largely on Tom Fillion's breathtaking 52-yard run. The Cats added another marker in the third quarter on Parilli's quarterback sneak from the 1, climaxing an 82-yard drive.

"And so now, it appeared once more that Kentucky would come out on top despite Ole Miss' two last-quarter scores. Parilli, not at his best in the first half, revealed his All-American talent in guiding Kentucky from its own 22 to the Ole Miss 8 with a spectacular display of hurling. He also contributed a 15-yard run.

"Then came the final heartbreaking 45 seconds. Babe tried three passes, hit on one to Cliff Lawson for a meager two yards. Finally, fourth down with 15 seconds to go, and 20,000 near hysterical fans waiting for the dramatic clutch play.

"Passing off the short punt, Parilli faded back to the 22 and as he looked for a receiver, he spotted Jim Proffitt in the end zone and tossed a perfect strike to his big end. For a moment, Kentucky partisans joyfully whooped it up. But they slumped in stunned silence when Proffitt dropped the ball after being brushed and then hit by a Rebel.

"Parilli today tossed 36 passes and completed 20 for 219 yards. None of the aerials were intercepted. And the exhibition was all the more impressive because the Babe completed nine of his last 15 heaves from the short punt—a tipoff to the defense that an aerial is en route.

"What's more, Parilli's passing record would have been fabulous indeed if seven or eight of the tosses had not been dropped.

"Once again today as in last week's 7-6 loss to Texas, it was the distressing story for the Wildcats of winning in almost all departments but not on the scoreboard. And again there were the agonizing frustrations of fumbling at critical times and dropping Parilli's passes when it hurt.

"The hard-charging, bruising tacklers of Ole Miss caused the Cats to fumble eight times, and the alert Rebels captured four of them.

"On the other side of the ledger, Kentucky outdistanced Ole Miss in total yardage, 394-244; rushing yardage, 175 to 136; passing yardage 219-108; first downs, 20-10."

* * * *

Once only since Bryant became head coach at Kentucky had the Wildcats lost three games in a row. That had occurred in 1948 against Ole Miss, Georgia and Vanderbilt when the Cats finished 5-3-2. After losing back-to-back games they should have won against Texas and Ole Miss, no one expected it to happen this time around against visiting Georgia Tech, although the Yellow Jackets were ranked 11th nationally.

But then no one expected what happened on the second play of the fourth quarter either.

The Cats, leading 7-6, had the ball, fourth down, on their own 36-yard line.

Clearly a punting situation.

Babe, as sportswriters had speculated he would, had taken over the punting duties and this day, in this fierce defensive battle, was kicking better than he had all season. He already had punted seven times and was averaging 44.6 yards per kick.

But Kentucky did not punt. Parilli, under center in the T formation, handed the ball to halfback Tom Fillion

Fillion was stopped short of the first down.

Tech took over and after a Tech receiver caught a pass, fumbled and UK defender Jim Proffitt recovered, officials ruled it incomplete and charged Proffitt with interference. Tech quarterback Darrell Crawford then tossed a short touchdown pass to give his team what turned out to be a game-winning 13-7 lead.

When the game ended angry UK fans, convinced that inept if not biased officiating had cost Kentucky the game, swarmed onto the field and surrounded the officials. State troopers rushed in and escorted them off the field.

Kentucky had been penalized 138 yards. Georgia Tech, 20

* * * *

After the game, the Bear issued a statement taking full responsibility for making the call that second-guesser blamed for Kentucky's defeat.

"It just turned out wrong," he said, "but if I had to do it over again, I'd make the same decision. If it had worked, I think we could have retained possession and would have protected our lead.

"I thought we had a play that would work there, but it went wrong. As it turned out, I guess we should have punted, but if it had worked, Parilli would have been a hero for taking the gamble.

"The squeeze play is one of the prettiest plays in baseball—when it works. But when it doesn't, it makes the manager look like a chump. Well our 'squeeze play' just didn't work."

* * * *

Who had called the ill-fated play that had led to Tech's scoring the game-winning touchdown—Babe or the Bear? From the sound of his post-game comments, he seemed to be shouldering the blame to take the heat off his star quarterback.

What really happened?

"I called it," Babe said in an interview years later. "What happened was, The Bear sent Tom Fillion into the game and I asked him, 'What play does he want?'

"Fillon didn't say anything. He just shrugged. We only had a few plays for circumstances like that and I called the one I thought would work. It was time and distance, the kind of situation we had rehearsed time after time for three years playing that board game in his office. But as soon as the ball was snapped, Fillon slipped and his knee hit the ground and he was late getting there and I had to wait to hand him the ball.

"Twenty years later, at a reunion, I asked The Bear:

"'Why didn't you send in a play?'

"He said, 'I did.'

"'Well, Tom didn't tell me. He just shrugged.'

"The Bear smiled.

"'I sent in the same play you called.'"

* * * *

A week before the Cats lost to Georgia Tech, a headline in *The Louisville Courier-Journal* had said:
**Butterfingers Kentucky Team
Gives Mississippi 21-17 Win**

In the lead paragraphs of his Georgia Tech game story, *Lexington Herald-Leader* reporter Ed Ashford sounded a mite testy too.

"Who wants to go to another bowl game, anyway?

"Kentucky's Wildcats, who gained bids to the Orange Bowl and Sugar Bowl in successive years, probably will spend next New Year's Day listening to bowl games on the radio, for the Wildcats' losing streak now has reached three, and thrice-beaten teams rarely get bids to major bowls.

"Georgia Tech's Yellow Jackets, coached by the personable Bobby Dodd, one of UK Coach Paul Bryant's closest friends, stung the Wildcats for Kentucky's third straight lacing yesterday before 35,000 fans at Stoll Field.

"The Cats lost to Texas, 7-6, when they muffed an extra point try and failed to hang onto a touchdown pass. They lost to Ole Miss, 21-17, when their fumbles gave the Rebels two scoring chances in the last quarter and a Kentucky touchdown was dropped.

"After those two games, Bryant decided his team was not aggressive enough and sent them through a stiff week of practice.

"So the Wildcats, who had had a big advantage over their conquerors in the statistical department, found a new way to lose a game yesterday—they were too aggressive.

"Kentucky's aggressiveness on several plays resulted in numerous penalties being assessed by the whistlemen, and the result was a 13-7 setback, giving UK a record of three straight losses by a total of 11 points."

If Ashford's story sounded a smidgen acerbic--and it did: "lacing," like "rout," was a cliché routinely reserved for contests about as close as Custer's Last Stand – there was no arguing with its accuracy.

The Wildcats were guilty on all counts.

And yet, there was just as much of an upbeat upside for the rest of the season as there was free-fall downfall. They were not a bad team. They were a team that had played well most of the time but not well enough all of the time. A couple of not-dropped touchdown passes here, a couple fewer fumbles there, and they would have been, if not should have been, undefeated.

There was still plenty of time, plenty of opportunities, to save their season.

The question wasn't whether they could, but would, do it.

Their fans were about to find out.

* * * *

LEXINGTON, KY.
October 13, 1951

"Just a day after Columbus Day, Kentucky discovered itself," *Courier-Journal* reporter Larry Boeck wrote.

"And it was a block-and-sock Kentucky that gave a good Mississippi State a sound lesson in football fundamentals here tonight while overpowering the Maroons 27-0.

"While Gen. Bob Neyland of Tennessee, long considered the finest exponent of sound football, looked on, the Wildcats found themselves.

"They came back from three close, heartbreaking defeats and tonight realized their football potential. Blocking crisply, running hard and playing near-flawless ball, these aroused Wildcats wore down a beefier Mississippi State with sheer power.

"Kentucky struck forcefully for single touchdowns in each quarter. Babe Parilli's clutch passing (he tossed for two touchdowns), the running of such backs as Bunky Gruner, Larry Jones, Tom Fillion and Ed Hamilton, plus keen play by both the offensive and defensive lines spurred Kentucky."

* * * *

It was a season, when a lot of things that weren't supposed to happen happened.

On Oct. 13, Dartmouth beat Army 28-14.

A week later, Indiana went into The Horseshoe in Columbus and throttled Ohio State 32-10.

On Nov. 10, Ivy League Cornell went into Ann Arbor and beat the Michigan Wolverines 20-7. Three weeks earlier, Princeton's Tigers had pounded Cornell 53-15.

The same day Cornell beat Michigan, Michigan State white-washed Notre Dame 35-0.

But of all the surprises, the shockers that season, none equaled, let alone surpassed, the remarkable, out-of-the-gate start of Villanova's Wildcats.

On Sept.29, they traveled to West Point and beat Army 21-7.

On Oct. 6, they beat Penn State, at Penn State, 20 -14.

On Oct. 12, in Tuscaloosa, they romped over Alabama 41-18.

Next up: Kentucky.

* * * *

LEXINGTON, KY.
October 19, 1951

"Villanova threw a pre-game challenge at Babe Parilli," *Courier-Journal* reporter Larry Boeck wrote, "and the Babe answered tonight by throwing the football. This was not the right answer as far as Villanova was concerned. Kentucky thrashed the Main Liners 35-13.

"Before tonight's encounter, word had gone from the Villanova bailiwick that the Main Liners, the nation's 12th ranked football team, was ready to knock down whatever Parilli could throw.

"It was Villanova that was knocked to the floor, staggered by four hay-makers for touchdowns from the unerring right arm of the Babe.

"It was not all the Babe tonight, of course. Sharp blocking, vicious tackling Kentucky turned in another team victory in winning its second straight and making a strong bid for the national recognition that has been denied it.

"Of Parilli's four touchdown tosses—one short of the Southeastern Conference record he owns—three were caught by Steve Meilinger, a speedy, bruising end. The other was accepted by Emery Clark.

"Kentucky's offensive line, opening holes crisply, sprang loose damaging runners in Tom Fillion, Emery Clark, Ed Hamilton and Bill Leskovar.

"Parilli called an excellent game, too, in using his runners as powerful jabs to set up the Main Liners for his knockout punches—demoralizing passes at critical spots.

"Coach Paul Bryant, who had been criticized in the Georgia Tech game for a daring fourth-down try for first down that failed, should be credited for his pre-game planning for tonight.

"'We aim to pass a great deal off spreads and the like to try to loosen up that big Villanova line,' said Bryant this afternoon.

"Parilli loosened them up—and then, when the Main Liners played a five-man line, Parilli sent Kentucky's slashing runners through the middle.

"This two-fisted attack had the Main Liners groggy at the half, when they trailed 21-7. However, Villanova drew first blood in the first quarter of a rough, wide-open game featuring passing."

* * * *

At the beginning of the season, one of the concerns had been lack of defensive depth. And yet, through the first six games, UK's defense had been anything but flimsy. The Wildcats' three losses had resulted more from dropped passes–two potential game winners in the end zone-- and fumbles deep in their own territory. The defense's only glaring contribution to those three losses had come against Georgia Tech in the form of unnecessary roughness and interference penalties in a game in which UK was whistled for 138 yards and Tech, 20. Although they had not rung up a string of goose eggs as had the 1950 team—UK had held five opponents scoreless, allowed only one touchdown in four other games and 69 total points -- 6.2-per-game – for the season, any worries about its defense so far had proved to be unwarranted.

Besides, in their two most recent games, the offense had caught fire, scoring 27 points against Mississippi and 35 against Villanova.

On the ground, as well as through the air, UK appeared to be on a momentous roll.

Then came the Florida game at Gainesville.

And a few days before it, news that made headlines in Florida as well as Kentucky.

Babe Parilli was ill, a patient in the UK infirmary and might not play.

* * * *

On Friday, Oct. 26, the headline that appeared in Jacksonville's *Times-Union--* **Babe Parilli Will Play Against Florida** --no doubt created mixed emotions. Babe, sidelined with a cold, had returned to practice after a one-day stay and had appeared "none the worse for wear."

Without Babe in the lineup, Florida's chances of beating UK and atoning for a 40-6 drubbing the year before would have increased considerably. But with him playing, Florida fans would have a chance to see a passing duel they were eagerly awaiting between Babe and their own flashy quarterback, Haywood Sullivan.

Sullivan, by completing seven passes against Vanderbilt the week before, had increased his two-year total to 132, eclipsing the all-time Florida career record of 127 set by Doug Belden 1946, 1947 and 1948.

Entering the Kentucky game, Sullivan needed to throw only 33 more passes to match Belden's record of 300 attempts in three seasons.

* * * *

"Vito Parilli," The Associated Press reported, "was the Kentucky Babe if he ever was, throwing a pair of long touchdown passes for a 14-6 victory over Florida.

"Five Florida fumbles, one within eight yards of the Kentucky goal, cut down the Gators' threats except for one 46-yard touchdown march.

"Kentucky's identical twins, Larry and Harry Jones, shared victory honors with Parilli early in the game. Larry got behind Florida's defense and caught a scoring pass of 56 yards and Harry Jones kicked both extra points. Parilli threw 38 yards to Harold Gruner in the last period to cinch the win.

"Sam Oosterhoudt ran seven yards for Florida's touchdown after Buford Lee set it up with a 30 yard scamper.

"The 80-degree temperature appeared to be softening up the big, strong Kentucky defense in the second half and Florida's capable defensive line was living up to its rating of fourth in the nation.

"But just when it looked bright for the Florida Gators and their 31,000 backers, Parilli came up with the stopper.

"Just as he found Larry Jones in the first quarter, he found Gruner behind the defense and racked up some insurance points.

"Parilli tried 15 passes, completed 10 of them for 166 yards.

"That was all the difference."

* * * *

The lead of the United Press story said:

"Babe Parilli threw two touchdown passes and his mates stopped Haywood Sullivan at 10 net yards as Kentucky beat Florida 14-6 and settled the argument over which was the better tosser.

"It was the third straight triumph for the rebounding Blue Grass Wildcats, who dropped three in a row at the start. The Kentucky Babe was never more efficient, both in passing and in shuttling the ball."

Sullivan attempted 10 passes, completed five and for the first time in two years with him at quarterback, did not have a single passing first down.

* * * *

"LEXINGTON, KY. (AP) --Kentucky, gradually rebuilding its national football stock, takes on once-beaten Miami (Fla.) here Saturday in what may prove to be a severe test of the vaunted Kentucky passing game

"The weather, and the Miami pass defense, third nationally, pose a threat to the sharp passing of Babe Parilli, Kentucky's All-American candidate.

"Temperature of freezing or thereabouts is forecast for the homecoming tilt expected to draw upward of 30,000. A light snow fell most of the day, finally leaving a light coating on the ground, but was due to stop overnight. No precipitation is forecast for the game.

"The weather kept Miami from getting in a final pregame drill. Unable to land at the Lexington airport, the squad flew to Evansville, Ind. some 200 miles away and started the Lexington jaunt by bus. The squad was due in town about bedtime.

"Kentucky meanwhile spent a portion of the afternoon studying movies and then went to a girls' hockey field for a limbering up drill in sweat clothes. The playing field is covered and mud kept the gridders from the regular practice lost."

* * * *

The weather remained frigid all day.

So did Miami, most of all its highly touted, nationally third-ranked pass defense.

The Wildcats thrashed Miami 32-0.

"Lexington, Ky. Nov. 3 (AP)—Kentucky's Babe Parilli tossed three touchdown passes today to pace a 32-0 football victory over Miami (Fla.) and pull within nine scoring heaves of his own national record.

"The Babe passed for 23 touchdowns last year. Today's production gave him 14 for the year with three games to play.

117

"He was the master of an easier-than-expected situation in which the Kentucky offense rolled at will and the defense stopped Miami's attack as cold as the 28-degree temperature. Miami finished with a net seven yards rushing and 15 passing.

"The Kentucky Babe twice pitched to end Steve Meilinger and once to halfback Ed Hamilton in penetrating the pass defense ranked third nationally. He passed to Emery Clark to set up another score and Kentucky stayed on the ground for its fifth tally.

"Kentucky, improving with each game and gradually working its way back into the national grid picture, kept Miami in a hole except for a pair of first-period threats. A homecoming crowd of 28,000 attended.

"It was Kentucky's fifth win against three narrow losses.

"Overall, the Babe hit 12 of 21 passes for 103 yards, bringing his completions to 98 for the year in 178 attempts and a grand total of 1,182 yards for the year."

* * * *

Two days after the game, the headline on an Associated Press story said:

Parilli Threatens All-Time College Passing Record

"Lexington, Ky., Nov. 5 (AP)—Babe Parilli, Kentucky's fabulous dispenser of touchdown passes, carried on a serious courtship today with other collegiate football records to go with the ones he already holds.

"The Kentucky Babe, a precision bomber with 23 payoff pitches for a national mark last season, appears certain to better the figure for scoring passes in three varsity years.

"His pass completions have erased the career record held by Sam Baugh, formerly of Texas Christian, and he is in a duel with Don Klosterman of Los Angeles Loyola for the all-time collegiate honors.

"Parilli, an All-American candidate, is on a par with his 1950 record performance though three narrow defeats lowered Kentucky's stock at the season's outset.

"The Babe last week scuttled Miami, the country's third best team on pass defense with three touchdown passes and brought from his coach, Paul Bryant, this appraisal:

"'Parilli is without a doubt the greatest T quarterback who ever put on a pair of football shoes, college or pro.'

"Always one to let the opposition to deal with the superlatives about Kentucky personnel, Bryant continued:

"'Miami had a great pass defense, but that boy Parilli hits against the best of them when he goes out there.'"

Andy Gustafson, the Miami mentor, had the same opinion.

"Babe is the finest T quarterback I have ever seen. He is absolutely a magician," said Gustafson.

"There is no doubt he is the backbone of the team. Two or three times we rushed him 15 or 20 yards and then he got his pass off. How that boy can stand back there when he's trapped and then pass is just uncanny.

"If Kentucky doesn't get a bowl bid he is my first choice for the North-South Shrine game at Miami Christmas night.

"Undefeated through eight games last year, the Babe was showing a mark of 72 completions in 132 attempts for 1,147 yards and 15 touchdowns. This season, on a thrice-beaten team that is working its way back into the national scene, he has 98 completions in 178 throws for 1,182 yards and 14 touchdowns.

"Parilli in his varsity career has 293 completions for 3,890 yards and 45 touchdowns, the latter only three below the four-year mark and two below the three-year record, both held by John Ford of Hardin-Simmons.

"To Parilli's record, though, you can add 15 completions, 233 yards and two more payoff pitches for his two bowl appearances, the Orange and the Sugar."

* * * *

Given the fact that Tulane entered its Nov.10 game against Kentucky having lost four straight, there was little reason to believe the Green Wave would not lose again.

119

They did.

But the real story wasn't the outcome. It was Babe's setting one new all-time college football passing record and equaling another one.

The *Courier-Journal's* Larry Boeck covered the game this way:

"NEW ORLEANS, La., Nov, 10-- Army Chief of Staff General J. Lawton Collins, a Tulane alumnus, provided words of encouragement for the Greenies in homecoming festivities preceding today's game with Kentucky.

"What the general should have provided for the slaughtered Greenies was some anti-aircraft to repel the record-breaking passes of Babe Parilli and some weapons of offense to combat the strength of an unyielding Kentucky defense.

"Tulane had neither and Kentucky had both. And so the alert Wildcats bettered the helpless Greenies 37-0 in scoring an impressive victory before 37,000 patrons this comfortable but overcast day.

"The Babe, who is becoming a man of almost monotonous brilliance, smashed one more national record and tied another. At that, he rested much of the time in the second half after the Wildcats had amassed a conclusive 28-0 halftime lead.

"Parilli attempted only 18 passes and completed 13 for 172 yards and two touchdowns. This assault on the harassed Tulane defenders allowed the Babe to crack the passing yardage mark of Georgia's Johnny Rauch. Rauch had compiled 4,004 yards in three seasons of college football and the Kentucky bombardier now has 4,062.

"In throwing two touchdown passes, the shy, modest Italian from Pennsylvania posted his 46th and 47th scoring aerials. This tied the record of 47 for three seasons of work set by John Ford of Hardin-Simmons several years ago.

"The Babe, who awed observers with spectacular exhibition, already has toppled the pass completions mark held for 15 years by Sammy Baugh of Texas Christian. 'Slingin' Sammy' had 267 completions. Babe, with two tussles ahead before completing a magnificent collegiate career had 306."

* * * *

It was neither accidental nor incidental that George Washington was UK's next opponent. Contrary to what their record—two wins, a tie and four losses-- suggested to some, Bear Bryant had not scheduled the Colonials because they would be a soft touch before UK's annual rivalry game with Tennessee.

The reason was their offense.

Going into the George Washington game, UK's defense was ranked second in the nation. It had allowed only one touchdown in the last three games, held three of UK's most recent five opponents scoreless and given up only 19 points in five games, an average of only 3.8.

But all of them were T formation teams. Like the Vols, George Washington operated out of the old-fashioned and fast-disappearing single wing. And, in Andy Davis, they had a tailback who made it work. Davis was rapidly approaching the Southern Conference rushing records of 4,871 yards set by North Carolina All-American Charlie "Choo Choo" Justice.

And so, like North Dakota State the year before, The Bear had scheduled an opponent before facing Tennessee based on how they played, not necessarily how well they played.

As expected, UK won handily, 47-13. The Colonials' only two scores came in the second quarter on a 59-yard pass thrown by Davis and a two-yard run in the final quarter after an 80-yard drive against Kentucky's substitutes.

Although playing less than half the game, Babe threw three more touchdown passes to set another all-time collegiate passing record. The 48th, 49th and 50th of his career, broke the record of 47 previously held by John Ford of Hardin-Simmons.

For two weeks, the emphasis in both pre-game and game day newspaper coverage had been on the all-time passing record Babe had already broken and those he was about to break.

Now, the spotlight focused on THE game.

Next Up: the Volunteers of Tennessee.

Maybe this time, at long last, the Wildcats would do something no Kentucky team had been able to do: beat a Tennessee team coached by Gen. Bob Neyland.

* * * *

As was predictable, there was no shortage of pre-game speculating and handwringing.

From Knoxville, the Associated Press reported:

"Tennessee's pass defense worried Gen. Bob Neyland today as he began preparing his Volunteers for Saturday's joust with Kentucky's Babe Parilli—one of football's foremost passers.

"Neyland has ample reason to be worried about Tennessee's air fortifications. The Sugar Bowl bound Vols have yielded nine touchdowns to eight opponents this fall and seven resulted from passes.

"'Our pass defense has been shaky all fall,' said Neyland, acknowledging it was high on the list of his worries for this week's showcase game.

"'Babe Parilli is the finest passer in collegiate football,' Neyland continued. 'We are well aware of what we are up against. But we are hoping to strengthen all our defense—especially our pass defense.'"

Neyland wasn't the only one wondering if his team was as good as its undefeated record and No. 1 national ranking suggested.

From New York, International News Service reporter Pat Robinson wrote:

"Time was when the Harvard-Yale was the big event of the football season. Time was, too, when it decided the national championship.

"Those days are gone, perhaps forever. Of course, the boys and girls will still show up with their blue and crimson hat feathers, raccoon coats, luncheon hampers and a little something in the thermos bottle.

"But the game itself means nothing to the general public and perhaps not too much even to the countless thousands of Yale and Harvard old grads.

"There are traditional games coming up all over the map this Saturday but the most interesting of them all will be the clash between unbeaten Tennessee and disappointing Kentucky.

"Nobody seems to know just how good Tennessee may be because of its not-too-testing schedule. Now we shall get a real line on them because Kentucky has come a long way since its wobbly opening and is good enough to give any team a battle.

"If Tennessee can give Kentucky a decisive trimming we will be ready to admit it must rank at least as good as any of the other four unbeaten gridiron powers—Maryland, Princeton, Stanford and Michigan State.

"Stanford may have its hands full with an aroused California outfit which has been a big disappointment to its supporters.

"Michigan State, which lost some of its luster last week when it barely nosed out Indiana, should handle Colorado in handy fashion.

"Maryland should be able to call its shots against West Virginia. The only doubt about this game is the size of the score Maryland may want to run up against a rival which has been swamped by Washington and Lee, Penn State, South Carolina and Pittsburgh.

"Princeton should wind up its season with its record still intact by trimming Dartmouth.

"Unbeaten Illinois, which was held to a scoreless tie by Ohio State last Saturday, can get to the Rose Bowl by taking Northwestern. With such an incentive, the Illini figure to rebound fiercely against the Wildcats."

* * * *

It wasn't even close.

Tennessee scored seven points in each quarter; Kentucky none in all of them.

Tennessee rushed for 307 yards; Kentucky, 43.

Only in passing did Kentucky hold the edge. The Vols completed four of eight passes for 38 yards; Babe, 15 of 25 for 172 yards.

* * * *

"It was quiet, but not morgue-like," the *Herald-Leader's* Bob Riegner reported.

"Coach Paul (Bear) Bryant walked slowly around the Kentucky dressing room, trying to smile when he didn't feel much like smiling. Occasionally, he would stop to whisper to one of his players or to place a hand reassuringly on the shoulder of one of his half-dressed athletes.

"'Guess you might call 'em (Tennessee) a pretty fair country team,' as he shook his head as if to ask, 'Where can one team get all that power?'

"Calling the Vols 'the best Tennessee squad I've ever seen,' Bryant said he guessed 'the only way to keep them from scoring is not to give them the ball.'

"One of the dressing room visitors told Bryant that he had heard a fan say that the best defense against Tennessee was prayer. The Bear smiled.

"There was no gnashing of teeth in the Wildcat den. The Cats were beaten and they knew it. They were virtually unanimous in their appraisal of the Volunteers—'great.'

"But although they were willing to concede that the Knoxville wrecking crew was the better team, they weren't inclined to think the Volunteers were four touchdowns better.

"'We should have scored once, maybe twice,' co-captain and All-American Babe Parilli said as he stood before his locker.

"'I guess I was pretty lousy,' the Rochester, Pa. Rifle said. 'When we were at the one, I called a sneak and couldn't make it. I'd call the same play again under the circumstances.'"

* * * *

Despite the crushing defeat, there was one consolation. After beating George Washington and before playing Tennessee, the Cats had received word that they had been selected to play in the Cotton Bowl.

Their opponent would be Southwest Conference champion Texas Christian.

TCU had lost four games too.

CHAPTER 9

If "thrice-beaten teams" rarely receive major bowl bids, as *Lexington Herald-Leader* columnist Ed Ashford had bemoaned back in early October after UK had lost three of its first four, how did two teams with four losses end up in the Cotton Bowl?

In the case of the Texas Christian Horned Frogs, it wasn't how many they had lost but to whom—and when. Three of their losses had been to non-conference teams: in their Sept. 22 season opener against Kansas, 27-13; in mid-October at Texas Tech, 33-19; and on Oct, 27 at Southern California. Their only SWC loss had come on Nov. 17, at Texas, 32-21.

Thus, three of the Frogs' losses had come relatively early in the season, two of them on the road, and they had won the SWC title with a 5-1 record and had beaten the second-place team Baylor (4-1-1).

Prior to their disappointing, and embarrassing, 28-0 loss at home to Tennessee in their regular season finale, the Wildcats' other three losses had occurred early in the season too.

Although no one said so, though, there was perhaps another reason the Wildcats' had been invited to play in the Cotton Bowl against SWC champion Texas Christian.

Babe Parilli.

After all, Babe was not exactly an unknown commodity in Texas. Two years before, as a sophomore, he had played in the Cotton Bowl against Southern Methodist and earlier in the 1951 season against the Texas Longhorns in Austin. And, he had just broken three all-time national passing records—two of them held by Texans: most career yards, by John Ford of Hardin-Simmons, and most career completions, previously held by none other than Texas Christian legend Slingin' Sammy Baugh.

Meanwhile, whatever the reason Kentucky received the bid, there was growing talk across the country that no college, no matter what their record, had any business playing in any bowl games— and that all bowl games should be discontinued. The NCAA was already conducting hearings that some saw as a rubber- stamp first step in that direction.

There seemed to be a very real possibility that UK, along with everyone else, might never play in a bowl game again. But for now, for the Wildcats, the only one that mattered was the one they were about to play. And after losing 28-0 to Tennessee, it mattered a lot.

* * * *

At halftime, with UK holding a precarious 13-7 lead, Babe remembered what the Bear had said at halftime in New Orleans the year before.

"Babe, don't throw the ball. We'll get 'em on defense."

Babe hadn't been so sure that day. Oklahoma was a high-scoring team, averaging more than 30 points a game. Was it realistic to believe, or even hope, that the Sooners would not break loose and score at least once more, and perhaps more than once?

As he sat in the locker room at the Cotton Bowl, he wondered too.

Through two quarters, the defense had been magnificent, stopping three TCU scoring drives, one inside the 10-yard line, another at the one. But TCU, while not able to score, had been moving the ball well between the 20 yard lines. And while not as prolific as Oklahoma, which had averaged more than 30 points a game, the Horned Frogs had scored three or more touchdowns in seven of their 10 regular season games.

And then as he and his teammates trotted back out onto the field, Babe felt a lump in his throat, chills down his spine as he gazed at what more than 75,000 other people were looking at too.

Out in the center of the field, the UK band had formed a large, blue-and-white block formation that spelled:

BABE

"*We can't lose this one,*" he said to himself. "*Not now.*"

* * * *

"DALLAS, Tex., Jan. 1 (AP)-- Vito 'Babe' Parilli's swan song to college football was a tune of touchdown passes today as the great quarterback of Kentucky shot down Texas Christian , 20-7, in the Cotton Bowl.

"Playing one of the greatest games of a glorious career, the celebrated Kentucky Babe passed, faked and ran the Horned Frogs into submission for the enjoyment of at least a third of the 75,000 fans.

"An iron-bound defense thwarted three mighty Frog drives, one of which reached the Kentucky one –yard mark, and the great man of the Wildcats was Doug Moseley, the All-American center.

"Moseley went out with a possibly serious injury late in the second period, but he was sure in there long enough to spear the defense against those three Frog surges.

"Gilbert Bartosh, the little man who couldn't make the TCU team this season, came off the bench to drive the Frogs to their only touchdown in the third period, and he did it in only four plays. Taking two of the touchdown passes from Parilli was Emery Clark who also intercepted passes and did great punt returning.

"The Texas Christian defense fell completely apart in the fourth period, and, after a short TCU punt, the Wildcats marched 26 yards to another touchdown when Ed Hamilton smashed over from the Frog four.

"And as time ran out, Kentucky had the ball deep in TCU territory again after Glenn Jones fumbled the kickoff and the Wildcats recovered on the 14.

"The Frogs never were in the ball game except for the few minutes Bartosh lashed the Wildcats for the TCU touchdown. The Frogs rolled from their own 20 to the Kentucky 41 the next time they had the ball, but the drive was stalled, and from then on, TCU was on the defensive.

"Parilli actually passed for only 85 yards but his throws were in the clinches.

"The first Kentucky touchdown came shortly after TCU took the opening kickoff and paraded to the Wildcat 11. Moseley led the staunch Kentucky barrier and the Wildcats took over. After a punt exchange and a fine return by Clark, the Wildcats swept 53 yards for their score. The payoff was a pass into the end zone by Parilli to Clark from the Frog five. Harry Jones converted.

"The next Kentucky score came in the second period after Clark intercepted Mal Fowler's pass and ran 30 yards to the Kentucky 43. The touchdown was on a 13-yard pass from Parilli to Clark in the end zone. Jones missed the conversion. He kicked the one after the third Kentucky touchdown, however.

"The Frog score was on a 43-yard dash around left end by Bobby Jack Floyd, the crashing TCU fullback. Keith Flowers, a defensive standout, kicked the extra point.

"Kentucky rolled up 213 yards on the ground and 85 in the air. The Frogs got 201 rushing and 99 passing.

"Tom Fillion led the Kentucky ground attack with 73 yards.

"Fears that the crowd wouldn't be near capacity were not realized. There were only a few empty seats.

"The game was supposed to be a wild offensive affair and produce touchdowns galore but Kentucky had too much defense."

* * * *

An Associated Press sidebar story said:
"You ask Kentucky's coach and players what it was that licked Texas Christian, 20-7, in the 16th annual Cotton Bowl.

"'Defense,' they chorus.

"You ask Texas Christian's coaches and players what beat it.

"'Defense,' they chorus, then in the same breath, 'Parilli."

"A savage defense and the magnificent work of Vito (Babe) Parilli were the twin efforts that assistant TCU coach Abe Martin said 'just shot us down.'

"'TCU is as good a ball club as we have ever faced,' said Kentucky Coach Paul (Bear) Bryant as he stood in the steaming bedlam that was the Wildcat dressing room.

"But I thought our defense was the reason,' he said, adding that it was a 'team' victory.

"Parilli, named the outstanding back of the game by sportswriters, said his passing was 'off.' He said 'good receivers' accounted for his two touchdown passes in eight completions out of 20 efforts for 85 yards.

"Gibert Bartosh, who quarterbacked TCU to its only score, disagreed.

"'That Parilli is the best passer I've ever seen,' he said.

* * * *

Only once during his three-year career at UK had The Bear ever said anything to Babe even remotely approaching negative. During a game when everything seemed to be going wrong— it was so insignificant Babe could never even remember which game it was—the Bear had told him:

"Parilli, don't you turn horsesh. .. on me too."

And yet, not even once had he ever praised Babe. To The Bear, "good' was nothing more than a down payment toward the high price of achieving greatness. Playing "well" was but a first step along the endless road that led to unachievable perfection.

But after the win over Texas Christian, Babe's final game at UK, The Bear walked up and reached out and straightened the Texas-style string tie Babe was wearing.

Then he smiled and said: "You played pretty well today, boy."

* * * *

Shortly after the Cats returned to Lexington, the Bear announced that Babe's jersey would be retired permanently.

No Kentucky player would ever again wear No. 10, Bryant said," Unless it's Parilli's son."

* * * *

The day after the game, *Lexington Herald-Leader* sports writer Ed Ashlford's column, *It Says Here*, included the following item:

"There was much criticism in New Orleans in November 1950 when the Cats were chosen for the Sugar Bowl after their 7-0 loss to Tennessee. But Kentucky silenced the critics with a 13-7 win that snapped Oklahoma's 31-game string.

"There were more complaints this year in Texas when Kentucky, beaten three times at the time it was invited, got the Cotton Bowl bid. One man, writing in a Dallas paper, said the selection of Kentucky was an insult to the Southwest Conference.

"Shortly after the loss to Tennessee, Ed Danforth of *The Atlanta Journal* proved a good prophet when he said 'The only way Kentucky will embarrass the Cotton Bowl is by beating their Southwest Conference champions."

* * * *

Two days after the New Year's Day Rose, Sugar, Cotton and Orange Bowl games, the controversial proposal to ban all bowls games surfaced again.

Among those who offered an opinion was Babe.

"MOBILE, Ala. Jan.3 (AP) –If college crusaders plotting the death of bowl games are doing it for the sake of the players, they might as well forget it

"The boys love 'em.

"Stars of three major bowls, gathered here for the annual Senior Bowl game Saturday, urged that the post-season events be kept alive as an incentive for players and an experience not soon forgotten.'

"Battered performers just in from battle of New Orleans, Dallas and Miami joined in a unanimous chant: 'Keep the bowls going.'

"It's an experience I wouldn't have missed for anything,' said Kentucky's Babe Parilli, who played in the Orange, Sugar and Cotton Bowls in successive years and who was voted the outstanding player in Kentucky's 20-7 triumph over Texas Christian this week.

"I think bowls are wonderful things for the boys. We all look forward to them and are proud when we are chosen. It's something we can tell our grandchildren.

"Ed (Mighty Mo) Modzelewski, Maryland's chief executioner in the 28-13 rout of top-rated Tennessee added:

"'It's sort of a reward for a good season. Our boys certainly are all for them."

He got a quick seconding vote from Bob Ward, Maryland, the All-American guard, who said:

'We didn't miss a day of class. The bowl didn't hurt us at all as far as school work is concerned and it was a great experience.'

"'It gives us something to play for,' chimed in Tennessee's All-American Halfback Hank Lauricella. 'Some of the boys on the squad who don't get to play much may resent losing time over the holidays but the regular players certainly don't, they love it.'"

* * * *

Four days later, an Atlanta sports editor had a few somewhat more emphatic words on the subject.

"ATLANTA, Ga., Jan. 7 (AP)—Sports Editor Ed Danforth of *The Atlanta Journal* called a proposed ban of bowl games by the National Collegiate Athletic Association 'the most monstrous fake issue yet devised.'

"Writing in his column, "*An Ear to the Ground*," Danforth said:

"'If the NCAA undertakes to declare bowl games out of bounds for its members, its members should assert their manhood, if any, and tell the NCAA which exit to use and urge the NCAA to pass out quietly.'

"Asserting that if any college felt that playing in bowls is unwholesome it could refuse invitations, Danforth commented: 'It is as simple as that. No college is ever compelled to play in a bowl.

"'If bowl games are an evil influence,' he continued, 'let the colleges foolish enough to risk it take a chance.

"Bowl games are not for Princeton, Yale, Harvard, Army, Navy, Virginia Military, North Carolina, Duke, Oklahoma and Michigan State. All right, let them skip bowl games. But what in the name of suffering Ph.D.'s is it to them if Alabama, Kentucky and TCU like to play in a bowl game every few years?

"If that weakens the general well being of intercollegiate football, more evidence should be advanced.'

"Danforth called recent action of the Southern Conference in banning and suspending Maryland and Clemson for accepting bids to the Sugar Bowl and Gator Bowls as ' as the most ridiculous of all the recent "me too" actions.'

"'Who are these characters who have just experienced a deathbed conversion and hear the rustle of angels' wings?" Danforth wrote.

"'North Carolina, of all people, three times in a big bowl but never a bowl winner, joined the rebels.

"'Duke, a two-fisted recruiting outfit, once Rose Bowl host, s'help me, voted against bowl games.

"'The charge that bowl funds provide a war chest to assemble stronger teams falls flat when the records of North Carolina and Duke are examined. It is a cinch the Tar Heels and Blue Devils were gipped out of several sorely needed football players if their old bowl checks were supposed to help corral talent.'"

* * * *

For all the talk, two questions never asked, let alone answered, were these:

Other than the possibility, if not the probability, of a few perennial powers such as Texas, Oklahoma, Michigan, Ohio State and Tennessee collecting more money than their conference rivals and therefore continuing to dominate because they could attract more of the best players, what exactly made bowl games so evil?

And if money from bowl games was the root of all success on the football field, how did Notre Dame, which had never played in one despite numerous invitations, become and remain such a perennial powerhouse?

Another question also never raised, let alone addressed: What exactly was the original purpose of bowl games?

Still another: Did anyone, including the NCAA, have anything approaching a vague idea how pervasive bowl games had become all across America?

As far as most newspapers and fans were concerned, "bowl game" meant the big four played on New Year's Day: the Rose Bowl, billed as "The Granddaddy of them all"; Sugar Bowl, Cotton Bowl and Orange Bowl.

But three other bowl games were played on New Year's Day too: the Gator Bowl, Salad Bowl and Sun Bowl.

Then there were the far less, or not at all, publicized "minor" bowl games that most people did not even know existed including the Mineral Water Bowl, Burley Bowl, Corn Bowl, Pear Bowl, Pretzel Bowl, Orange Blossom Classic, Cosmopolitan Bowl, Golden Isles Bowl, Lions Bowl, Iodine Bowl, Refrigerator Bowl, Pythian Bowl, Brandeis Bowl, Tropical Bowl, Aztec Bowl, Tangerine Bowl, Pineapple Bowl, Prairie View Bowl and Vulcan Bowl.

And the junior college Potato Bowl, Oleander Bowl and Junior Rose Bowl.

Plus the military Electronics Bowl, Cigar Bowl and Cherry Bowl.

During the 1951 season, all were played, at locations all over the country, between Nov. 22 and New Year's Day.

Was the NCAA going to abolish them all?

If not, which ones?

And how would it decide which survived and which didn't?

CHAPTER 10

The first week in August, Babe went to a two-week training camp in Delafield, Wis. to prepare for the annual College All-Star game. Officially known as the Chicago Charities All-Star Game, it matched a select roster of college seniors against the NFL team that had won the league championship the year before. Inaugurated in 1934 at the suggestion of *Chicago Tribune* sports columnist Arch Ward, it attracted huge crowds to Soldier Field and received national television and nationwide newspaper coverage.

This year, the collegians would meet the Los Angeles Rams, led by quarterback Norm Van Brocklin. In the 1951 NFL championship game, the Rams had beaten Cleveland 24-17, avenging a 30-28 loss to the Browns in the 1950 title game.

In August, 1951, the Browns had routed the College All-stars 38-7.

But the 1952 All-Star roster was loaded with talent, including All-American guard Les Richter of California; tackles Don Coleman of Michigan State; Jim Weatherall of Oklahoma; Bob Toneff of Notre Dame; center Doug Moseley of Kentucky and ends Gino Marchetti of San Francisco and Bob Carey of Michigan State.

Their roster included plenty of outstanding backs too. 1950 Heisman Trophy winner Vic Janowicz of Ohio State; Hank Lauricella of Tennessee; Ollie Matson of San Francisco; Johnny Karras of Illinois; Hugh McElhenny of Washington; John Petitbon

135

of Notre Dame; Ed Modzelewski of Maryland; and Frank Gifford of Southern Cal.

Rams coach Joe Stydahar told reporters:

"In all sincerity and frankness and not merely trying to set up an excuse, I am convinced that we are about to meet the strongest all-star team in the history of the annual game. It is a team without a weakness simply because the coaches were first selected and then told to pick their own players.

"The collegians may be amateurs but they aren't boys."

* * * *

For each of the 54 college players selected, it was a chance for those who been named to the All-American team and gone high in the draft to show that they were as good as advertised; for those who weren't and drafted much lower, an opportunity to demonstrate that they were as good, if not better, than those who had been.

Meanwhile the coaching staff faced a problem any coach would love to have: choosing a starting lineup from such a wealth of talent. For Georgia Tech's Bobby Dodd, the Stars' head coach, the most difficult job of all would be deciding on a starting quarterback.

There were four from which to choose: One was Al Dorow of Michigan State who had led the Spartans to an undefeated season, including wins over Notre Dame (35-0), Ohio State (24-20) Penn State (32-21) and Pittsburgh (53-26), as well as an 8-1 record the year before, also beating Notre Dame and Michigan in 1950.

Then there was Billy Wade of Vanderbilt, chosen first in the first round of the 1952 NHFL draft by the Rams; and Darrell Crawford, Dodd's own quarterback at Georgia Tech.

And Babe.

Cincinnati Post sports columnist Pat Harmon dissected Dodd's dilemma -- and how he resolved it.

"There was considerable comment last fall that Wade was a better quarterback than Parilli, especially on situations that called for a long, accurate pass. And the comment about Crawford vs. Parilli was loud.

An Atlanta sportswriter was so struck with Crawford's superiority he refused even to recommend Parilli for All-American.

"The All-Stars began practicing two weeks ago. Best guess, at the start, was that Coach Dodd would use all three. . . . Parilli, Crawford, Wade . . .in some assignment.

"Crawford for his familiarity with the Dodd system. Parilli for his ball handling perhaps. Wade for his long-passing ability.

Dodd had two weeks to look them over at close quarters. . . To test them in scrimmage. It was man-to-man competition.

And Parilli today is No. 1.

"Vito Parilli's feat of winning the starting assignment on the College All-Star football team Friday night must stand as one of his most notable achievements.

"Babe won many honors as quarterback for Kentucky but none has been so dramatic as this."

* * * *

CHICAGO, Aug. 14 (AP)-- The favored Los Angeles Rams, champions of the National Football League, catapult against one of the best-balanced collegiate squads ever assembled in the 19th annual all-star football game at Soldier Field Friday night.

"A throng of 90,000 will pack the huge arena on the fringe of Lake Michigan, but millions more will be tuned in on a national telecast and broadcast of the colorful classic which traditionally kicks off the grid season.

"Dumont's network of 53 television stations and 400 stations of the Mutual broadcasting system will handle the game which starts at 8:30 p.m. eastern standard time."

* * * *

And when it was over, Pat Harmon wrote:

"For 51 minutes here last night, pro football's fledglings—the College All-Stars who are no longer in college—ran the show against the National Football League champions, the Los Angeles Rams.

"Then Bob Waterfield place kicked a 33-yard field goal and it was all over. The Rams won, 10-7.

"An audience of 88,316 at Soldier Field and uncounted millions on the TV range saw a closely fought game. So closely fought that at one moment the All-Stars and the Rams almost erupted into fist fighting.

"The sympathy of the crowd was so strong for the All-Stars that the spectators booed the Rams when they ran onto the field for the second half. They booed loudly again when Tom Fears, Los Angeles end, was thrown out of the game for unsportsmanlike conduct in the fourth quarter.

"In the moments the all-Stars were in control, their hero was "the Sweet Kentucky Babe," Vito Parilli. At times, his performance transcended the finest play ever before seen in 18 of these all-star-pro games. On a couple of other occasions, he was hopelessly stymied.

"Linemen knocked down his protection, slammed him around and knocked the ball out of his hand.

"But Parilli was the all-star among the All-Stars. If there are any red faces in the football ranks today, they belong to those seasoned experts who said last fall that Parilli wasn't an All-American.

"He was an All-American last night. He was placed in charge of a squad that included his two great rivals for All-American honors last fall—Darrell Crawford of Georgia Tech and Bill Wade of Vanderbilt.

"He threw the pass that had the All-Stars ahead almost all the way. He also fumbled and lost the ball four times. But that couldn't be entirely his fault. The center of the Rams' line was grinding the All-Star forwards to shreds, charging through and pawing at Parilli on every play.

"In the first quarter, the All-Stars drove down to the Rams' 20-yard line, where Parilli was hit by three monstrous Ram linemen and lost the ball.

"The All-Stars were back in a moment at the Ram 28 and lost the ball the same way as before.

"In the second quarter, Parilli burst forth not only as a passer but as a runner. He swept around his right end, faked a pitchout to a fleeing halfback, kept the ball and ran 10 yards the 50. On the next play he again kept the ball around right end, cut back to his left, and gained 32 yards.

"Then Parilli passed to Bob Carey, Michigan State, on the three yard line. Parilli then faded to the right, kept the ball as long as he dared on what looked to be a pass play, then pitched out to Ohio State's Vic Janowicz who drove hard to the goal line and over.

"Janowicz place kicked the extra point and the All-Stars led 7-0.

"The All-Stars had their shutout for three periods. But on the first play of the last quarter, Frank Gifford, All-Star back, committed a costly interference foul on his six yard line. The Rams took over. Van Brocklin passed to Paul Younger and Waterfield place kicked the tying point.

"Later, a squirming, dodging run by Elroy Hirsch gained 21 yards and set the Rams' up for their winning play. From 33 yards out, Waterfield place kicked a field goal with eight minutes to play and the Rams had won, 10-7."

* * * *

And so, things had not turned out quite the way sportswriters and fans had expected. Instead of stopping, the rain that had begun soaking the field when the game started continued intermittently until the end. Rather than a high-scoring shootout, it had been a defensive battle. Instead of throwing a barrage of passes, the All-Stars had attempted only seven. Instead of using their superior size, strength and experience to run through the All-Stars' defense, the Rams had thrown 15 passes, the result being that the All-Stars ended up with more rushing yards (178) than the Rams (107) and the Rams more passing yardage (170) than the collegians (104).

What did turn out as expected was the result of a post-game poll among 100 sportswriters to select the All-Stars' most valuable player.

Babe Parilli.

Second was California linebacker Les Richter, who had been a major factor in keeping the Rams out of the end zone. Also receiving votes were defensive back Ollie Matson of San Francisco and Ohio State's Vic Janowicz who had scored the All-Stars' only touchdown.

The story announcing the outcome of the voting did not side-step Babe's miscues.

"Parilli," it said, "committed fumbles of the rain-slicked ball that possibly denied the collegians an otherwise deserved triumph. But the Kentucky ace who is tabbed to play pro ball with the Green Bay Packers was going away from his position on two of these bobbles and thus missed a chance to recover."

"Defeat was bitter for the All-Stars. They had dominated play in the first half which, barring fumbles, might have wound up with them ahead by as much as 21-0."

"The most serious blow to the collegians, though, came at the start of the second half. Parilli whipped the ball to Washington's Hugh McElhenny who raced 58 yards to the Rams' 12. On a split T lateral play, Parilli fumbled and Larry Brink recovered for the Rams to turn the tide."

What the story did not say, however, was what did have not to be said.

Because even playing in the rain, without the kind of Secret Service protection his offensive line at Kentucky had given him all season, against the defending National Football League champions, Parilli had demonstrated that being a great quarterback required more than just being a strong-armed passer with high-percentage accuracy.

Against the Rams, as he had for three seasons at UK, he had shown that he also was a calm and cool leader unfazed by pressure and adversity; a crafty tactician calling the right plays at the right time; a master of deception, keeping the Ram defense off balance with his now-you-see-it, now-you-don't faking; a runner willing and able to absorb brutal punishment to pick up vital yardage when his team needed it.

And, like the great baseball hitters, Babe Ruth, Ted Williams, Joe DiMaggio, Mickey Mantle, who struck out more than anyone else, he had been able to keep his poise and persevere despite his miscues. While costing the All-Stars two opportunities to score and perhaps put the game out of reach, his fumbles had occurred deep in Ram territory, not in his own. They had not directly led to in-close LA scores and strictly from a field position standpoint, had been the equivalent of long, well placed punts.

The two missed scoring opportunities were profit lost, not ill advised, cumbersome debt.

On the other hand, on the Stars' one successful scoring drive, had he not run for 10 yards and on the next play, 32 more, had he not then hit Michigan State end Bob Carey at the three, Vic Janowicz would not have been in a position to power across the goal line to give the All-Stars the 7-0 lead they held for three quarters.

Had not his ball faking left the Rams' defense standing flat footed, had he not then flipped the ball to Hugh McElhenny at the split-second, just-right moment, McElhenny could not have raced 58 yards to give the Stars a chance for a second touchdown.

Yes, as Kentucky fans had known all along, Babe was more than just a passer.

He was, as Bear Bryant had so succinctly said, "a coach's dream."

By any standard, under any circumstance, at any level, a most valuable player.

* * * *

After the game, The Bear walked into the locker room.

"I didn't know you could run that way," he told Babe. "We could have gained thousands of yards."

* * * *

As a college student, Babe still had not been able to overcome his fear of public speaking.

He decided to face the lions by taking a speech course. Wally Briggs, his speech professor, repeatedly took Babe to a large, auditorium. There, he spoke to empty seats.

"If somebody walks in," Briggs told him, "keep right on going."

A year after being named Most Valuable Player in the 1952 College All-Star game, Babe returned to Soldier Field.

There, as was customary for the previous year's MVP to do, he gave a speech—the first of his entire life.

In front of 93,818 people.

Chicago Tribune sports columnist Arch Ward, creator of the game, told him afterward that it was the best he had ever heard.

**Babe and Bear Bryant playing simulated football game
the coach invented**

Babe and Bear Preparing for 1949 season opener

"Best passer in the country" : Tennessee Coach Gen. Bob Neyland

**Babe, Bear and All-American tackle and Outland
Trophy winner Bob Gain**

Babe's passing stakes UK to 13-0 lead in Sugar Bowl

1951 UK Wildcats: starting lineup. Front row, from left: Jim Proffitt, Bob Fry, John Ignarski, Doug Moseley, Gene Donaldson, John Netoskie and Steve Meilinger; back row, Ed Hamilton, Babe, Bill Leskovar and Harry Jones.

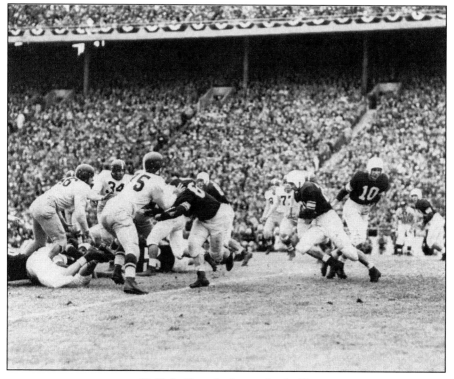

Ball, ball—who's got the ball?

UK band salutes Babe at Cotton Bowl , his final collegiate game

Wildcats celebrate 20-7 Cotton Bowl victory over Texas Christian

Babe, Bear, Ed Hamilton and Emery Clark

Green Bay Coach Gene Ronzani signs Babe to three-year contract

**Otto Graham, legendary Cleveland Browns' quarterback, crowns
Babe, his chosen successor. At left is coach Paul Brown.**

Babe with Patriots' teammate, end Tony Romeo

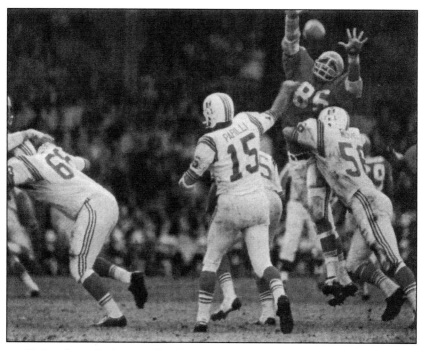

Babe threads the needle through arms of 6-foot 7 Kansas City
Chiefs' defensive tackle Buck Buchanan

Babe with Joe Namath during the New York Jets' 16-7 upset win
over the heavily favored Baltimore Colts in Super Bowl III

With Babe holding, Jim Turner kicks three field goals and an extra point to account for 10 of the Jets' 16 points in Super Bowl III

CHAPTER 11

On Jan. 17, two weeks plus after Kentucky had beaten Texas Christian in the Cotton Bowl, the National Football League held its 1952 draft. By the time the selection process was over, the 12 member teams—the Cleveland Browns, Green Bay Packers, Detroit Lions, Chicago Bears, Chicago Cardinals, Pittsburgh Steelers, Philadelphia Eagles, New York Giants, New York Yanks, Washington Redskins, San Francisco 49ers and Los Angeles Rams—had scavenged their way through 30 rounds involving 360 players.

Among them were two Heisman Trophy winners, Vic Janowicz (1950) of Ohio State and Princeton's Dick Kazmaier (1951). Kazmaier (Maumee) like Janowicz (Elyria) had played his high school football in Ohio.

Underutilized, hobbled by injuries, Janowicz, the Buckeyes' triple-threat winner as a junior, had struggled his senior season, as had his teammates during Woody Hayes' first season at OSU. The Buckeyes had finished 4-3-2. Their fans were so outraged that when the marching band began playing *Carmen Ohio,* the school's oldest, most somber and revered song, some sang:

"Oh, come let's sing Ohio's praise
"And say goodbye to Woody Hayes"
Then concluded with:
"Time and change will surely show
"That Woody Hayes has got to go"
Janowicz was selected 79th.

Kazmaier's was the 176th name called. He chose to enroll at the Harvard School of Business and pursue a career in business over pro football.

It was, however, a draft loaded with lots of other outstanding, nationally known players, including Maryland fullback Ed Modzelewski (6th); Washington fullback Hugh McElhenny (9th); Southern California halfback Frank Gifford (11th); San Francisco end Gino Marchetti (14th) ; Oklahoma tackle Jim Weatherall (17th); Notre Dame tackle Bob Toneff (22nd); Michigan State quarterback Al Darow (31st); Texas A & M defensive back Yale Lary (34th); Washington quarterback Don Heinrich (35th); Arkansas placekicker Pat Summerall (45th) and Notre Dame quarterback John Petitbon (74th). Of that group, four, McElhenny, Gifford, Marchetti and Lary, were future Professional Football Hall of Fame. Inductees.

Meanwhile, when Kentucky fans began to scan the long list of selectees, they did not have to look far to find Babe's name. He was drafted fourth, behind only quarterback Billy Wade of Vanderbilt (1st), California guard Les Richter (2nd)' and San Francisco fullback Ollie Matson (3rd). Richter and Matson also were destined to be inducted into the Hall of Fame.

Jim Mutscheller, the Beaver Falls star who became an All-American end at Notre Dame, was the 134th player chosen.

Skippy Doyle, once the apple of Bear Bryant's eye as well as everybody else's, 318[th..]

Babe and Doyle would never be NFL teammates, but their paths would cross again—for Babe, in a most satisfying manner.

* * * *

It would have been perfectly understandable had Babe been, as Damon Runyon would have phrased it, "dismayed more than somewhat" when he learned that he had been drafted No. 1 by the Green Bay Packers. Many NFL players, including some of the Packers themselves, considered Green Bay the Siberia of professional football. Its bitterly cold winters, made even worse by the gusting, punishing arctic winds that blew in off Lake Michigan, were not the only reason. Since the end of World War II, the Packers had been a ne'r do well, ugly duckling team only their own rabid fans could love. Even then it wasn't easy. In both the 1946 and 1947 seasons, the Packers had managed to finish a mediocre. 6-5. Considering what happened the next four seasons, those seemed like the good ol' days. In 1948, they finished 3-9; in 1950, slid to 2-10; and in both 1950 and 1951, finished 3-9. Meaning, over their most recent six seasons, they had won 23 and lost 47 and in the most recent four, won 11 and lost 37.

Another factor was pay. Some of their linemen, who endured more than their share of black eyes, missing teeth, broken fingers and noses, bruises, contusions, concussions and assorted other injuries and ailments, were paid as little as $3, 500 a year.

Nor would anyone have been shocked if Babe had refused to play for Green Bay. Babe's former teammate, All-American tackle and Outland Trophy winner Bob Gain, had. Gain had been the Packer's No. 1 pick in 1951. Instead of accepting what he considered to be the Packers' miserly offer, Gain had gone instead to Ottawa, where had played in the Canadian Football League. After one season, the Packers relinquished their rights to Gain by trading him to the Cleveland Browns.

But Babe wasn't in the least discouraged by the prospect of playing on one of the NFL's worst teams in its smallest, most remote and frigid city.

Not after talking with Bear Bryant.

"Tell 'em you want $15,000 a year, for three years," the Bear growled. "If they won't give it to you, you and I will open up a string of hamburger stands."

When Packer coach Gene Ronzani arrived in Lexington to sign his No, 1 draft pick, Babe, embarrassed even to talk about such things as salary let alone make such a bold demand, told Ronzani over lunch how much money he had to have in order to sign.

Ronzani nearly choked.

But with a pale, pained grimace, he reluctantly accepted Babe's terms.

Then there was the new car.

* * * *

After his senior season. Kentucky fans said thank you for all the thrills, fun and enjoyment he had given them during his three-year collegiate football career.

They gave him a brand new, powder blue, 1952 Pontiac Catalina.

It wasn't a gift from a well heeled, fat cat booster. Rather, it was the result of a pass-the-hat fund raiser that included a dollar here, a couple of bucks there from waitresses and store clerks and bus drivers and all kinds of ordinary fans all over the city.

And so, on a bright, sunny, muggy summer morning, Babe whistled as he headed northwest through the cities and towns that dotted the Indiana and Illinois countryside and across the flat farmland that surrounded them.

And why not?

Here he was, the son of first-generation Italian immigrant parents, a kid who had grown up in a gritty, grimy western Pennsylvania industrial town who, at the age of 22, thanks to Bear Bryant, was one of the highest paid rookies –if not the highest paid rookie-- in the National Football League, driving a new car with his whole bright future ahead of him.

Best of all, he had just been given a chance to continue doing what he loved to do most.

Play football.

* * * *

Shortly after he arrived in Green Bay, however, he saw first hand that life in the NFL was not so rosy for everyone.

Lloyd McDermott, a former teammate at Kentucky, was among those unfortunate, underpaid linemen he had heard about.

McDermott had just been traded by the Chicago Bears to the Packers. And now here he was, standing in the hallway outside Babe's open door at the Northland Hotel. McDermott and his wife and three children had just driven in from Chicago.

They had no place to stay.

"Get a big room here and charge it to the team," Babe told him.'

Lloyd did.

The next day, he was released.

Back into the car he and his family climbed. Back they went to Chicago.

Two years after McDermott, a defensive tackle, had been drafted in the sixth round by the Philadelphia Eagles and then been peddled to Chicago and on to Green Bay, his NFL career was over.

* * * *

A few days before, when Babe had arrived in Green Bay, he didn't know a soul. But then despite the tens of thousands who saw him play at Stoll Field and far more who listened on the radio and read about him in the newspapers, he hadn't know many people in Lexington either. With football and classes taking so much of his time, with the intense focus Bear Bryant had demanded that he and his teammates devote to both, there just hadn't been much left for anything else.

Sometimes, it took someone not accustomed to the Bear's driving passion for perfection to make Babe realize how intense it was. Such as when Gay Brewer, whose dream was to become a professional golfer, showed up at practice.

UK did not offer scholarships in golf so the Bear, in order to make it possible for Brewer to attend UK, gave him one for football. And just to make it look good, or good enough, Brewer was to show up for football practice once in awhile.

Once was enough.

After 20 minutes or so, and right before he turned in his football gear, Brewer told Babe: "I never realized what you guys go through."

Evenings, now and then, he and a few teammates would stop in at the Three O'Clock Club for a beer or two. Go downtown to the movies, where they always got in free. Loaf at Jack Cook's little gas station down on South Limestone. But before, during and after classes, he had not felt, nor had he been treated, like the Big Man on Campus. No one asked for his autograph and besides, if they had, he would have felt embarrassed. He would rather hide than have to deal with that.

Still, he was not ignored. Hazel and Tracy Neal, who owned The Springs Motel down on Harrodsburg Road, practically adopted him. They invited him to dinner, although his presence, like that of all of his teammates, was required at the football training table. They took him to Harrodsburg for delicious chicken and country ham at the Beaumont Inn. They attended all the games, including the 1952 College All-Star classic against the Los Angeles Rams at Chicago's Soldier Field and later, traveled to Green Bay to see him play.

He had dated Sue Wetherby, whom he had met on campus. She was the daughter of Kentucky Governor Lawrence Wetherby. That had led to dinner invitations at the governor's mansion. It also led to something that Babe had found more embarrassing than stage fright.

Sometimes, when the team traveled, the governor went along. He insisted upon carrying Babe's suitcase.

"Save your arm," he always said.

Then there were invitations to the Kentucky Derby and the galas and parties leading up to it. Babe had never attended. He didn't like big crowds.

He didn't lack for suitable clothes if he had wanted to go though.

More than once, when he dropped in to see Phil Angelucci, brother of the UK team doctor and proprietor of Angelucci & Ringo's downtown clothing store, a wealthy customer would walk in and Phil would say:

"Why don't you buy Babe a shirt or a sports coat?"

That was embarrassing too, but so was acting like he did not appreciate it.

Had anyone been interested enough to go through the news-paper files covering the 1949, 1950 and 1951 football seasons, they would have found something else to show how personally anony-mous Babe had been.

Even after a game, reporters did not interview him or any of his teammates.

The Bear didn't allow it. Didn't tell reporters they couldn't talk to his players. Didn't need to. Same way for glad-handing boosters. Adoring hangers-on and gushy well wishers. Just as he kept his players away from them, he kept them away from his players.

"They were afraid of the Bear," he recalled.

Nor did he or any of his teammates ever celebrate after scoring a touchdown.

"That's what you're supposed to do," the Bear growled.

But that was all behind him now. He was in a new place, with a new team, playing for a new coach, in a totally different atmosphere.

Freedom.

He smiled when he remembered the night he was in the bath-room at the football house at 147 Washington Street washing his socks when the door slowly opened and the Bear peered in. It was after 10 o'clock curfew.

"Where is everybody?" he asked.

"They went out," Babe replied.

"*Out?*"

"Remember? You gave us the night off."

The Bear thought about that for a moment, then said:

"Well, they ought to be here studying."

Freedom.

He welcomed it. Because of the Bear, he had grown into it; was far better prepared to handle it. And yet, he was still the quiet, modest kid from a smoky, obscure little factory town in western Pennsylvania.

And always would be.

* * * *

As he moved about Green Bay, he discovered that everybody seemed to know who he was. They had seen his photo in the newspaper; read about his two-time, first-team All-American career at Kentucky. Things, they said, sure were looking up. And if everyone he met acted so proud of the Packers and adored them so much that they talked like they owned them, well, they did. The team was community-owned—the only major professional team in any sport that was—and had been since it had been formed way back when. In the weeks and months that followed, he would learn more and more about the Packers' storied past.

How in 1919, Earl "Curly" Lambeau, one of the team's co-founders and long-time coach, had gone to the Indian Packing Company soliciting funds for uniforms and equipment and had been given $500 with only one condition: that the team be named the Packers.

How in 1935, Don Hutson, an All-American end at Alabama, had joined the team and over the next 10 years, not only had led the Packers to NFL championships in 1936, 1939 and 1944 and led the league in receptions eight seasons but when he retired in 1945, held 18 all-time league records, many of which still stood.

Don *Hutson?*

From *Alabama?*

Then he remembered hearing the name back at UK and why it rang a bell.

Don Hutson had played one end at Alabama and Bear Bryant –The Bear!—his coach at Kentucky-- the other!

He also learned about the Packers' abrupt, depressing and continuing decline. How after the Hutson glory years had ended in 1945, not even Green Bay icon Curly Lambeau could keep the Packers from sliding into mediocrity and, even sadder to see and say, inferiority.

Now, Gene Ronzani, the man who had followed Lambeau, was about to begin his third season as the Packers' coach. His teams had finished 3-9 in both 1950 and 1951.

Perhaps 1952 would be better.

* * * *

A week or so after Babe arrived in Green Bay, the Packers headed for Grand Rapids, Minn. to begin pre-season training camp. Grand Rapids, located 70 miles or so west of Duluth and 100 or so south of International Falls, was a paper mill town with a population of about 7,000. Its chief claim to fame was that it was the birthplace of actress-singer Judy Garland and a faint second, that it was the home of the University of Minnesota North Central Agricultural School.

Why the Packers chose Grand Rapids was an enduring mystery rivaled only by how they found it in the first place. For the Packers' coaching staff, its chief attribute seemed to be that it was close to next to nothing and possessed next to nothing to entice people to come there. Ideal, then, to conduct six weeks of practice with no distractions.

* * * *

Like the other 11 NFL teams, the Packers would begin the regular season with a 33-man roster. As with the other teams, there would be only two quarterbacks, meaning only two dozen in the entire league. While it was permissible to have more than two, it was not practical. Carrying, say, four quarterbacks, two of whom, barring major injuries, were not likely ever to play even a single down, meant diluting depth, already shallow, at other positions.

Former Rice star Tobin Rote had been the Packers' starting quarterback the season before. From the outset, Ronzani considered Rote and Babe equally good enough to play regularly. And, as it turned out, an equal amount of time. When the season opened, if Rote started, he played the entire first quarter; Babe, the second; Rote, the third; and Babe, the fourth. Same pattern if Babe started. It was a strategy, a routine, that worked so well that Rote and Babe, combined to lead the NFL in net passing yardage that season.

One reason it worked was that the two young quarterbacks, one two years out of college and other, just out, became close friends. Although both were highly competitive, there was no jealousy; no animosity on or off the field.

* * * *

If there was little to do for fun and amusement in Green Bay, and there wasn't, there was even less in Grand Rapids. The players were not allowed to have cars. The only way they could get from camp to town seven miles away was to ride a school bus.

Nor were they allowed to have beer at camp. The only way one of the Packers could enjoy a cold one after practice was to finish first in the team's daily foot race. In the beginning, Tobin Rote sometimes won; others, Babe Parilli. Then, they devised a way to share the coveted daily been prize the same way they did playing time.

They agreed to cross the finish line at the same time. That way, they both received a cold beer.

A joint attempt to increase their supply proved less successful, however. One day, they sneaked a six-pack onto the bus and when they got back to camp, buried it. But the next day, when they were in the process of digging it up, head coach Gene Ronzani caught them in the act.

He confiscated the beer and, Rote and Babe were quite sure, proceeded to take it back to his room and drink it all himself.

Perhaps not though. As Babe found later after they returned to Green Bay, Ronzari seemed to be as straight-laced as a football. One day when Babe, once again with nothing to do, wandered into Ronzani's office, the coach, with a little time on his hands himself, suggested that they go to a movie.

They went to see "*The Moon Is Blue.*" starring William Holden, David Niven and Maggie McNamara. It was the story of two aging playboys pursuing the same attractive young woman who thwarts their advances by telling them that she intends to remain a virgin until she marries.

When one of them persisted and tried, cautiously, but in Ronzani's opinion, inappropriately, to change her mind, he turned to Babe and said, "Come on, let's get out of here."

Babe followed, trying to keep from laughing out loud.

* * * *

No matter how many games Gene Ronzani's teams won or lost, Babe quickly saw that he had to be a better football coach then he was a motivational speaker.

When he gave a pre-game talk, he never looked at his players. When he stood before them in the Packers' dressing room, he gazed at the floor, sometimes his voice so low, he seemed to be talking to himself.

A partition with a large blackboard divided the locker room from the showers. Before one game, through the open door connecting the two, they all could hear one of the showers dripping. Ronzani kept on talking. The shower kept dripping. Then, still talking, Ronzani walked over to the open door, through it and began trying to tighten the shower handle.

The shower continued to drip. Ronzani, out of sight, continued to talk.

Babe and his teammates leaned in their seats, trying to peer around the corner as Ronzani, still out of sight, continued to talk.

* * * *

One of Babe's daily forms of entertainment was watching William Fritz Afflis eat. Afflis, a gruff, brawny left guard with a 56-inch chest, devoured his food like a starved grizzly. He also went about in a way Babe had never seen before. First he wolfed down his desert. They he gulped a milkshake or several, each containing a dozen eggs.

Then, and only then, did he begin the main course, or in Afflis' case, coarse.

As a pro football player, Afflis never became a household name, but he did, beginning in the late 1950s in the Midwest, as a professional wrestler known as "Dick The Bruiser." Every Thursday night, he appeared on live TV in Detroit, body slamming and pinning one hapless opponent after another. His only live TV defeat was to Cowboy Bob Ellis.

In two rematches, Afflis, who billed himself as "The World's Most Dangerous Wrestler," won both.

As fascinating as it was to watch Afflis eat, no one ever got around to telling him how funny it was too. Somehow, it just didn't seem like such a good idea.

* * * *

For Afflis, packing away a few thousand calories or felling a defensive tackle like a telephone pole struck by a semi was one thing; remembering the snap- count directions Babe called, something else.

Afflis, snarling, was so intent on destroying the defensive man opposite him, he forgot to listen.

Which was why, as Babe crouched in the huddle and called the play-- *blah-blah-blah-blah* "on *TWO*," he looked right at Afflis.

And held up, near his face, two fingers.

"That really helps me a lot," Afflis told Babe.

* * * *

That season, two other Packer linemen also achieved a measure of lasting fame in the annuals of Packer lore. They were credited with originating what became known as the Lookout Block.

It began with one of them attempting, with only occasional success, to stop a defender from streaking into the backfield. Then failing—again—they would shout to Babe or Tobin Rote, whichever had dropped back to pass:

"LOOK OUT!"

* * * *

Having just completed three highly successful seasons playing for The Bear, it would have been easy for Babe to second guess Ronzani's personality, his system, his handling of players, his play calling, his entire approach to the game. Understandable, too, to think, at every turn: *That's not the way the Bear would have done it.*

But he didn't. Right away, he realized there was so much more to learn; so much more to memorize until it became second nature; so many more offensive options. So much more flexibility.

It all boiled down to one word: freedom. True, as a college quarterback at Kentucky, he had called all the plays. But he had called them all exactly as he knew Bear Bryant wanted them called given the circumstances at the moment-- down, field position, the score, time remaining and on occasion, weather conditions.

Having played question-and-answer board-game football every lunch hour in the Bear's office for three years, he now knew, he had, in effect, been "brainwashed." He had been free in the same way that a well trained race horse or an obedient K9 dog is free: free to do exactly, precisely, automatically what he knew he was supposed to do.

Creativity, spontaneity had nothing to do with it.

And yet, it was not a realization that reflected unfavorably on the Bear or diminished even a little bit the deep affection he felt for his college coach or his appreciation of everything the Bear had taught him. Bear Bryant and his assistant, Ermal Allen, had taught him everything he knew about handling the ball, footwork, passing, team leadership. Utilizing his abilities, his love of the game, they had taught him *how* to play. And in the process, they had taught him lessons, enduring values, that would stay with him long after he had played his last game. Now, so equipped, it was time to think for himself. To play the cards life as well pro football dealt him.

Whatever they might be.

* * * *

Off the field, Babe was enjoying his new-found freedom too.

No more regimentation. No more day after day of doing the same things, at the same times, in the same way. No more going to class. No more tutoring sessions. No more curfews. No more doing without a car. Money. Clothes.

Off as well as on the field, he was having fun.

* * * *

One afternoon, NFL Commissioner Bert Bell appeared in the Packers' locker room. His message, delivered to players on all of the 12 league teams, concerned the dangers and evils of gambling.

Although Bell did not say so, in the wake of the collegiate point-shaving basketball scandal the year before involving more three dozen or so players from City College of New York, Manhattan, Long Island University, New York University, the University of Kentucky and Bradley, Babe sensed that Bell was concerned about the possibility of a similar scandal rocking the National Football League.

Babe smiled when he recalled what had happened in August at the College All-star game in Chicago when he had met Frank Gifford, the Southern California star who had been the first player drafted by the New York Giants.

When they talked about an exhibition game scheduled the next day in Milwaukee between the Packers and Giants, one of them kidded:

"I'll betcha dollar we beat you."

"You're on," the other replied.

Because Babe had not had time to learn his team's offense, he was in the game for two plays. For the same reason, Gifford did not play at all. Babe would never forget the first play he ever called as pro quarterback:

"Two right 39 toss Tess Ed crack 26 on two."

Huh?

After the game, won by the Giants, Babe suggested he be given a chance to even the score when the two teams at the Polo Grounds during the regular season.

The second time around, the Packers beat the Giants.

Neither Babe nor Gifford won or lost any money.

Nor did any money change hands.

Both promptly forgot it, as well they should have. It was nothing more than a fleeting, joking, harmless incident.

Bet on a football game, especially one in which he was playing?

Babe couldn't even imagine it.

But that day in Green Bay, from the look on his face, the tone of his voice, Bert Bell left no doubt that he certainly believed it could happen if NFL players were not careful what kind of places they frequented and with whom they associated.

* * * *

In their first exhibition game of the 1952 season, the Packers played the Washington Redskins in Kansas City. Playing pre-season games in such league- remote places as Kansas City, Spokane, Wash. and Bangor, Maine was a marketing tool to attract more fan interest nationwide. At the time, pro football, like pro basketball, was nowhere close to being in the same league with baseball, the National Pastime.

Babe was awed.

Not because he was starting for the Packers but because of who was for the Redskins: his collegiate idol, Slingin' Sammy Baugh, the former Texas Christian star whose all-time national passing records Babe had broken the year before.

Baugh, 38, was beginning his 16th professional football season.

Sixteen years. . . .

Babe couldn't even imagine how someone could play that long.

* * * *

After losing three of their first five regular season games, the Packers enjoyed a rare spree of prosperity by winning three in a row, the third, 17-3 over the New York Giants in New York.

When they emerged from the stadium and started to board their bus, Coach Gene Ronzani was so elated he pointed to a bar across the street: :

"Come on, let's all go have a drink."

* * * *

Later that month, Babe learned there was one place he would gladly never frequent again and 33 people he would just as soon not associate with either.   On a bitterly cold day, the Packers boarded a four-engine prop plane and headed for Detroit to play the Lions on Thanksgiving Day.

From November through late spring, Green Bay wasn't exactly Miami Beach, but as they trotted out onto the field at Briggs Stadium in downtown Detroit, blinding snow, racing horizontally across the field, felt like a desert sandstorm as it lashed their faces. The ground was frozen. Their feet were numb. And so, while the rest of America was heading over the river and through the woods to Grandmother's house for a big, juicy Turkey Day dinner with all the trimmings, here they were, having already lost to the Lions 52-17 in Green Bay on Oct. 27, about to take another drubbing, this time 48-24, as Detroit merrily frolicked it way on toward an 11-3 season and the NFL championship.

Although there was more than a smidgen of poetic justice in their Arctic Circle discomfort, it didn't help a bit to know that the way they felt that day was exactly the way everyone else in the league did every time they had to play a late-season game in Green Bay.

* * * *

Before losing to Detroit for the second time, the Packers had been cruising along with a 6-3 record. Now, they had only two games left, on Dec. 7 against the Rams in Los Angeles and on Dec. 14, with the '49ers in San Francisco. They had to win only one to finish with a winning record, their first since—who knew when?

The records said 1947, but for long-suffering Packer fans, it seemed like 1847.

At least they could settle back and enjoy a nice, long, relaxing flight out to the West Coast. At least they would be warm again.

Alas, Gene Ronzani was not a big fan of flying. He preferred traveling by train. So off they went, clattering across the country on what seemed like a ride to forever. Along the way, the veteran players whiled away the time playing cards. Whenever the train stopped, Babe and the other rookies had to bound down the steps and go searching for the nearest liquor store and then, somehow, sneak a bottle of booze onto the train and deliver it to the veterans before Ronzani intercepted them.

Because of the long train trip, the Packers did not arrive in time to work out.

They lost to the Rams, 45-27 and a week later, to the '49ers, 24-14.

Perhaps a lack of practice had had nothing to do with their second consecutive loss. The Rams were a good team, finishing first in the league's National Division with a 9-3 record. As the comparative scores indicated, the '49ers (7-5) had been the Packers' best hope of winning one of the two games necessary to finish 7-5.

* * * *

Bill Reichardt, fullback and backup placekicker, scored only one touchdown during the Packers' 1952 season. Seeing as how he played only one season in the NFL, it also was the only one he scored in his entire career.

But it was a touchdown Babe would never forget because of how it came about.

On Dec, 7, in Los Angeles, with the Rams leading the Packers 45-14, Reichardt raced onto the field and into the huddle. The

171

regular fullback, thinking Reichardt had been sent it to replace him, trotted over to the sidelines.

Babe, thinking Reichardt had been sent in with a play, asked what it was.

"Two C trap!" Reichardt said.

Reichardt's play.

Babe took the snap, handed the ball off to Reichardt and off he went— 57 yards to the Rams' two- yard line.

On the next play, seeing as how Reichardt had put the Packers in a position to score, called Reichardt's number again.

This time he plowed across the goal.

Only later did Babe learn that the person who sent Reichardt into the game was . . . Reichardt.

He had simply rushed out onto the field.

* * * *

Back home in the taverns, the glass-half-full crowd pointed out that all things considered, the 1952 Packers had done reasonably well. Until this time around, no Packer team had won six games in a season since 1947.

The half-empty bunch, well, where was Don Hutson when they needed him?

And the way things were going, and had been going, they sure needed him now more than ever.

* * * *

On Sept. 27, the Packers opened their 1953 season at home against the Cleveland Browns. The previous year, Cleveland had been good enough to finish the regular season 8-4 before losing to the Detroit Lions 17-7 in the NFL championship game. They figured to be even better this time around and if anyone doubted it, it wasn't the Packers.

Cleveland won 27-0. The loss was the beginning of a disastrous 1-4 beginning, and an even worse 0-5 ending. The Packers finished 2-9-1, their only wins both coming over the Baltimore Colts who didn't fare much better (3-9).

The year before, Babe and Tobin Rote, alternating starts and minutes played, had combined for 159 completions in 334 attempts and accounted for 2,684 yards and 26 touchdowns. In 1953, they connected on 146 of 351 for only 1,835 yards and nine touchdowns. For the season, the Packer's scored only 200 points in 12 games compared to 295 the year before.

Meanwhile, the defense, which had allowed 312 points in 1952 had surrendered 338, second worst in the league

With two games to go, Gene Ronzani resigned. Hugh DeVore and Ray (Scooter) McLean served as interim coaches for the final two games. They did no better. The Packers lost both.

For Ronzani, a legendary three-sport star at Marquette in the 1930s, it was an ignominious end to a valiant attempt to resurrect the Packers' proud tradition. His biggest contribution to that cause, however, was not in how his teams performed, but the uniforms they wore. Before he became the head coach in 1950, Green Bay teams had worn blue and gold, Curly Lambeau's tribute to his alma mater, Notre Dame. But Ronzani had switched to green because, he said, we are the GREEN Bay Packers."

Given how poorly they had performed in 1953, some cynics snickered that a more fitting color scheme would be black and blue.

For Green Bay, the prolonged drought that had begun in 1946 would continue in 1954.

Mercifully, Babe would not be a part of it.

CHAPTER 12

If everyone else in the country was not obsessed with what Wisconsin Senator Joseph McCarthy insisted was a growing communist threat to the nation's very survival, it wasn't his fault. Reds, commies, fellow travelers, pinkos, spies— McCarthy toured the country in the early 1950s declaring that there was one behind every tree, entrenched in the highest levels of every branch of the federal government, aided and abetted by movie stars, authors, college professors, nuclear scientists—all despicable subversives and traitors guilty of treason.

Many of those he vilified were ruthlessly smeared, some blacklisted, their careers and lives ruined, nearly all outraged by what they considered to be unbridled demagoguery by a man drunk with power, not to mention possessed of a propensity for consuming more than his share of a certain product aged, bottled and distributed by distilleries.

Among his targets were what he termed "pampered" professional athletes, who, because of mindless hero worship and schmoozing with the rich, the elite, received special treatment and were exempted from military service.

Perhaps because of McCarthy, perhaps only through coincidence, Babe, being a Green Bay quarterback and therefore one of Wisconsin's most prominent athletes, suddenly was notified in the spring of 1954 that he was being called to active duty seeing as how he had been enrolled in the ROTC while a student at the University of Kentucky.

He reported to Tyndall Air Force Base 12 miles east of Panama City, Fla. There he met Tom Brookshier, a defensive back for the Philadelphia Eagles who also been called to duty. What they ought to do, Brookshier said, was get themselves assigned to a base where they could play or coach football.

Brookshier did. Babe didn't.

When he completed training as an aircraft intercept controller,

Babe was given a choice. But it wasn't play or coach football. He could go either to Korea or Europe. He chose Europe, although when he stepped off the plane, he wasn't in Europe.

He was in Casablanca, Morocco.

* * * *

After enduring two icy, arctic winters in Green Bay, he now found himself wilting in the scorching Sahara heat.

As the merciless sun beat down on the hot, blowing sand, even memories of stepping off a plane in Detroit and trotting out onto the frozen Briggs Stadium turf for a shivering, teeth-chattering Thanksgiving Day football game against the Lions suddenly sounded appealing.

Morocco was every bit as hot as Green Bay was cold.

That night, he flew to Rabat, the capital, then rode a bus to an encampment several miles away. He spent the night in a tent. When he awoke, he stepped outside and saw he was standing in what someone said was a cork tree forest.

Cork trees?

Yeah, someone explained, they're where that stuff comes from that's used to make cork stoppers for wine bottles.

Oh.

* * * *

Babe wondered when they were going to report to headquarters in the city.

This *is* headquarters, he was told.

This? This God forsaken place that's nothing but wind-whipped tents, leaning outhouses, and constantly blowing sand and poker-faced Arabs walking around armed with huge swords?

Then came a powerful wind followed by a sudden rainstorm that whipped the sides of the tent like someone beating a rug. Rain dripped inside, creating puddles on the tent floor.

What next?

A flood?

Not to worry, someone said. A new officer's hotel was being built in Rabat. They would move there when it was finished.

Finished when?

In about six weeks.

Six weeks? Meaning we're going to be living out here in this terrible heat, in a tent with our eyes and ears full of sand for *six weeks?*

Oh, boy. It sure was going to be a long, long two years.

* * * *

Out in the trackless western Sahara, forming an electronic arc to guard against unidentified aircraft, were four early warning stations. If they detected anything suspicious, they notified headquarters. If the identity of the aircraft was not immediately made known, the next step was to send fighter jets scrambling to intercept it.

Everyone on the headquarters staff overseeing the 200 or so men stationed there also has secondary duties. Babe's was to serve as French Education officer. Communicating in French was essential because the base was under French control.

Babe Parilli? From Rochester, Pa.?

A *French Education Officer?*

A young woman working there happened to be fluent in five languages. Fortunately, one of them was French. She handled all of his calls, correspondence and conversations requiring it, including, after he had moved to Rabat, ordering from the menu when they went to dinner at a French restaurant.

Babe's only remaining duty as French Education Officer was signing diplomas —in English—when other airmen completed their French classes.

* * * *

When the officers' hotel was completed and he moved into Rabat, life became much easier. Before reporting to Tyndall Air Force Base, he had traded in the powder blue 1952 Pontiac Catalina Kentucky fans had given him. He now owned a brand new, mint- green Pontiac convertible with green vinyl seats and interior.

He had it shipped to Rabat.

Driving through Rabat and out to air intercept headquarters, he felt like he had that day in 1952 when he drove out of Lexington en route to Green Bay. Like then, he had a new car. Not just a new car, but in all likelihood the best looking car in Rabat. He had money and nearly no living expenses. His room at the hotel cost only $15 a month.

He never locked the car. He knew that if he did, thieves would slit the convertible top or break the glass to get in. Often, when he came out, the doors were standing open. Nothing had been taken though because he never left anything in the car to take.

* * * *

In another way, he felt like he was back in Green Bay too. He was in a remote place, with time on his hands and little to do for fun.

What about sports?

Soccer, he was told.

The base had a soccer team and nothing else.

Babe decided to do something about that.

Soon he had organized a flag football program. Basketball too. A pretty good basketball team at that. Good enough, in fact, to warrant flying to Germany to compete against other military base teams scattered across Europe.

While there, he learned that there was an All Armed Forces team and that its coach was looking for an assistant.

Would he be interested?

Babe, who had excelled in basketball as well as baseball and football back home in Rochester, Pa., said he would be.

After spending four months in Germany, he flew with the basketball team to Cairo.

* * * *

During his stay in Cairo and Alexandria, an Egyptian, Cambridge-educated army captain was assigned to be his escort. He had been involved, he said, in the overthrow of Egyptian dictator King Farouk.

One afternoon, he took Babe to a mansion that had been the home of the king. Among its lavish amenities was a swimming pool.

Would Babe like to go for a swim?

Yes, he sure would.

As they walked out to the pool his escort told him that its contents would be different than when the king had gone in for a dip.

Different?

How could it be different? Water was water.

"Sometimes," his escort said, "he had it filled with milk."

Then added:

"At a time when many of our people were starving."

* * * *

During the basketball tournament, a man walked up, smiled, and shook Babe's hand.

He name, he said, was Gamal Abdel Nasser.
The president of Egypt.

* * * *

When he learned that an air force plane was scheduled to fly from Rabat to Naples, Italy, Babe received permission to go along. South of Naples was Sparanise, the little farming village where his father and mother had grown up. His grandmother and other relatives, none of whom he had ever met, still lived there.

It was a joyous visit, but one that proved to be somber as well.

When Babe saw a street sign that said, "October 22 Way," he asked what it meant. Then they told him the story.

* * * *

Although Italy, at Axis ally of Germany during World War II, had surrendered on Sept. 3, 1943, German troops continued to occupy parts of the country. One of them was Sparanise, a farming village near Naples where Babe's grandparents lived. Mary Feola, Babe's mother's younger sister had lived there too.

Mary Feola was 17 and beautiful. Carlo Cappuzzuto, a loud bully and wheat farmer, was twice her age. Carlo wanted to marry Mary. Wanted her bad enough that he threatened her parents. He would kill the whole family, he told them, if she didn't marry him. Frightened, her parents consented.

One day, Mary went down to the village well for a bucket of water. Carlo was loafing nearby. Their baby was at home with Mary's mother. Two Germans riding a three-wheel motorcycle approached. The one driving had a sub-machinegun draped diagonally across his chest. His passenger was holding a briefcase over the edge of the side car.

When they got closer, Carlo stepped out into the street and pulled out a gun. He shot and killed the passenger and wounded the driver. He then snatched the briefcase, apparently thinking it contained money, and fled. Soon, German soldiers began round-ing up village residents, 39 in all.

They were ordered to dig a long ditch, then stand beside it. Then the Germans opened fire, killing them all. Among them was Babe's aunt, Mary, and his grandfather, Vito Feola. Two young cousins were wounded but played dead and survived.

Later, a monument was erected and the street renamed Vic-tims' Way.

* * * *

Babe's two years of active duty weren't exactly flying by, but his military duties and directing and participating in the basketball and flag football programs he had created kept him busy.

Then came the best news he could imagine. As part of a com-prehensive manpower reduction, his 24-month hitch had been reduced to 18. His time was nearly up. Soon, he would be heading home. And, at long last, back to doing what he loved most: playing football.

* * * *

Had he known about it, there was other, older news that would have lifted his spirits sooner and perhaps even more.

On August 6, 1954, a story originating in Hiram, Ohio, where the Cleveland Browns held pre-season training camp, announced:

"The Cleveland Browns today traded Bobby Garrett, Stanford's great 1953 quarterback and bonus draft choice of the Cleveland club to Green Bay in a six-player deal.

"In exchange, the Browns, runner-up for the pro grid title the last two years, received Babe Parilli, former Kentucky quarterback, and Bob Fleck, former Syracuse tackle, from Green Bay.

Joining Garrett in the shift from the Browns to Green Bay were Johnny Bauer, former Southern Methodist quarterback Don Miller and Chet Gierula, Maryland tackle.

"Parilli, a big star at Kentucky, is in the Army now and may not be available until the 1956 season. He played with Green Bay in 1952 and 1953.

"Garrett is expected to play this season but then faces two years in military service.

"A spokesman for the Browns said it was believed that a new quarterback would be needed more in two years than at present. Otto Graham is the club's star at the post now, and has been with the club since 1946 but there has been talk of his retiring. His understudy is George Ratterman.

"We are swapping someone who will be of immediate value to the Packers for someone we will need in two years," the spokesman said.

What the spokesman did not say was that there was another reason for the trade.

Too late, Coach Paul Brown discovered that he had spent his first draft selection and paid bonus money to boot for a quarterback who stuttered so badly he had trouble calling signals.

Too late, after consummating the deal, Green Bay discovered Garrett's handicap too.

As a backup for Tobin Rote, Garrett had played in nine games, completed 15 of 30 passes for 143 yards with no touchdowns and one interception and ran once for minus three yards.

After the 1954 season, he never played another down in the NFL.

Not until he arrived home from North Africa did Babe learn of the trade.

Then, he received a letter from Browns' coach Paul Brown.

It said:

"You have inherited a throne."

* * * *

During Babe's two years away from the National Football League, the Packers, as usual, had not done so hot. But Tobin Rote, with whom he had shared the quarterbacking duties in 1952 and 1953, had.

In 1954, although the Packers had finished 4-8, Rote had completed 180 of 382 passes for 2,311 yards and 14 touchdowns to go along with 18 interceptions. He also had rushed 67 times for another 301 yards.

In 1955, when Green Bay finished 6-6, he had attempted 342 passes, completed 157 for 1977 yards and 17 touchdowns with 19 interceptions.

Had Babe brooded about all of that, he could not have helped but think that he could have done every bit as well, perhaps even better, if he, like Rote, had had the job full time for two full seasons instead of sharing it 50-50 as Gene Ronzani had insisted. And now he had lost two full seasons, two full seasons to show what he could do, two full seasons of valuable experience, because of military duty.

Babe did not brood, however. Nor was he any more interested in looking back at where he had been than he was about what might have been. His future was in Cleveland and, wow, what a future it appeared to be.

For when he had read Paul Brown's message—"*You have inherited a throne*"—he didn't have to wonder what it meant. Otto Graham, the Browns' legendary quarterback, was retiring and Paul Brown expected Babe to be his successor.

By any measure, it would be a tall order.

Over a 10-year period, Graham had led the Browns to seven championships—four straight in the now defunct All-America Conference and three in the NFL as well as three NFL runner-up finishes. All totaled, the Browns had played for a championship all 10 years Otto Graham was their quarterback.

Since joining the NFL in 1950, the Browns, with Otto Graham under center, had appeared in the championship game every year, winning it three times (1950, 1954 and 1955) and finishing runner-ups three times (1951,1952 and 1953). Over a four-year period,

1952, 1953, 1954 and 1955, he had completed 612 of 1092 passes for 9,442 yards and 62 touchdowns.

But the numbers also showed that over the past two seasons, his production had decreased significantly. After passing for 2,816 yards in 1952 and 2,722 in 1953, he had only 2,092 in 1954 and 1,721 in 1955.

And now, like so many of his illustrious teammates who had already done so or soon would, Graham had concluded his career.

For Babe it was a golden opportunity, the chance of a lifetime, but it came at an inopportune time. He had played only two seasons in the NFL and neither year had he been a full-time starter. He also had not played in two seasons, a long time to be away from the game.

On the other hand, he did not seem to be facing stiff competition for the job. Graham's backup, George Ratterman, was a candidate, but he too was aging and had played only sparingly in each of the preceding seasons.

Nor had the Browns selected any quarterbacks in the 1956 draft. The 1955 collegiate season had not produced many good ones. Other than Colorado's Gary Glick, a bonus pick awarded to the Pittsburgh Steelers; Earl Morrall of Michigan State, chosen second by the San Franacisco '49ers; Southern Methodist's John Roach, the Chicago Cardinals' third pick; no other major- school quarterbacks were drafted in the first 10 rounds.

Overall, only a dozen or so quarterbacks were drafted, and most who were way down the list, including George Welsh of Navy (186); Bart Starr of Alabama (200); Eagle Day of Mississippi (203) and Wisconsin's Jim Miller (330).

So now after spending nearly two years of his life literally as well as figuratively in the desert, Babe was going back. Back to America. Back to Rochester, Pa. Back to what he loved doing best.

Only this time, not for one of the NFL's most consistently inconsistent teams but for the one that since joining the league in 1950, had been its year in, year out absolute best.

At long last, things were looking up.

CHAPTER 13

Long before Paul Brown formed his own professional football team in the mid 1940s, he had established himself as an uncommonly successful coach.

In 1932, at the age of 23, Brown had returned to his alma mater, Washington High School in Massillon, Ohio where he had played as a scrub quarterback, to become its head football coach. A Washington High graduate at 16, from Miami (Ohio) University at 21, Brown had begun his coaching career two years earlier at Severn Prep in Maryland. During his two seasons at Severn, a Naval prep school, his teams won 16, lost one and tied one.

During the decade prior to his return to Massillon, the Tigers had been good but not great. In 1922, they won all 10 games, outscored their opponents 378 to 29 and were named state champions. But they had two losing seasons during that 11-year stretch and most years, finished with six to eight wins and two or three losses. One of the losing seasons occurred the year before Brown arrived when Massillon won two, lost six and tied two.

Paul Brown's first season at Massillon was nothing to shout about either. The Tigers didn't score a point in their final three games, only one touchdown in their last four and only 79 points all season while allowing 98. The Tigers finished 5-4-1.

But after winning 8 of 10 and outscoring their opponents 311-52 the next season, Paul Brown's 1934 team rolled up 427 points and did not allow a single point until their final game when arch-rival Canton McKinley beat them 21-6.

After that, Massillon was all but invincible, winning six straight state championships . In 1935, they went undefeated and out-scored their 10 opponents 483-13 then went undefeated again in 1936 when they outscored the opposition 443-14.

In 1939, they rang up 460 points and gave up only 25, and in 1940, did even better. They pummeled their opponents 477-6.

In nine seasons, Paul Brown's record at Massillon was 80-8-2; combined with his two seasons at Severn prep in Maryland: 96-9-3.

The following year, Brown became the head football coach at Ohio State and after winning six, losing one and tying one, led the Buckeyes in 1942 to their first national championship. The follow-ing, having lost 18 seniors to graduation and almost every incom-ing member of what was called their greatest recruiting class to military service, the Buckeyes won three, lost six and tied one.

The next season, Brown entered the service too and for two years, served as head coach of the Great Lakes Naval Station Blue-jackets with a 15-5-2 record. One of those wins was over Notre Dame, 35-0.

In 1946, he then became general manager and part owner of a new professional team called the Cleveland Browns. Before joining the NFL in 1950, the Browns played in the All-America Conference win-ning four straight championships and 47 games while losing only four.

* * * *

Whether they knew it or not, whether they acknowledged it or not, by 1956, when Otto Graham retired and Green Bay traded Babe to Cleveland, Paul Brown and his Browns were already begin-ning to stand in the considerable shadow of their own success. Since those unforgettable days between 1946 and 1949 when they had totally dominated the All-America Conference and continu-ing into the early 1950s in the NFL, fewer and fewer of the players who had made it all possible were still around.

Fullback Marion Motley, halfbacks Dub Jones and Edgar "Special Delivery" Jones, ends Mac Speedie and Dante Lavelli, center Frank "Gunner" Gatski, guard Abe Gibron, middle guard Bill Willis, defensive end Len Ford, tackle Chubby Grigg, guard Lou Saban, punter Horace Gillom—most were gone. Those who remained were approaching or had already reached the twilight of their career.

But the loss of Otto Graham was more significant than any of the others. For a decade, he had been their leader; their instant offense; their steadying hand when the pressure was on.

Could others, particularly this guy Parilli, step in and provide the continuity, the productivity they would need to remain if not the best, among the best, teams in the NFL?

They and along with Coach Paul Brown would soon find out.

So would Babe.

* * * *

Paul Brown made no secret of his conviction that Babe was the right man to provide the leadership, the passing, the continuity necessary to perpetuate his team's unbroken decade of success. He even staged a press and photo conference with Babe standing in the middle with Brown on one side of him and Otto Graham on the other. In one published picture, reminiscent of Brown's message, "You have inherited a throne," Graham was placing a Browns' helmet, like a crown, on Babe's head.

Although Babe did not know it at the time, he and Otto Graham had more in common than quarterbacking the Browns. During World War II, Graham, a star at Northwestern, had been drafted in 1944 by the Detroit Lions, but instead, served two years in the U.S. Coast Guard, at the time, still part of the U.S. Navy.

During that time, his football coach had been Bear Bryant.

* * * *

Behind the scenes, their discussion about salary also reinforced Babe's impression that Brown was sincere about his becoming Otto Graham's exclusive and sure-fire successor.

When Babe told Brown he had been paid $15,000 for each of his two seasons at Green Bay and his contract had called for a third $15,000 season, Brown replied:

"Oh, I think we can do better than that."

He offered Babe a two-year contract paying $16,500 the first season and $17,500 the second.

At long last, for the first time as a pro, Babe was about to play full time. No more alternating, every other play, every other quarter, as he had for two years at Green Bay.

* * * *

The Browns did not get off to a rousing start. On Sept. 30, they lost their season opener to the Chicago Cardinals, 9-7. Starting quarterback George Ratterman connected with end Ray Renfro for a 46-yard TD to give Cleveland a 7-0 lead. But they did not score again and three field goals by Pat Summerall made the final score 9-7.

A week later, Ratterman ran one yard for a touchdown and fullback Ed Modzelewski 13 yards for another as the Browns beat the Steelers 14-10. The Browns accumulated 336 yards rushing and only 122 passing.

On Oct.14, The Browns lost to the Giants 21-9, finishing with only 94 yards passing and 40 net yards rushing and a week later, lost to the Redskins, 20-9. To make matters worse, Quarterback George Ratterman was injured.

Then in their second matchup with the Steelers, although Cleveland lost 24-16, Babe provided a glimpse of what Cleveland fans hoped would be a long parade of great things to come. He connected with Ray Renfro for a 68-yard touchdown pass.

Until then, Cleveland had produced only one passing touchdown --and that had come in the season opener.

* * * *

On Nov. 4, Babe struck again, this time on a 26 yarder to Renfro and the Browns beat the Packers 24-7

The following week, in a 21-7 loss to the Baltimore Colts, Babe hit Renfro with a 27-yarder, his third touchdown pass in three games.

But that day, the Browns lost more than the game. Mike McCormick, the Browns' all-pro missed a block, and Colts end Gino Marchetti thundered past him. Just as Babe cocked his arm to throw a pass, Marchetti blindsided him. Pain, pain the likes of which he had never experienced before, raced through his shoulder like a hot wire.

Unable to lift his arm, writhing in pain, he was helped to his feet and led, looking like someone who had been shot, to the Browns' bench.

Just when he had seemed to be getting into a flow, a rhythm, just as he was beginning to show bright flashes of why Paul Brown had anointed him to be Otto Graham's successor, Babe had suffered a severe injury to the rotator cuff on his right shoulder.

His season was over.

* * * *

With Ratterman ailing and Babe lost for the season, Paul Brown quickly signed former Illinois quarterback Tommy O'Connell. O'Connell, chosen 212th in the 18th round of the 1952 draft, had played only one season in the NFL. In 1953, as backup to ex-Kentucky star George Blanda, he had been used sparingly, completing 33 passes in 67 attempts for 437 yards, one touchdown and four interceptions. While appearing in seven Browns' games that season, starting five, O'Connell would complete 33 of 67 passes for 437 yards and one touchdown with four interceptions.

In the four games he played and started in, Ratterman completed 39 of 57 passes for 398 yards with one touchdown and three interceptions.

In the five games in which he played, starting three, Babe had completed 24 of 49 passes for 409 yards, three touchdowns and seven interceptions.

Combined, they accounted for 1,244 yards and only five passing TDs.

As a rookie at Green Bay, Babe alone had completed 77 of 177 passes for 1,416 passes and 13 touchdowns, most ever for a first-year Packer; he and Tobin Rote combined, 159 of 334 for 2,684 yards and 26 TDs.

While no one was saying so, the 1956 Cleveland Browns looked more like the Green Bay Packers than they did the Browns of old.

* * * *

Try though he might, Babe could not throw a football across the locker room. But Paul Brown insisted that he suit up for every game and stand next to him when he called the plays.

Theoretically, it was a teaching tool. But it also seemed like displaying a Trojan horse, a player who might not be as badly injured as had been reported and who might come trotting out onto the field at any time.

But the truth was, even if Ratterman, still hurt, could not spell O'Connell in a pinch or if O'Connell got hurt too, what would – what could--Babe do if he did go back out on the field?

Certainly not pass. The longer the season went—and the way the Browns were playing, it was far too long already—and the colder the weather got, the stiffer his shoulder became and the more it hurt. All he could possibly do was hand the ball off and hope he did not get injured further in the process.

As a rookie at Green Bay, Babe had never made comparisons between the personalities and coaching styles of the Packers' Gene Ronzani and UK coach Bear Bryant.

But as he stood next to Paul Brown on the sideline, he could not help but think how different Brown was from the Bear both on and off the field.

By conducting one-on-one football board game sessions with him every lunch hour for three years, the Bear had allowed him to use his own judgment, to improvise within the framework of time and distance, to call all the plays.

Paul Brown called all the plays.

Babe also learned from Blanton Collier, who had served on Brown's staff from 1946 until 1953 when he replaced Bear Bryant as head coach at Kentucky that Otto Graham had also worked under the same tight-fisted control.

"If Otto wanted to change a play," Collier told him, "he knew it had better work."

And yet, as he listened to the plays Brown ordered and saw the results that followed, Babe had doubts about some of the calls.

As he had seen demonstrated countless times playing that football board game during lunch hour at Bear Bryant's office, some sure were different from what the Bear would have chosen.

* * * *

Unlike the Bear, Babe believed, Brown was not a players' coach. He was more like a CEO, aloof, apart from his team. Not only did he never seem to get close to his players, he never seemed to want to relate to them.

Whereas the Bear never browbeat or criticized a player in front of his teammates for making a mistake during a game, talking privately instead with him later, Brown was a needler, prone to berate, to humiliate, with sarcasm.

When Babe first reported for practice, Brown told him he would have to run a foot race against George Ratterman.

"If you can't beat him, I'm going to get rid of you."

Perhaps Brown meant to be humorous, but it seemed to Babe like he was berating Ratterman, known, like George Blanda, Babe's quarterbacking predecessor at UK, to be anything but swift afoot.

As the Browns watched film of the Giants game, Brown ridiculed all-pro tackle Mike McCormick, who had missed the block that resulted in Babe's injury, by saying:

"That's a *fine* block. We lost our quarterback."

Nor was it the only time he brought it up.

He reminded McCormick all season long about the costly price of his rare mistake.

Nor did he express any concern, any empathy for Babe's injury or offer words of encouragement. Like with everything else, Brown seemed emotionally detached. On those rare occasions when he said anything all about it, he would remark, as if it were Babe's fault that he got hurt:

"You're having a *great* year."

And yet, Paul Brown had had enormous success throughout his coaching career.

It was difficult to argue with success.

But at the same time, Babe knew that much of that success had come because Brown had surrounded himself with such an enormous wealth of talent.

As a quarterback at Green Bay, Babe had experienced it first hand.

When the Packers played the Browns, every time he dropped back to pass, it was more like running for his life. Pursuing him from one side faster than he could retreat was 6- foot 8 defensive end Doug Atkins; on the other Lenny Ford, the Browns' equally if not more ferocious defensive end, both destined to be inducted into the Pro Football Hall of Fame.

He especially remembered the time back in 1953 when the Green Bay Packers were the absolute worst team in the league and the Browns the best; when he and Tobin Rote, as was always the case at Green Bay, alternated playing every other quarter and it was Rote's turn to play the first quarter. After Atkins and Ford had repeatedly bear hugged and thrown Rote to the ground like a rodeo steer, he called time and slowly walked over to the Packers' bench.

"Go get 'em, Babe," he croaked.

"No," Babe replied. 'You stay in there. It's your turn."

'Nah," Rote said. "Go on in there and see what you can do."

Babe, having seen how much punishment Rote was absorbing, declined again.

"For heaven's *sake*! Will *some*body go in there? 'exasperated Packer coach Gene Ronzani shouted.

* * * *

But that was three years ago and a lot had changed since then and as their 2-5 start and their 5-7 finish clearly showed, Brown and the Browns no longer had a copyright on outstanding talent.

And somehow, that "throne" Babe had been told he had inherited seemed badly tarnished.

* * * *

Throughout his career, Paul Brown had always been an innovator as well as a winner. In his 1994 book *The Massillon Tigers Story: The First Hundred Years,* author John E. (Jack) White declared that Brown was "responsible," apparently meaning the first, or one of the first, to pioneer the following firsts:

"Employ a year-'round staff.

"Use notebooks and classroom techniques extensively.

"Set up complete game film clip statistical study.

"Grade players from individual game clips.

"Keep players together at a downtown hotel the night before home games as well as on the road.

"Call plays from sidelines by rotating guards as messengers.

"Develop detailed pass patterns which opened specific defense areas.

"Make major contributions to improve science of defensive plays to counteract pattern passing by others who followed his lead.

"Switch some fine running backs to defensive specialists and explain 'They were so good, I didn't want to waste them on offense.'

"Invent face bars for helmets.

"Use intelligence tests as a clue to a player's learning potential."

Whether Brown was indeed "responsible" for any, some or all of the revolutionary approaches White listed may be open to question, but Babe witnessed one first that White did not list.

It was an attempt to make obsolete one of Brown's other accredited firsts: the use of alternating guards as messengers to bring in plays.

And it the process, he became the first to have his play calling, transmitted from a hand-held microphone on the sidelines to a receiver in the quarterback's helmet.

It happened in a 1956 against the New York Giants.

* * * *

In 1953, the Cleveland Browns had drafted Gene Filipski, a Villanova halfback in the seventh round. He was the 83rd player selected.

But Filipsi did not play until the 1956 season, apparently because of serving in the military, having attended West Point before enrolling at Villanova. Paul Brown then had peddled him to the Giants.

Brown apparently had forgotten that Filipski knew about his revolutionary head phone, play-calling system that made obsolete shuttling guards in and out as messengers.

Nor did Brown know that when the game began, Filipski somehow had collaborated with someone on the Giants' staff and figured out a way to intercept every play Brown called.

Befitting his imperious personality, it was a one-way communication system. Paul Brown was not interested in discussing or debating the merits of the plays he called. The Cleveland Browns' system was not a democracy.

And so, each time Paul Brown called a play from one side of the field, Gene Filipsi, standing on the other side, was yelling to

Tom Landry, the Giants' defensive captain and future Dallas Cowboys coach, telling him what Brown had called.

Brown was beside himself. No matter what play he called, the Giants were all over it.

Years later, at a football reunion, Babe reminded Landry about the play-calling interceptions, Landry smiled and said:

"Best day I ever had."

* * * *

A few months after the season ended, as Babe was driving to Blacksburg, Va. to help a friend, Virginia Tech coach Frank Moseley, conduct spring practice, he turned on the radio.

"The Cleveland Browns announced today," he heard the announcer say, "that they have traded quarterback Babe Parilli back to the Green Bay Packers, where he played his rookie season in 1952 and again in 1953."

* * * *

His shoulder still hurt. It was still stiff. He still could not throw a football across the living room.

Babe returned to Lexington, this time to talk with Dr. O. B. Murphy, the UK football team physician. Wasn't there something—anything?—that could be done to make it heal?

Dr. Murphy injected his shoulder with two tubes of cortisone.

He also told Babe to start throwing.

"Throw. Keep on throwing. Throw as hard as you can. That's what it's going to take to break up all that scar tissue."

It was painful. Monotonous. Discouraging. Progress was slow. But little by little, as the days and weeks went by, his shoulder began to get better. By the time it was time to report to the Packers' preseason training camp, Babe was firing the ball as if he had never been injured.

So what if he was going back to Green Bay? Back to sub-zero weather and a sub-par football team?

Babe didn't care where he played. All that mattered was that he was being given another chance to play. But as the 1957 season and those that followed unfolded, he couldn't help but wonder what might have been had Paul Brown given him a chance to show that he had recuperated fully from his should injury. And, to team up with the Browns' No. 1 pick in the 1957 draft: Syracuse fullback and future Hall of Fame great Jimmy Brown who over the next nine seasons would rush 2,359 times for 12,312 yards and 106 touchdowns before abruptly retiring in 1965 at the age of 32.

CHAPTER 14

Upon Babe's return to Green Bay for the 1957 season, the first order of business was to take care of business. The year before, when he had signed with Cleveland, his two-year contact had called for a salary of $16,500, a $1,500 increase over what he had made at Green Bay before going into the service, and the second year, $17,500. Having acquired him, The Packers had to assume his contract as well.

Or so he thought.

But Packer officials said they had never received a copy of a two-year contract from Paul Brown. They therefore had no proof that such a contract ever existed.

Their offer: $12,500— a decrease of $2,500 from what he had been paid as their first- round draft choice in 1952.

"That's what we're paying Paul Hornung," he was told.

Hornung, the 1956 Heisman Trophy winner at Notre Dame, had been the Packers' No. 1 draft pick a few months before.

Babe didn't believe it. And, was right. He later learned that Hornung was making $17,000—plus a $15,000 bonus.

* * * *

Gene Ronzani was long gone as the Packers' coach. In late 1953, the second of Babe's two seasons with the Packers, Ronzani, after going 2-7-1, had been replaced with two games left by co-coaches

Hugh Devore and Ray McLean. It didn't help. The Packers lost both games.

Lisle Blackbourn, who had coached Marquette from1950 to 1953, took over in 1954 but had not fared much better than Ronzani. The Packers had finished 4-8 in 1954; 6-6 in 1955; and 4-8 in 1956; for the three seasons, 14-22.

But there had been a major personnel subtraction and a couple of even more significant additions that eventually would help propel both the Packers and the Detroit Lions to NFL championships.

The Packers had traded Tobin Rote, with whom Babe had shared quarterbacking duties in both 1952 and 1953, to the Lions. That season, 1957, Rote would serve as Bobby Layne's backup and together, they would lead Detroit to a 10-4 record and a 59-14 thrashing of the Cleveland Browns in the NFL championship game. Layne would complete 87 of 179 passes for 1,169 yards with six touchdowns and 12 interceptions and Rote, 76 of 177 for 1,070 yards, 11 touchdowns and 10 interceptions.

The Packers also had signed their first-round 1957 draft pick, Notre Dame Heisman Trophy winner Paul Hornung. The year before, deep in the 1956 draft, they also had selected Alabama quarterback Bart Starr, the 200th player chosen, in the 17th round.

During the 1956 season, Starr had played sparingly behind Tobin Rote, completing 24 of 44 passes for 325 yards with two touchdowns and three interceptions, but with Rote gone to Detroit, figured to play a lot more in 1957.

Babe knew both Hornung and Starr. As a college senior, Babe had gone with the Bear to Louisville to help recruit Hornung. He recalled the Bear telling him he believed that both Paul and this kid down in Alabama, a quarterback named Bart Starr, would commit to Kentucky, but Hornung had enrolled at Notre Dame and Starr at Alabama, decisions that perhaps changed the history of Kentucky football as much as signing Babe had.

During Bart's visit to UK, Babe also had worked with him several days, teaching him what Ermel Allen had taught him about taking snaps, footwork, ball handling and ball faking.

So now Babe was back where he started, making less money that when he started, once more facing the prospect of having to be a Packer co-quarterback.

Once again though, he was doing what he wanted to do. He was playing football. Everything else would take care of itself.

* * * *

Off the field, some things had not changed since his 1952 rookie season. Other than an occasional movie, there was little to do for entertainment.

Hang around the Northland Hotel perhaps. Shoot the breeze with "Mr. Chauffeur," a pleasant, uniformed self-employed valet of sorts who leaned against the side of the old Astor Hotel. He always lit up like a Christmas tree every time someone stopped to talk with him; even more so when they asked him to park their car or drive them somewhere. Packer placekicker and fullback Fred Cone, who had played college football at Clemson, always made a point of befriending him. Sometimes, Cone hired Mr. Chauffeur to drive him around the block and then gave him a good tip.

Still took their meals at the YMCA across the street from the hotel. Still stopped in now and then, after recuperating from the last visit, at Chili John's for a piping hot bowl strong enough to strip all the chome off the grille of a Cadillac.

The cost of housing had doubled though. During the 1952 and 1953 seasons, Babe, center Jim Ringo and end Bill Howton had rented the upstairs of a private residence for $7 each per week. This time around, it cost Babe, Ringo, Howton and rookie Paul Horning $15 a week each to room at the Astor.

It might be scorching hot in Green Bay in mid-August.

At least it was boring.

* * * *

Since 1945, when Don Hutson retired, hope had continued to spring eternal in Green Bay. But then so had bitter disappointment.

Not since 1944, when they finished 9-2, had the Packers won an NFL championship—or come even close. In the following three years, their record dropped to 6-4, 6-5 and 6-5-1.

Then began the precipitous plunge. They fell to 3-9 in 1948; 2-10 in 1949; 3-9 in 1950; and 3-9 in 1951. During Babe's first season, the Packers had climbed to 6-6, but the next year, nosedived again to 2-9-1.

Over in the 11 seasons since their last title, the Packers had won 51, lost 88 and tied two.

But Sept. 29, 1957, opening day of the 1957 season, was a special day in Green Bay. The Packers were about to play their very first-ever game at City Field, a new 32,000-seat stadium built as a result of a voter-approved $960,000 community fund-raising drive. Later, it would be known as Lambeau Field.

What happened during that game that day also offered a glimmer of hope that things might be about to get better. Babe threw two touchdown passes—the first, the first ever in the new stadium-- to give the Packers a 21-17 victory over the Chicago Bears.

It was only the third time in a decade that the Packers had won their opening game.

The next week, the visiting Detroit Lions jumped out to a 14-0 lead in the first quarter, increased it to 17-0 by the end of the first half and in the fourth quarter held a commanding 24-0 lead. Two Packer touchdowns made the final score, 24-14, look more presentable than it was.

Whatever else it was, the game was not a passing clinic. Between them, Babe and Bart, spending most of the day running for their lives, completed only 11 of 29 passes for 107 yards, no touchdowns and five interceptions—one for a touchdown. Even with far better pass protection, the Lions' Bobby Layne and Tobin Rote, didn't do much better, completing nine of 20 for 84 yards, no touchdowns and one interception.

On Oct. 13, again playing at home, the Packers fell behind 7-0 in the first quarter, held a 10-7 lead at the half and then collapsed like an accordion as Johnny Unitas and the Baltimore Colts romped to a 45-17 victory.

Once again, gloom hung over Green Bay like an impending blizzard.

* * * *

On Oct. 20, in their fourth straight home game, the Packers, as they had against the Colts the week before, played well, or at least well enough, in the first half against the San Francisco 49ers.

In the first quarter, former Minnesota Golden Gophers' star Gordy Saltou kicked a field goal to give the 49ers a 3-0 lead. In the second, after Babe sneaked in for a touchdown and a 7-3 lead, 49er quarterback Y.A. Tittle threw a 19-yard touchdown to regain the lead 10-7, at the half.

In the third quarter, Tittle connected on a 12-yard TD pass and in the fourth, scored from the one on a quarterback sneak to put the game out of reach. Paul Hornung's nine-yard run closed out the scoring, the 49ers winning 24-14.

Packer fans always looking for, but rarely finding, something to be optimistic about, pointed to the Packers' rushing total for the day: 194 yards. In their first three games, the Packers had run for only 97, 98 and 47.

Yeah, the critics countered, but they passed for only 61.

* * * *

On Oct. 27, there was plenty of shouting in the amen corner though. Two weeks after absorbing a 45-17 thumping at home at the hands of the Baltimore Colts, the Packers travelled to Baltimore – and won.

Down 14-0 going into the final quarter, Green Bay had outscored the Colts 24-7 to pull out a 24-21 victory.

Paul Hornung had ignited the comeback by scoring two touch-downs, one from three yards out, the other from two, and Fred Cone had kicked a field goal to put the Packers in front 17-14.

Then Johnny Unitas had hooked up with Lenny Moore, the former Penn State star, on a six-yard touchdown pass to enable to Colts to regain the lead at 21-17.

Then, with only 28 seconds remaining and no time to warm up— or way to anyhow, what with freezing rain falling and snow swirling – Babe trotted out onto the field to make his first appearance of the day.

The ball rested on the Green Bay 25.

Babe took a quick snap, dashed back, dodged one onrushing defender, sidestepped another, and threw it as far as he could.

Though the worsening rain and snow and mist, the ball sailed past mid field, past the 40, past the 30—and right into the hands of wide receiver Bill Howton who didn't even break stride as he raced into the end zone for a game-winning, 75-yard touchdown.

Green Bay 24; Baltimore 21.

* * * *

Prosperity, however, was as fleeting as a Green Bay winter was unending.

The following week, the visiting New York Giants took a 24-10 halftime lead and went on to win, 31-17, despite the fact that the Packers piled up 225 yards rushing and 185 passing compared to 123 rushing and 153 passing by the Giants.

Two Packer blunders, the first in the first quarter when line-backer Sam Huff scooped up a Packer fumble and ran for a touch-down, the other in the final quarter when Emlen Tunnell inter-cepted a Packer pass and ran 52 yards, were the difference.

* * * *

On Nov. 10, at Soldier Field, after the Packers fell behind 7-0, Bart Starr threw two touchdown passes, one for 47 yards to end

Bill Howton in the first quarter, the second in the second 28 yards to Don McIlhenny to give the Packers a 14-7 lead over the Bears.

Then Harlon Hill hauled in a pass from Zeke Bratkowski for a 35-yard touchdown and the game was tied. It stayed that way until the final quarter when Rick Caseres scored from nine yards out to give the Bears a 21-14 win.

* * * *

On Nov. 17, in Green Bay, against the Los Angeles Rams, the Packers played like they were someone else.

In the first quarter, Fred Cone kicked a 39-yard field goal and Bart Starr connected with Don McIlhenny for a 29-yard touchdown to give the Packers a 10-0 lead.

After Paige Cothern sliced the lead to 10-3 with a 13-yard field goal, the Packers' Al Carmichael scored from the four and Bobby Dillion converted an interception into a 52-yard touchdown.

At halftime, the Packers owned a 24-3 lead.

The Rams then scored 28 points, held the Packers scoreless and walked away with a 31-14 victory.

It was a bitter defeat on a bitterly cold Green Bay day. Any hope of a winning season, let alone a breakthrough season, was all but gone.

That faint hope stayed alive a week later in Pittsburgh though. Following a scoreless first quarter, the Packers scored three touchdowns, all by rushing. Babe slithering in from the three for one of them to take a 21-3 halftime lead.

This time, they did not blow it.

Two field goals in the fourth quarter, one of 24 yards, the other of 12, offset a Steeler touchdown in the third quarter to preserve a 27-10 victory.

Seven Steeler turnovers, including three lost fumbles and four interceptions, helped.

* * * *

On Thanksgiving Day, at Detroit's Briggs Stadium, a place so cold, the ground so frozen that even the Packers, hated to go there, only one touchdown was scored all day.

Five field goals and a safety accounted for the rest of the points. Detroit won 18-6.

The Packers were 3-7 with two games left, one at Los Angeles, the other at San Francisco.

They lost both.

For Green Bay, the city as well as the team, it was an unmerciful end to another unmerciful season.

Surely the one to follow would not be as bad.

It wasn't.

It would be worse.

* * * *

In his first full season back after suffering what could have been a career-ending shoulder injury and despite being used primarily as a backup and having completed only 39 of 102 passes for 690 yards with four touchdowns, Babe had had his moments.

He expected to do even better during the upcoming season—and did.

Not the Packers, however.

They won one, lost 10 and tied one—the worse in Green Bay history.

Babe finished the 1958 season with 68 completions in 157 attempts for 1,068 yards and 10 passing touchdowns. Against the Philadelphia Eagles, he had thrown for four, leading the Packers to their only win, 38-35.

Bart Starr, although starting eight of the 12 games, completed 78 of 157 for 875 yards and three touchdowns, down from the year before when he had thrown 215 times and completed 117 for 1,489 yards and eight touchdowns.

But even their most devoted fans had to admit that the '58 Packers were downright atrocious. In winning one, losing 10 and tying once, they scored only 193.

Their opponents: 382.

The Packers rushed for 1,421 yards.

Their opponents: 2,041.

They passed for 2,118 yards.

Their opponents: 2,655.

Even a coaching change had not helped. Like his predecessor, Gene Ronzani, Lisle Blackbourn had been unable to lead the Packers back to respectability. In three seasons, his teams had won 17 and lost 31.

Like Ronzani, Blackbourn was fired.

Ray McLean, who had served with Hugh Devore as interim co-coach for two games at the end of the 1953 season, was hired to replace him. For many Packer fans, it was not an inspiring hire. More like recycling than rejuvenating.

Meanwhile, although it might not have seemed readily apparent at the time, the Packers had done exceptionally well in the 1958 draft. In the first round, they had selected Dan Currie, a linebacker from Michigan State, the third player chosen; in the second round, LSU fullback Jim Taylor (15th); the third, Illinois linebacker Ray Nitschke of Illinois.

Both Taylor and Nitschke would be inducted into the Pro Football Hall of fame.

Their fourth-round choice was Idaho guard Jerry Kramer, who would start every game that season and be become an all-pro during his 11-year career.

The Packers also added another quarterback, Joe Francis of Oregon State.

Because, in part, of the drafting of Taylor, Nitschke and Kramer, combined with the earlier selection of Bart Starr and Paul Hornung, better days were indeed awaiting for the long-suffering Packers and their fans.

Not yet though.

Things had to change.

Immediately.

On Feb. 2, 1959, the Packers announced the hiring of a new coach and general manager.

His name was Vince Lombardi.

* * * *

Off the field, 1958 had been a banner year for Babe. He had met and married Priscilla Perkins, Miss Wisconsin USA, 1956. Priscilla had grown up in Depere, a small town right outside Green Bay.

Babe and Priscilla purchased a two-story home across the street from the East High School field where the Packers had played their home games before City Field was built.

Green Bay to Morocco, Morocco to Cleveland, Cleveland back to Green Bay—perhaps now, at long last, Babe could settle down in one place; and play for one team for the rest of his career.

* * * *

Babe and Vince Lombardi had more in common than their Italian ancestry. Both hungered for a long-overdue opportunity to demonstrate what they could do under the right circumstances.

For both, that meant directing their own team.

Beginning with his rookie NFL season, Babe had had to share playing time, with the Packers' Tobin Rote (1952 and 1953) and with Bart Starr (1957 and 1958). In between, he had been out of pro football for two seasons because of military duty, then at Cleveland, just when he was beginning to blossom as Otto Graham's successor, he had suffered a severe shoulder injury and had missed the rest of the season.

Although Babe had served mainly as a backup to Starr during the 1957 and 1958 seasons, he had passed for more yardage than Starr (1,068 to 875) and more touchdowns (10 to three). Whereas Babe's figures had gone up from the previous season, Starr's had gone down.

In addition to Starr, there were two other candidates: Larmar McHan and Joe Francis.

McHan, 26, had played college football at Arkansas and had finished ninth in the 1953 Heisman Trophy voting. In the first round of the 1954 NFL draft, he had been the second player chosen, by the Chicago Cardinals. Before arriving in Green Bay, McHan had played five seasons for the Cardinals, averaging more than 1,000 yards and 10 touchdowns in each.

Francis, who had led Oregon State to the 1957 Rose Bowl, had played sparingly during the Packers' 1958 season, throwing only 31 times and completing 14 for 175 yards and two touchdowns.

* * * *

For Lombardi, 46, the Green Bay job meant receiving the chance he often believed he would never have. After serving as an assistant at Fordham, where he had played college, at West Point and with the New York Giants, where he served as what would become known as offensive coordinator, he and defensive coordinator Tom Landry, future coach of the Dallas Cowboys, helped lead the Giants to the NFL championship by beating the Chicago Bears. Lombardi had applied for several collegiate head coaching jobs, including at Wake Forest and Notre Dame. Despite letters of recommendation from Giants' head coach Jim Lee Howell, he received no offers and in some cases, no replies. Lombardi   wondered aloud whether he was being discriminated against because of his Italian origin.

So now he had his chance. As both head coach and general manager, he assumed full responsibility for the success or failure of the Packers.

After the disastrous, one-win 1958 season, there seemed to be only one way to go.

Up.

* * * *

Babe and Lombardi shared another interest: golf.

One hot, late-summer day, they played 18 holes.

They even agreed to a friendly wager.

$1.

But when Babe won, the payoff wasn't so friendly.

Lombardi reached into his pocket and peeled off a dollar bill.

Then, scowling, he tossed it at Babe.

"That's the last dollar you will ever get from me," he said.

* * * *

For Starr, McHan and Babe, the Packers' pre-season exhibition games became a chance to audition for the starting job.

Starr started one and McHan another.

The Packers lost both.

"Don't worry," Lombardi told Babe. "You'll get your chance."

Babe started the third game.

On one series, within scoring distance, Babe called time out and trotted over to the sidelines.

"What play do you want to run?" he asked.

Unlike Paul Brown who called all the plays, Lombardi called none of them.

"Well, you can pass or you can run," he replied.

Babe returned to the huddle.

"What did he say?" Paul Hornung asked.

"He said to give you the ball and for you to run the damn thing into the end zone."

Babe did and Horning did.

The Packers won.

After leading Green Bay to a victory—even if was an exhibition game, any victory was a major victory in those days—it therefore came as something as a surprise when an assistant coach told Babe he was being released.

When he broke the news to Priscilla she said:

"You should punch him in the nose."

Babe went to Lombardi's office.

Babe looked directly at Lombardi.

"Why?"

Lombardi did not look directly back. He never did look Babe in the eye. Nor did he ever answer Babe's question.

"Philadelphia is interested in you," he said in a low, near-whisper monotone.

"You can go play for the Eagles . . . ."

Babe knew what that meant. Play backup to Norman Van Brocklin.

No, he was through playing backup.

Babe stood up and walked out.

* * * *

The next day, the telephone rang.

The caller was Frank Clair, coach and general manager of the Canadian Football League's Ottawa Rough Riders.

"I hear you're a free agent," Clair said.

He'd read it on the overnight waiver wire, he said.

Would Babe be interested in playing for the Rough Riders?

Clair offered to match Babe's $12,500 Green Bay salary.

Babe agreed to start packing his bags.

As he later discovered, he had just been given a $1,000 raise because at the then going rate of exchange, an American dollar was worth $1.08.

* * * *

It took a little getting used to, this business of playing football, Canadian style. Twelve men on a team. The 12th was an "anywhere player," because that's where he could play: anywhere. Only three downs instead of four. The field was 110 yards long. The middle of the field was the 55-yard line. It was wider too. Punt the ball into the other team's end zone and if they did not run it out, you got a "rogue"—one point. Ditto if you punted it clear out of the end zone so they couldn't run it out.

Send a man in motion? Why, help yourself. Send as many as you like.

Most important of all, the keys to winning were quickness and speed, not brawn and brute force. Line up in a T formation, scatter receivers all over the field and let 'er fly.

Babe did well, and so did the Rough Riders. One more win and they would have qualified to play in the Gray Cup championship game.

Alas, the Rough Riders lost 14-12 to the Hamilton Tiger-Cats.

Babe was not only gracious in defeat, he was downright ecstatic.

For the first time in his life, he was happy *not* to win. The ground was so frozen, his cleats-- more like sharp-pointed spikes—didn't even penetrate the iron-like turf.

Besides, each member of the Gray Cup- winning team received only $500.

He never bothered to find out what the losers received.

If anything.

* * * *

Meanwhile, for both Babe and Priscilla, living in Ottawa had been an exciting adventure. They wandered all over the city. Visited its historic sites. Its museums. Dined at its best restaurants. Attended movies and plays.

And never did they feel exiled.

From NFL football.

Or anything else.

* * * *

No team in the Canadian Football League was allowed to have more than a dozen Americans on its roster. The NFL had no similar restriction. But then a Canadian player appearing in an NFL uniform was about as rare as a balmy winter day in Green Bay.

And so, the next spring, if it did not set a precedent, it sure sounded like one when Clair called to inform Babe that he had just been traded to the Oakland Raiders.

Who?

"The Oakland Raiders. In the new football league."

"*What* new football league?"

"The American Football League. They're going to start playing their first season in September."

Later, he would learn that Jack Vanisi, former business manager of the Green Bay Packers and newly hired general manager of the newly formed Raiders, had engineered the trade.

Babe never had a chance to thank Vanisi. Before heading to Oakland to begin his new job, Vanisi, not yet 40, suffered a heart attack and died.

* * * *

Babe nearly did not go to Oakland though. The Raiders wanted to pay him less than the $12,500 he had been making in Ottawa.

Babe said no.

"You don't want me badly enough."

Pay what he demanded or lose him.

They decided to pay him.

The Bear would have been proud.

CHAPTER 15

If the owners of a newly awarded American Football League franchise in Minneapolis had not decided to join the NFL instead and form a team that would become known as the Minnesota Vikings, the Oakland Raiders never would have existed.

Not in 1960 anyhow.

But they did because suddenly, after the Minnesota group's unexpected about face, AFL officials were frantically searching for a place to establish an eighth team to join the all-new, yet-to-play Boston Patriots, Buffalo Bills, Dallas Texans, Denver Broncos, Houston Oilers, Los Angeles Chargers and New York Titans.

Oakland seemed like an unlikely prospect. Not only did it not have an ownership organization in place or a stadium—the closest available were in Berkley and San Francisco—but had never even asked to join the league. Besides, there was already a thriving NFL team, the San Francisco 49ers, right across the bay.

But when Barron Hilton, who owned the Los Angeles Chargers, threatened to abandon his Los Angeles franchise unless a second AFL team was established on the West Coast, league officials chose Oakland anyhow. Then began a hectic scramble to transform a team that existed only on paper to one ready to play when the 1960 season began.

All Oakland had was a sheet of paper listing the names of the college players the Minneapolis group had chosen in the annual 1960 draft. Even that didn't look like it amounted to much seeing as how the long-established NFL teams—the nearby 49ers, Rams, Lions, Browns, Bears, Giants, Eagles, Steelers, Redskins, Colts, Cardinals and Packers --were all after the same cream-of-the-crop college seniors.

Although an abundance of investors rallied to the cause and *The Oakland Tribune* launched a "name the team" contest, a furor arose when the winner—the Oakland Senors – was announced. Critics charged that the contest was fixed because Y. Charles (Chet) Soda, the investment group's managing general partner, was well known to call his numerous business acquaintances "senor."

A few weeks later, the Senors became the Raiders.

Meanwhile, after the University of California refused to allow the Raiders to play their home games at Memorial Stadium in Berkley, their owners chose San Francisco's Kezar Stadium as their home field.

As the season opener, scheduled for Sept. 11 against the Houston Oilers, approached, forming and organizing a team seemed tantamount to rounding up passengers and taking boarding passes on Noah's Ark.

* * * *

Although their rival neighbor, the San Francisco 49ers, had been a member of the National Football League since 1950 and the Los Angeles Rams since 1946, expansion of the nation's three major spectator sports, baseball, football and basketball, to the West Coast thereafter had been a slow and sporadic process.

The Rams had joined the NFL when the Cleveland Rams moved west after winning the 1945 league title. The 49ers had been a charter member of the All-America Football Conference which, during its four years of existence, also had included the Cleveland Browns, New York Yankees, Brooklyn Dodgers, Buffalo Bisons, Miami Seahawks, Los Angeles Dons and Chicago Rockets. When the AAFC merged with the NFL after the 1949 season, the Browns and '49ers had joined the NFL and the LA Dons had merged with the Rams. All the others had disbanded.

Until then, pro football, except for the Green Bay Packers way out there in the frozen hinterlands of Wisconsin, had been concentrated wholly in the East and Midwest.

So had major league baseball. Although the Boston Braves had been the first major league team to scramble the old order when they moved to Milwaukee in 1953, it was the shocking transfer of the Brooklyn Dodgers to Los Angeles and the New York Giants to San Francisco in 1957 that made the game truly a coast-to-coast spectator sport.

Pro basketball had remained the exclusive domain of the East and Midwest prior to 1960 too.

But the winds of big change were blowing again.

The NBA Minneapolis Lakers had just pulled up stakes and relocated in Los Angeles. In the years to come, major professional sports teams also would locate in San Diego, Sacramento, Seattle, Portland, Salt Lake City and Phoenix.

Unlike the Dodgers, Giants and Lakers, however, the Raiders and the Chargers weren't longtime existing teams who belonged to a well heeled league. They were brand new, without an established fan base or an abundance of capital, and so was the AFL.

And now, for better or worse, the Oakland Raiders and the Los Angeles Chargers and the rest of the eight new AFL teams were about to challenge the heretofore unchallenged monopoly of the entrenched and storied NFL.

* * * *

Even before any of the AFL teams had played a single game, haughty NFL officials were dismissing the new league as inferior; comparable to triple A minor league baseball aspiring, if not pretending, to be the real thing: the majors.

But after both leagues had made their collegiate draft choices and began the process of collecting signatures on contracts, the results were surprising, if not downright shocking.

215

Of the 12 players selected in the first round of the NFL draft, six signed with an AFL team.

Louisiana State's Heisman Trophy winner Billy Cannon, the No. 1 NFL pick, passed up a chance to play for the Los Angeles Rams and signed with the Houston Oilers.

LSU defensive back Johnny Robinson, No. 3 in the NFL draft, chose the Houston Oilers over the Detroit Lions.

Penn State quarterback Reggie Lucas, No. 4, picked the Buffalo Bills over the Washington Redskins.

Texas Christian fullback Jack Spikes, No. 6, spurned the Steelers to play for the Texans.

Northwestern halfback Ron Burton, No. 9, chose the Boston Patriots over the Philadelphia Eagles.

Southern Cal tackle Ron Mix, a future Pro Hall of Fame inductee, went with the Chargers instead of the Baltimore Colts.

Overall, the AFL was credited with signing 75 per cent of the players whose names appeared on its draft lists.

Throughout the early and middle '60s, the NFL would continue to dismiss its ambitious rival like a red-headed stepchild.

And all the while, the AFL talent pool would become deeper and deeper.

* * * *

For Raiders head coach Eddie Erdelatz and his staff, as for all of the eight AFL coaches and their assistants, there was much too much to do and little time to do it. Erdelatz had faced a challenge before though—and succeeded. In 1950, after serving two years as defensive coordinator for the 49ers, he had returned as head coach to the U.S. Naval Academy where he had worked as an assistant. Before his arrival, Navy had won only four games in five seasons. That season, however, the Midshipman, despite a 2-6 record, had knocked off arch-rival Army, winners of 19 in a row and unbeaten in 28, by a score of 14-2.

After finishing 5-12 in his first two seasons at Annapolis, Erdelatz never had a losing season during the next seven. Navy also shut out Ole Miss in the 1955 Sugar Bowl and in 1958, beat Rice 20-7 in the Cotton Bowl.

After abruptly resigning from the U.S. Naval Academy in 1958, Erdelatz had been a leading candidate to replace Bear Bryant when he left Texas A &M to return to his alma mater, Alabama. While sitting out the 1959 season, Erdelatz also had turned down an assistant coaching job with the Washington Redskins, been mentioned as a top candidate to coach the Southern Cal Trojans and California Golden Bears and turned down the chance to coach the Los Angeles Chargers.

And so, considering how many other seemingly better opportunities he had passed up, it came as something of a surprise then when he agreed to coach the Raiders, a team created so late, in a city without a stadium and with a paper roster, like the rest of the teams in the upstart AFL consisting of nothing more than a list of unsigned names.

* * * *

One of Erdelatz's top priorities in trying to convert a roster filled with players he did not know into a team was to find a quarterback. The 1960 college draft list he had inherited from the Minneapolis franchise holders contained 52 names but included only four quarterbacks: Dale Hackbart of Wisconsin Fran Curci of Miami (Fla,) ; Bobby Lackey of Texas; and Sam McCord of East Texas State. But Hackbart had signed with the Green Bay Packers, Lackey had decided to forego pro football to begin a career in agriculture and Curci passed up a pro football career as well.

As the season opener neared, he had only three remaining possibilities. One was Paul Larson, who was 28 years old, had played only one season in the NFL for the Chicago Cardinals in 1957 and had attempted only 14 passes and completed six for 61 yards.

The second was 23-year-old Tom Flores, who had even less experience. Flores, who had played college football at University of the Pacific, had tried out but been cut by the Calgary Stampeders in 1957 and also failed the next year to earn a spot on the Washington Redskins' roster.

The third was Babe, back from playing a year with the Ottawa Rough Riders in the Canadian Football League after two years as a part-time starter for the lowly Green Bay Packers.

And, by now, he was 30 years old.

Youth or experience?

Experience or youth?

Erdelatz had both.

Only not together in the same player.

* * * *

From the beginning, Babe sensed that Erdelatz was not one of his admirers. It wasn't personal, although Erdeltz, as did Babe, clearly liked Tom Flores. Flores, like Bart Starr with whom Babe had shared quarterbacking duties for two seasons at Green Bay, was a fine, classy young man and a good passer to boot. Rather, it seemed to have more to do with Erderlatz wanting to imprint his own personal stamp on the program immediately by developing his own young quarterback with long-range possibilities. And, perhaps Babe's age had something to do with it too. The prevailing wisdom at the time held that it took five years to develop a solid NFL quarterback. At 30, Babe already had five years' experience; in five years, Flores would still be only 28.

Ederlatz' approach to coaching the Raiders also followed two other commonly, if not universally, practiced offensive philosophies.

The first was that the offense was built primarily around running the ball. Passing was considered much more risky then—and with good reason. There were no fun 'n gun formations, no multiple wide receivers to spread the defense all over the field. Most passes were thrown to the two ends, only occasionally to a halfback or fullback. One result: as both collegiate and professional records from the 1950s consistently document, even the best quarterbacks in both the NFL and AFL threw nearly as many, if not more, interceptions than they did touchdowns.

And, although no statistics were ever kept, quarterbacks, Babe included, often deliberately threw too short, too long, too wide, too high in order to make sure than the pass was not picked off, particularly within the 50-yard line.

The second: Each team in both leagues carried only two quarterbacks and both were used extensively, sometimes alternating after every play, or series of players, or even every other quarter. If one was not playing particularly well, the other might end up playing the rest of the game. Because of the risk of injury, neither the starting quarterback nor his backup ran the ball often.

So once again, as had been the case in 1952 and 1953 at Green Bay, in 1956 at Cleveland and in 1957 and 1958 when he had returned to Green Bay, Babe knew he would be a co-quarterback in his first AFL season. All things considered, though, it sure beat no playing time at all, especially considering that there were only 16 quarterbacks in the league and many times that number of ex-collegiate starters whose names had not been called during the 1960 draft or the two or three before that.

* * * *

Meanwhile, Babe and Priscilla had rented an apartment and were enjoying living in Alameda, south of Oakland. Even more so, going to San Francisco to shop, to visit museums and historical sites, to go out to dinner, to attend plays and movies. Living in the bay area, bathed in sunshine, was a dramatic change from the cold, bleak winters and the stifling sameness of Green Bay where the Packers were the sole source of entertainment and the most popular topic of conversation, even in the off season.

Nor did it hurt that Babe could play golf year 'round.

As she had in Green Bay and in Ottawa, Priscilla attended all the home games.

Things were looking up.

* * * *

The Raiders' first-ever game of their first-ever season was played on Sept.11 at Kezar Stadium in San Francisco. It turned out to be a passing duel between Houston Oilers' quarterback George Blanda and Tom Flores. Blanda completed 19 of 37 for 279 yards and four touchdowns; Flores, 13 if 32 for 232 yards and two touchdowns. After being tied 7-7 at the half, the Oilers rolled to a 37-22 victory.

* * * *

On Sept.18, at Kezar, the Dallas Texans held a 17-10 lead at the half and outscored the Raiders 17-6 in the final two quarters for a 34-16 win. Babe, who had passed only twice and completed one in the opener, threw 28, completed 14 for 196 yards, two touchdowns and was intercepted twice. Tom Flores completed six of 13 for 45 yards and also was intercepted twice.

In their first game, the Raiders were sacked three times for 23 yards; this time, four times for 56 yards.

* * * *

A week later, in Houston, Babe completed seven of 13 passes for 118 yards and Flores seven of 10 for 57 yards and one TD as the Raiders edged the Oilers 14-13. Oiler quarterback George Blanda completed 17 of 36 passes for 222 yards and kicked two field goals, but was intercepted three times.

This time the Raiders were sacked three times for 27 yards, giving them 10 in three games with losses totaling 106 yards.

For Babe, it was like that ol' Green Bay "Lookout!" pass protection -- or lack of it-- drill, all over again.

* * * *

On Oct. 2, at Bears Stadium in Denver, the Broncos scored three touchdowns in the second quarter, two thrown by former Notre Dame quarterback Frank Tripucka and the other on an interception return en route to a 31-14 win.

Tom Flores completed 10 of 15 passes for 124 yards and Babe, nine of 22 for 84 yards. Both were intercepted once.

The Raiders (1-3) were sacked five more times for 36 more yards.

* * * *

The following week in Dallas, the Raiders, trailing 7-0 at the half, the result of the Texans' Dave Webster picking off a Tom Flores pass and running 80 yards to score, erupted for 20 points in the third quarter and then held on in the fourth to squeak out a 20-19 win.

The Raiders (2-3) gave up three more sacks and lost another 25 yards.

* * * *

On Oct. 16, after playing three straight games on the road, the Raiders beat the Boston Patriots 27-14 to even their record at 3-3. Flores threw two touchdown passes in the second quarter to give his team a 21- 6 lead. He finished with 14 completions in 24 attempts for 161 yards with three interceptions.

This time, the Raiders gave up no sacks but had five turnovers; the Patriots, seven.

* * * *

On October 23, at Buffalo, the Raiders fell behind 14-0 in the first quarter, 28-7 at the half and lost 38-9. Former Tennessee-Chattanooga quarterback Johnny Green, drafted 233rd by the Pittsburgh Steelers in the 21st round of the 1959 NFL draft and subsequently cut, threw four touchdown passes--all in the first half.

Although giving up no sacks while passing 40 times, the Raiders completed only 16 for 134 yards, ran 22 times for only 85 yards and lost three fumbles and threw three interceptions.

Football? A game of inches?

For the Raiders, it was proving to be a game of perpetual mistakes. The offense, largely because of inadequate pass protection, was inconsistent, scoring 122 points, or an average of 17 per game while the defense allowed 186 or 26 per game. Too many fumbles. Too many interceptions—it was tough to beat another team when you were already beating yourself.

And yet, the Raiders were winning nearly as many as they lost. Not bad considering what was happening to the NFL's newest addition, the Dallas Cowboys. At the mid-point of their inaugural season, the Cowboys were 0-6, including lopsided losses to the Browns (38-7), Colts (45-7) and Rams (38-13). They later would lose to the Packers (41-7) and finish 0-11-1.

* * * *

To many, the NFL Cowboys' dismal beginning was all too reminiscent of the first time an attempt had been made eight years before to establish a pro football team in the Dallas-Fort Worth area, smack dab in the heart of one of the nation's hottest collegiate football hotbeds.

Dallas was the home the Southern Methodist Mustangs filled with lingering ecstatic memories of 1948 Heisman Trophy winner Doak Walker; his running-wild sidekick, All-American Kyle Rote. The Cotton Bowl, site of one of the nation's four premier New Year's Day collegiate classics and each fall, the bitter, the Red

River Shootout between the Oklahoma Sooners and the Texas Longhorns.

Neighboring Fort Worth was where the purple-clad Texas Christian Horned Frogs cavorted; where the echoes of Slingin' Sammy Baugh and Davey O'Brien, who had led the Frogs to a national championship in 1938, still resounded amid fond hopes of more Saturday afternoon heroes, more championships to come. The two cities also were the hub of a circled-wagons array of other hated rivals and intense rivalries. Texas Tech out in Lubbock. Texas A. & M. in College Station. Baylor down in Waco, Rice, in Houston. The neighboring Arkansas Razorbacks too.

In 1952, into this cauldron of collegiate football, enter the Dallas Texans, a moveable fast of a team if there ever was one, In their eight years of existence, the Texans, previously the New York Yanks, had already changed names so many times the lettering on their jerseys should have looked like a laundry list.

Formed, or deformed as it turned out, it was a team that began its trek down a long road to oblivion in 1944 and continued until 1948 as the NFL Boston Yanks. Owner Ted Collins called his team the Yanks because what he really wanted was a team in New York that played its home games in Yankee Stadium. Because of a wartime shortage of players, the Yanks were merged with the Brooklyn Tigers for the 1945 season, playing four home games in Boston and one in New York. Didn't matter. Attendance was sparse wherever they played.

Then in 1946, when Dan Topping decided to move his Brooklyn Tigers from the NFL to the newly formed All-America Football Conference, Collins saw his chance. He moved his team to New York, arranged to have them play in the Polo Grounds and renamed it the New York Bulldogs.

After the 1949 season when the AAFC disbanded, Collins absorbed a number of players from the newly disbanded AAFC New York Yankees team, and renamed his team the New York Yanks and moved its games to Yankee Stadium.

In 1952, Collins peddled his team back to the NFL and the franchise was awarded to a group of enthusiastic but misguided Texas businessmen headed by Giles Miller. The first big dose of oops came on opening day when a considerably –less- than- record crowd of 17,499 wandered into the 75,000-seat Cotton Bowl.

As the losses piled up, attendance declined even more.

With five games left, Miller, unable to pay his players, returned the franchise to the NFL, after which, for reasons known only to themselves, league officials 1) moved the team to Hershey, Pa. and 2) continued to call them the Dallas Texans. The Hershey, Pa. "Texans" played their final two games in Akron, Ohio's Rubber Bowl where in their season finale, they beat the Chicago Bears for the only win in their one disastrous season. The reason the Bears lost was because owner-coach George Halas was so sure his team could beat the hapless Texans that he took all of his starters out of the game. By the time he got them back in, it was too late. The Texans won 27-23.

Compared to the Texans' past and the Cowboys' present, the future of the Oakland Raiders didn't look so bad.

* * * *

None of which was the reason Babe remembered the Texans, however.

It was the kick. That kick during his rookie season, the likes of which perhaps had never been seen before and likely never would be seen again as long as the game was played.

With the Packers momentarily pinned back near back near their own goal, Babe took the snap in the end zone and sent a quick-kick spiral soaring high and long toward midfield. When it hit the ground, it began bounding wildly across the turf like a jackrabbit frightened by speeding passenger train. End over end it bounced, head higher and higher. Then it began rolling. Rolling and rolling and rolling.

By the time it stopped, the ball had traveled 93 yards.

But as the Packers stood and watched in awe, as they began to trot up the field, one of the officials tossed a flag into the air.

"Off sides," he said, point at Jim Keane, one of the Packers' ends.

Twenty years later, at a team reunion, Babe walked up to Keane and said, with an easy smile:"I've got a bone to pick with you."

Keane's eyes widened.

"Now, Babe," he said, "I know what you are going to say, but I'll tell you what really happened.

"I ran up to the ref and I told him: 'I wasn't off sides.'

"The ref smiled and said, 'I know. But they haven't won a game all season."

* * * *

On Oct. 28, despite being penalized 11 times for 119 yards, the visiting Raiders, trailing 24-14 going into the final quarter, scored two touchdowns, and edged the New York Titans 28-27 to even their record at 4-4.

Tom Flores completed only nine of 20 passes for 170 yards but two of them were for touchdowns.

* * * *

On Nov.4, The home team Boston Patriots jumped out to a 14-0 first-quarter lead, held it 20-7 at the half, then survived to beat the Raiders 34-28.

In the third, after the Raiders cut the lead to 20-14 on an eight-yard Tom Flores pass , the Patriots scored twice to go ahead 34-14. Two touchdown runs by Tony Teresa, who had played one season for the San Francisco 49ers in 1958 before joining the Raiders, cut the final margin to six.

Babe completed 11 of 20 passes for 121 yards and ran four times for 35 yards.

* * * *

Three weeks before, in Buffalo, the Bills had riddled the Raiders 38-9.

Not this time.

On Nov. 13, The Raiders' led 13-0 at the half, 20-0 after three quarters and the defense allowed the Bills only 90 yards rushing in 22 tries, created seven sacks for 48 yards and gave up only one touchdown as Oakland won 20-7.

Bill's quarterback Johnny Green who had burned them for four touchdowns in their first meeting didn't get any this time and the Raider offense, which had lost two fumbles and thrown three interceptions in their Oct.23 game, committed only one turnover, a harmless interception.

The Raiders were 5-5 with four games remaining.

* * * *

For what seemed like it should be the beginning of an intense rivalry between the only two AFL teams on the West Coast, the first-ever meeting between the Oakland Raiders and the Los Angeles Chargers was not exactly overrun with drama.

The Chargers instead overran the Raiders 52-28.

Chargers' quarterback Jack Kemp lit the fuse in the first quarter with a 69-yard touchdown completion to Don Norton and after the Raiders' J.D. Smith bulled over for a one -yard score, Kemp threw another TD pass, this one to Paul Lowe covering 63 yards to go back in front 14-7.

In the second quarter, the Chargers added two running touchdowns and a field goal to build a commanding 31-7 halftime lead. Each team scored once in the third quarter to make it 38-14 and in the fourth, the Chargers extended their lead to 52-22. Babe's eight-yard pass to Doug Asad completed the scoring.

The Chargers shredded the Raiders' defense for 541 net yards, 298 rushing and 241 passing and ran 65 plays to Oakland's 40.

* * * *

A week later, on Dec. 4, the Raiders and the Chargers met again, this time in San Francisco's new Candlestick Park in the first pro football game played there. The Raiders also would play their two remaining games in Candlestick.

Oakland trailed only 17-14 going into the final quarter. But then Chargers' quarterback, Jack Kemp, threw a 49-yard touchdown pass, ran in two more from inside the 10 yard line and Rommie Loudd scooped up a fumble to give Los Angeles a 41-17 win.

* * * *

Tom Flores connected on 15 of 27 passes for 170 yards and three touchdowns, but in the fourth quarter, with the Raiders leading 28-24, New York Titans' quarterback Al Dorow threw his third touchdown pass of the day to give his team a 31-28 victory.

Dorow completed 29 of 48 passes for 375 yards.

As had been apparent for some time, the Raiders' pass defense, like their pass protection, could use a little work too.

* * * *

In their season finale, after leading only 17-10 after three quarters, the Raiders scored 31 points to route the Denver Broncos 48-10.

While the defense was limiting the Broncos to 33 yards rushing on eight carries and 173 yards passing, the Raiders rang up 532 net yards of offense. Tom Flores' and Babe's passing accounted for 299 of it.

During that last-quarter scoring spree, Flores passed for one TD, then Babe passed for one, ran for one and passed for yet another.

* * * *

Although they finished the year with a respectable 6-8 record, there was more reason than ever to worry about the Raiders' future.

Despite playing their final three home games at Candlestick Park, attendance had declined rather than increased. The announced figure for the Dec.4 loss to the Chargers had been 12,061; their Dec. 11 loss to the Titans, 9,037; their season finale win over the Broncos, an estimated 7,000.

Meanwhile, the team was $500,000 in the red. Ralph C. Wilson, founder of the Buffalo Bills, came to the rescue with a $400,000 loan.

The Raiders would survive to play at least one more season.

* * * *

For both Tom Flores and Babe, it had been a good year.
Good enough, anyhow.
Flores had started 12 games, attempted 252 passes, completed 136 for 1,738 yards and 12 touchdowns with 12 interceptions. Babe had started two, attempted 187 passes, completed 87 for 1,003 yards and five touchdowns with 11 interceptions.

But what he would remember more than anything about that the entire season were two things that happened, one during, one after, the Broncos' game.

* * * *

Since going their separate ways to college, Babe to Kentucky and Skippy Doyle to Ohio State, their paths had rarely crossed. After failing to blossom as a big Buckeye offensive star as expected, as heir apparent to Heisman Trophy winner Vic Janowicz, Skippy Doyle had played as a defensive back throughout his pro career.

And on that day, shortly before the Raiders and the Broncos collided in Candlestick Park, the two former high school team-mates back in Rochester, Pa. had a little conversation.

"Say, Babe," Skippy Doyle said, a mischievous twinkle in his eye," how about laying one on me today? You know. Let me make an interception. Run for a TD. For ol' Time's sake."

Babe merely smiled.

He knew that Skippy Doyle knew, or ought to know, that Babe would not deliberately throw an interception to his own mother.

And so in the final quarter, when Babe trotted back out onto the field, he noticed Skippy Doyle grinning, making knowing nods in his direction.

The next play, Babe dropped back to pass. A receiver angled toward the sideline.

Babe planted his feet. Cocked his arm. And just as Skippy Doyle came tearing in between Babe and his receiver, certain he was about to pick off the throw and go racing , untouched, all the way for a touchdown, Babe pump faked.

His receiver glided free into the clear. Too late, Skippy dug in his cleats and tried to turn around.

All he could do was watch the ball sail float over his head and straight into the sure, waiting hands of the Raider receiver 15 yards all in the clear with nothing and no one between him and the goal line except white lines and grass.

Touchdown

Oakland.

As he trotted up the field, Babe grinned.

And said to himself:

"*There. I finally gotcha.*

"*That one's for Barbara and Eleanor.*"

* * * *

As their plane skied high over the Rockies, Babe and Coach Eddie Erdelatz sat together and talked.

"You know," Erdelatz said, "I tried to run you off."

Babe knew.

From the beginning, he had sensed that Erdelatz, as was his right, for whatever reason, had decided to go with Tom Flores as his prime quarterback. And to underscore that unspoken message,

Erdelatz, in the rigid manner of his devotion to the rigid military discipline he had learned and embraced during his coaching days at the U.S. Naval Academy, had tried to discourage Babe; to break him.

That was why, he told Babe, he kept ordering Babe to run sprints. Then more sprints. Then more and more and more.

But what Erdelatz did not know was what Babe had gone through during those agonizing, exhausting, blistering, suffocating pre-season boot camps the Bear had conducted at Millersburg Military Academy and again down in Cocoa Beach, Fla. the week before Kentucky's Orange Bowl game with Santa Clara.

Or how, while pushing his players to, and past their mental and physical limits the Bear had instilled in them the will to endure all of that and more.

Play hard. Play hurt. And no matter what, keep right on playing.

That was the Bear's credo.

And that had become Babe's.

And so he had survived.

Again.

* * * *

Long after he had played his last football game, Babe was frequently asked:

Who's the best quarterback?'

He knew being a good quarterback wasn't merely a matter of who could throw the ball the farthest. That could be ascertained simply by checking the yard markers; or the fastest; something that could be timed with a stop watch, or who was the biggest, by stepping on the scales; or who was the tallest, by checking the numbers on a tape measure.

He always answered:

"Who's got the best offensive line? The best supporting cast?"

For he knew, as the Bear had taught him, that football was a team game and individual statistics and records meant nothing ; working together as a team, everything.

And as he and the owners and lots of others learned following the first AFL season, what applied to quarterbacks also applied to football teams.

The ones who look the best, or even are the best, did not always survive.

Which was why, that year, despite finishing 0-11-1, the NFL Dallas Cowboys survived because they had solid financing, fan support and facilities.

And why, despite finishing 10-4, the Los Angeles Chargers didn't because they didn't.

The following fall, the Los Angeles Chargers became the San Diego Chargers.

And that look-to-the-future foundation Eddie Erdelatz had set out to pour?

In 1961, after his team lost the first two games, and in the process was outscored 99-0, Erdelatz was gone, replaced by Marty Feldman who won only two of the remaining 12.

In 1962, Feldman lost the first five and was replaced by Bill Conkright who lost eight of the remaining nine.

Mercifully, though, Babe was not around to endure those two horrendous seasons which produced a combined record of 3-25.

Before the 1961 season began, he was traded to the Boston Patriots.

CHAPTER 16

There was no reason to remain in Oakland. With the season over and Babe's teammates all gone, he and Priscilla decided to head on back to Green Bay. They still owned a home there. Priscilla's parents were still living in nearby DePere. She and the baby could spend a lot of time with them before pre-season practice began in mid-summer.

They didn't have to read the weather reports to know that driving east through Nevada, Utah, southern Wyoming, the Dakotas and Minnesota would be cold. Colder still the farther north they traveled. It would take them out of the way, but the only route that made any sense was to swing south to Los Angeles and then follow U.S. Route 66 across northern Arizona through Flagstaff, Albuquerque, Amarillo, Oklahoma City, Tulsa, St. Louis then swing north.

They had no winter clothes. Hadn't figured they would need them living in California. Yes. The southern route. It was the only way to travel.

But as they headed across northern Arizona, the sky darkened. The temperature began to fall. So did a light snow. The colder it became, the heavier the snow fell. The windshield fogged up. Slivers of ice began to form inside the car.

Some car.

Babe knew he never should have bought it.

It was a Peugeot and it was absolutely the worst automobile he had ever owned. It had no heater. Not to worry, the salesman had said. It's designed so the heat from the engine heats the car.

Only it didn't.

So now they rode along, shivering, squinting into the line-drive snow that peppered the windshield like a Sahara sandstorm.

Soon, of necessity, they developed a routine. Each morning before they checked out a motel or roadside tourist cabin, Babe called the AAA. Had to. Another of the Peugeot's quaint charms was that it would not start in cold weather. Every tow truck driver who answered Babe's call said the same thing:

"Hardest car I've ever seen to get started."

Before they left their room, they layered on as many of their lightweight clothes as they could and when they got into the car, piled and tucked the rest over and around the baby.

Come 4 p.m. they stopped at the first motel they saw. It was too cold, too dangerous, the Peugeot too undependable to continue any later. They did not see many as they drove across the empty, desolate, barren landscape that looked like photographs of the surface of the moon.

As they left the New Mexico high country and ventured out onto the vast, treeless Oklahoma plains, the snow became worse, the towns farther and farther apart.

Babe drove with one eye on the road, the other on the gas gauge.

One evening, out in the middle of nowhere, having found no place to stop, for food, gasoline or shelter, the needle inched toward E, then lay diagonally across it like power pole leaning against the roof of a two-story house.

House.

The light of a house.

Any house.

Babe glanced out the driver's side door window. He spotted a light off in the distance. Had to be a farmhouse. After struggling to push the door open against the howling wind, he stepped out in snow nearly up to his knees. The light looked to be a mile or so away.

He tried to run, but the snow was so deep, all he could do was slog, one step at a time.

When he knocked on the back door, a rancher answered. After pausing to grab a heavy coat off a hook on the back of the door, he led Babe to the barn, where he found a can of gasoline and gave it to Babe.

Numb, shivering, exhausted, Babe returned to the car and unscrewed the gas cap.

The neck of the can was too large.

He had to cup his hand to pour the gasoline, a palm full at a time, into the tank.

It took five days to get home.

But when they got there, Green Bay didn't seem so cold any more.

After what they had endured on the road, even the arctic wind whistling off Lake Michigan seemed downright balmy.

* * * *

Mrs. O'Brien sure was glad to see them.

Mrs. O'Brien – Babe always called her "OB"—rented the second floor of their house and had since right after they had bought it in 1958.

One day shortly after she had moved in, Babe told OB, who was nearing 70 and as cantankerously Irish as they came, that the rent she was paying, $60 a month, would never change.

Twenty years later, long after Babe's football-playing days were over, OB was still living there.

Still paying $60 a month.

After she was gone, Babe sold the house.

Green Bay, he discovered, wasn't exactly one of America's hottest real estate markets.

He had purchased it for $18.000.

He sold it for $18,000.

* * * *

Salary was still a frustration. As a modest rookie, embarrassed to talk about such things but with Bear Bryant's insistence, he had signed a three-year a contract with the Green Bay Packers for $15,000 per year. Upon returning from military service in North Africa, Paul Brown had increased his 1956 salary to $16,500 with a provision that it be upped to $17,500 the next year. Brown, however, had never forwarded a copy to the Packers and Babe had had to settle for their offer of $12,500, after being told, falsely, that that was how much Heisman Trophy winner Paul Hornung, their No. 1 draft pick out of Notre Dame, was receiving.

Now, as he had at Green Bay in 1957 and 1958, in Ottawa in 1959, in Oakland in 1960, he was still being paid only $12,500.

He always shrugged and said the money wasn't what mattered. What did was having the opportunity to play.

But it was irksome.

Because it was just plain, downright unfair.

* * * *

One of the now extinct provisions of the professional football drafting system was something called "territorial rights." That meant that a team, say the Cleveland Browns, could claim first rights to a college player who lived within reasonable proximity to Cleveland. The thinking was that fans in northeastern Ohio would like to see one of their own play and that players who wanted to play close to home would have the opportunity rather than being shipped clear across the country.

Behind the scenes, however, there was another not so altruistic reason team owners liked to sign local talent.

They didn't have to pay them as much.

If Butch Songin was not a territorial rights signee, he certainly fit the profile. Songin had played quarterback at Boston College between 1947 and 1949, finishing his career with 192 pass completions in 385 attempts for 2,534 yards and 30 touchdowns. He also had been an All-American hockey player at BC.

In 1953 and 1954, he had played professional football for the Hamilton Tiger-Cats in Canada and as a rookie, led his team to the Gray Cup, Canada's version of a league championship game and trophy.

But Songin had not played again until 1960 when he became the starting quarterback for the upstart Patriots, during their first season in the American Football League. He had performed well enough, completing 187 of 392 passes for 2,476 yards and 24 touchdowns with 15 interceptions. The Patriots had done well enough too, at least for a first-year team, finishing 5-9.

But going into the 1961 season, although Songrin was a good drawing card at the ticket window, he was 37 years old, a fact Patriot officials were not unaware of as demonstrated by the fact that they had chosen three quarterbacks in the 1961 draft: future Hall of Fame inductee Fran Tarkenton of Georgia; Paul Teheres of Bucknell and Bryant Harvard of Auburn. However, Tarkenton signed with the NFL Minnesota Vikings;, Teheres with the Baltimore Colts ;and Harvard was not on the Patriots' roster when the season began.

And, they had obtained Babe from the Oakland Raiders. Suddenly, Babe found himself in an unlikely role reversal. At 32, he was the Patriots' "young" experienced quarterback, perhaps even heir apparent to Songin's starting job in the not too distant future.

* * * *

It didn't take long to figure out that in order to increase attendance as well as minimize expenses, the Patriots were attempting to fill as many places on their roster as possible with local talent.

Including, apparently, Babe's.

When Priscilla showed him a newspaper story that said rumors were circulating that Babe might be traded or released in order to make room for former Boston College quarterback Don Allard, he headed straight for Head Coach Lou Saban's office.

A coaches' meeting was in progress when he arrived.

Babe walked in anyhow, holding the newspaper.

"What's this about my being traded?" he asked." If it's true, I'm gone. I don't need the money that badly."

Although he did.

"Give me 15 minutes," Saban replied.

An hour later, Saban emerged from his office.

No, he said, Babe would not be traded.

As Babe headed for the locker room to dress for practice, he passed Allard.

In street clothes, football shoes tied together and draped over his shoulder, heading out the door.

* * * *

As the 1961 AFL season unfolded, while Babe's old new team, the Oakland Raiders, were beginning a skid that would turn into a two-year avalanche of 25 defeats in 28 games, his new team, the Patriots, were ascending from not bad to pretty good. After finishing 5-9 the year before, Boston went 9-4-1.

It was a season in which both Babe and Butch Songin would prosper. Babe would start eight games; Songin, six. Babe would complete 104 of 198 passes for 1,314 yards; Songin, 98 of 212 for 1,429 yards. Babe would throw for 13 touchdowns and run for four more; Songin pass for 14.

But the strangest, and perhaps unprecedented, part of their two-headed season was *when* they played. At Green Bay, Babe and Tobin Rote had alternated every other quarter. The 1961 Patriots might as well have had a sideline revolving door.

Babe and Songin passed each other running onto and off the field after *every* other play.

In and out, in and out, in and out, in and out-- they probably expended more energy running to and from the sideline as they did on the field. And while it might have been comforting to have two quarterbacks, each capable replacing the other should one get hurt or experience an off day, a game-by-game review also suggests

238

perhaps how difficult it must have been for either to establish any
kind of consistency or continuity.

* * * *

In the season opener, after the visiting New York Titans had
taken a 7-0 lead in the first quarter, Babe sneaked in from the one
to tie the score.

In the third quarter, with the Titans leading 14-7, Babe fired
his first touchdown pass as a Patriot to tie the score again. Gino
Cappelletti's field goal gave the Patriots their first lead at 17-14,
but then the Titans were back in front 21-17. Cappelletti kicked
another field goal but the Patriots fell a point short, 21-20.

* * * *

On Sept.16, after leading only 10-3 at the half, the Patriots
erupted for 35 points to beat the Denver Broncos 45-17.

Songin completed 13 of 26 passes for 250 yards and four touchdowns.

* * * *

A week later, Gino Cappelletti kicked a fourth-quarter, 46-yard
field goal, his third of the game, as the Patriots beat the Buffalo
Bills in Buffalo, 23-21.

Songin completed 12 of 28 passes for 128 yards and one touchdown .

* * * *

On Oct.1, at the Polo Grounds, after trailing 20-9 at the half,
the Patriots rallied in the third quarter to tie the score at 23-23.
But the Titans scored two touchdowns in the final quarter, the
Patriots one, and they lost 37-30.

Songrin completed 10 of 23 passes for 131 yards and two touchdowns.

* * * *

On Oct. 8, the San Diego Chargers jumped out to 31-14 halftime lead to hand the Patriots their third loss in five games, 38-27. Chargers' quarterback Jack Kemp burned the Patriots' defense for three TD passes and ran for a fourth.

In the third quarter, Babe fired a 30-yard touchdown pass and in the fourth, another one for 47 yards.

* * * *

Two days later, Patriots' owner Billy Sullivan fired head coach Lou Saban and replaced him with Mike Holovak, one of Saban's assistants who had both played and coached at Boston College.

* * * *

Once again, the Patriots' pass defense, of lack of it, was the difference as Jacky Lee, a first-round choice in the 1960 AFL draft and backup quarterback for the defending AFL champion Houston Oilers, completed 27 of 41 for 457 yards and two touchdowns.

The Oilers' defense wasn't much better though and the game ended up in a 31-31 tie. While the Oilers were rolling up 540 net yards, they gave up 383—533, counting 140 yards on eight penalties.

Songrin completed nine of 15 passes for 152 yards and one touchdown; Babe, five of nine for 122 yards and no touchdowns.

* * * *

On Oct. 22, Babe threw three touchdown passes and Songin two as the Patriots zoomed out to a 38-0 halftime lead and smothered the Buffalo Bills 52-21.

* * * *

On Oct. 29, in Dallas, after trailing 17-7 going into the fourth quarter, the Patriots scored on a four-yard Butch Songrin pass, a two-point conversion run by Songrin and a Gino Cappelletti field goal to beat the Texans 18-17.

* * * *

On Nov. 4, they met again, this time in Boston and the Patriots won again, this time 28-21.

In the first quarter, Babe and Songin each threw a touchdown, but in the third, after the Texans had tied the score at 14-14, Babe picked up a Dallas fumble at its own one yard line and scored to give the Patriots a 21-14 lead. After the Texans tied it again the Patriots' Ron Burton returned the kickoff 91 yards and a 28-21 victory.

* * * *

At Houston, on Nov. 12, George Blanda threw a 16-yard touchdown pass, kicked two field goals, and the Oilers scored another touchdown on a 12-yard fumble return to take a 20-0 first-half lead.

Before the intermission, Butch Songin threw a three-yard TD pass and in the third quarter, Gino Cappellerti kicked a field goal to trim the lead to 20-9.

Then in the final quarter, Babe scored on a one-yard run and after the PAT attempt failed, the Patriots trailed the defending champions only 20-15.

But Blanda's backup, Jacky Lee, the former University of Cincinnati star, threw a six-yard touchdown pass to cinch a 27-15 victory.

* * * *

The following week, after former Northwestern star Ron Burton run for a six-yard touchdown in the first quarter, Oakland quarterback Tom Flores threw two touchdown passes in the second. A pair of Gino Cappelletti field goals cut the Raiders' lead to 14-13, at the half.

In the third quarter, a 16-yard field goal increased the Raider lead to 17-13, but in the fourth, defensive end Leroy Moore fell on a Raider fumble in the end zone for a touchdown, giving the Patriots their sixth win of the season, 20-17.

* * * *

Earlier in the season, in Boston, the Patriots had routed the Denver Broncos 45-17.

Not this time.

In the final quarter, with the Patriots leading 14-10, the Broncos' Al Frazier returned a punt 55 yards to give Denver a 17-14 lead,

Then Babe connected with Larry Garron on a 51-yard touchdown pass to regain the lead at 21-17 and then ran for a seven yard touchdown to give the Patriots a 28-17 lead.

The Broncos' Frazier then returned the kickoff 90 yards for a TD trimming the Boston lead to a final-score 28-24.

* * * *

On Dec. 9, at Candlestick Park in San Francisco, Babe threw two first-half touchdowns to offset one thrown by Raider quarterback Tom Flores to stake the Patriots to a 21-7 halftime lead.

In the third quarter, Flores threw for another touchdown to bring his team within seven, 21-14. Billy Lott then scored from the three to give the Patriots a 28-14 lead, but then the Raiders' Riley Morris scored on a 35-interception return and the lead was down to 28-21.

Babe then put the game out of reach at 35-21 with an eight-yard pass to Larry Garron.

* * * *

On Dec. 17, in San Diego, in the first quarter, Gino Cappelletti kicked a field goal, Babe threw a 33-yard touchdown pass and Don Webb ran an interception 31 yards to give the Patriots a quick 17-0 lead over the Chargers. . Billy Lott scored from five yards out and Cappelletti kicked another field goal to stretch the halftime lead to 27-0.

In the third quarter, Babe threw a seven-yard TD pass to Cappelletti and Ward returned a blocked punt 20 yards for another to make the final score 41-0.

Chargers' quarterback Jack Kemp, who had blistered the Patriots earlier in the season by tossing three touchdowns and running for a fourth, completed only nine of 26 passes for 163 yards and had four interceptions.

* * * *

So now it was over. Nine wins, four losses and a tie, including seven wins and only one loss in their last nine games.

Nine wins, four losses, one tie and two quarterbacks, both doing well, although apparently not well enough to confine the other to the bench.

There was no reason to believe that things would be any different the next season.

CHAPTER 17

AMHERST, MASS.
July, 1962

Ten years had gone by since Babe had led the Kentucky Wildcats to a 20-7 victory over Texas Christian in the Cotton Bowl, been chosen fourth in the first round of the NFL draft, named most valuable player in the College All-Star game and reported to his first Green Bay Packers' pre-season training game.

In some ways, it had been a productive as well a rewarding decade. His world was far bigger, his experience much broader. He had traveled to North Africa, Italy, Germany and Egypt while serving in the military, had a wife and son, purchased a home, and played eight seasons of pro football, four in Green Bay, one in Cleveland, one in Canada, one in Oakland and one in Boston.

The three collegiate stars who had been chosen ahead of him in the 1952 NFL draft, quarterback Billy Wade, guard and linebacker Los Richter and fullback Ollie Matson were still playing. But many, if not most, of the other 356 other college seniors selected in the draft no longer were. Nor were Leon Hart, Vic Janowiz and Dick Kazmaier, the Heisman Trophy winners during Babe's three seasons of varsity football at UK.

Hart had played for the Detroit Lions from 1951 through 1957. Janowicz had passed up professional football in order to play major league baseball, but after two seasons with the Pittsburgh Pirates, had spent two seasons with the Washington Redskins before being seriously injured in an automobile accident that ended his career. Instead of playing pro football, Kazmaier had elected to enroll in the Harvard School of Business and pursue a business career.

But Babe's pro football career had not blossomed the way he had hoped. He had missed two seasons because of being called to active duty in the Air Force, most of a third because of a serious shoulder injury and during the seven others, been limited to sharing quarterbacking duties with another part-time starter. For that, he had been thankful. With only 12 NFL teams, each carrying only two quarterbacks, and a new batch being drafted every year, there was little job security. The formation of the American Football League had changed all that. Now, more players were needed at every position, especially at quarterback.

Although Babe wished he had played more over the past eight seasons, he knew that even at the age of 32, he could still play as well if not better than ever.

And now, all of a sudden, he was about to get his chance.

The Patriots had just traded Butch Songin to the New York Titans. Although Patriots head coach Mike Holovak did not say so, the implication was clear. This time, there would be no shuffling quarterbacks in an out, sometimes every other play.

For the first time since the 1952 Cotton Bowl, Babe had his own team to lead.

All by himself.

His backup would be former Michigan State star Tom Yewcic, who also doubled as a punter and sometime receiver and running back.

* * * *

In his Sept. 8 debut as the Patriots' full-time starter, Babe completed 16 of 31 passes for 204 yards and one touchdown and ran for another.

But the host Dallas Texans piled up more than 200 yards both passing and rushing, Abner Haynes ran for four touchdowns and Len Dawson passed for another to beat the Patriots, 42-28.

* * * *

At home, on Sept.16, Babe threw two touchdown passes, one for 63 yards, and ran 32 yards for another one as the Patriots beat the defending champion Houston Oilers, 34-21.

He completed 15 of 34 passes for 207 yards.

* * * *

Against the visiting Denver Broncos, on Sept.22, Babe threw for two more touchdowns as the Patriots rampaged to a 41-16 win

Babe completed nine of 19 passes for 143 yards.

Denver attempted 56 passes and completed 27 for 433 yards, but gave up two interceptions and lost three fumbles.

* * * *

On Oct. 6, at the Polo Grounds, the Patriots beat the New York Titans, 43-14.

Babe completed 14 of 23 passes for 234 yards. He also ran twice for 29 more.

Once again, the Patriots' rushing defense was as tight as their pass defense was porous. The week before, the Denver Broncos had rushed 14 times for 31 yards; the Titans, 16 for 48. They threw 46 times and completed 24 for 352 yards, but lost two fumbles and two interceptions.

In two games, the Patriots' opponents had thrown 102 passes and completed 51 for 785 yards but only three touchdowns.

Babe had thrown for five.

* * * *

The following week, Babe completed 17 of 31passes for 253 yards and one touchdown against the visting Dallas Texans.

Len Dawson riddled the Patriots' pass defense for 306 yards on 17 completions in 32 tries. The Texans won, 27-7.

* * * *

As he had playing for Bear Bryant at Kentucky, Babe was calling all the plays.

* * * *

After trailing 20-3 at the half, Babe threw two touchdown passes, both in the third quarter, as the Patriots rallied to beat the San Diego Chargers, 24-20. He completed 14 of 26 passes for 166 yards.

* * * *

The Patriots' offense was not complicated. Or creative. A few running plays going this way here, a few passing plays going that way there . . .

Sometimes, as he kneeled in the huddle, Babe created his own plays.

Using his finger.

To sketch them out in the dirt.

* * * *

On Oct. 26, in Boston, Gino Cappelletti kicked four field goals and hauled in Babe's 13-yard touchdown pass as the Patriots beat Oakland 26-16.

It was the Raiders' seventh straight loss.

Babe attempted 23 passes and completed 16 for 197 yards.

* * * *

In addition to play calling, bewildering defenses with his decep-tive faking and ball handling, and passing, Babe also was the sure-handed holder on all of Cappelletti's field goal and extra point attempts.

All season, they never had one blocked or a hold botched.

* * * *

On Nov. 3 in Buffalo, in a game that ended in a 28-28 tie, Babe completed 20 of 33 passes for 296 yards for three touchdowns.

Buffalo completed four of 17 passes for 46 yards.

* * * *

A week later, Gino Cappelletti kicked four field goals and Babe threw two touchdown passes, one covering 67 yards, as the Patriots beat the Broncos in Denver, 33-29.

Babe completed 15 of 23 passes for 236 yards.

* * * *

Houston.

Nov. 18

In the first quarter, Babe tossed a 28-yard touchdown pass to end Jim Colclough to give the Patriots a 7-0 lead. It was his 18th of the season. He also completed four of 10 other passes for 51 more yards, moving him to within the 2,000- mark for the season.

And then it happened.

As he double faked handoffs and froze the linebackers and dropped back to pass, a defensive end barreled in, unblocked, and smashed him to the ground. Writhing with pain, he could not get up. When trainers rushed onto the field, it didn't take long to see what was wrong.

His collar bone was broken on the left side...

Babe was done for the season and so, it appeared, were the Patriots.

His backup, little-used Tom Yewcic, trotted out onto the field.

For the season, Yewcic, primarily a punter, had passed only eight times, completing five for 61 yards and no touchdowns. He had not thrown a single pass in the Patriots' last six games.

In Michigan and Ohio, Yewcic was remembered, fondly in East Lansing, considerably less so in Columbus, not for passes he had thrown for Michigan State but the one he caught against Ohio State in 1951.

It became known in Michigan State folklore as "The Transcontinental Pass."

In the closing minutes, the Spartans, trailing 20-17, lined up in their customary winged T formation. The snap went directly to the fullback, who pitched it to the right halfback who appeared to be headed for an end sweep. Suddenly, he stopped, whirled and fired the ball clear across the field to Yewcic, the quarterback, who was streaking down the sidelines. Yewcic raced in to score and the Spartans won 24-20.

Since completing his career at Michigan State, however, Yewcic had not played football again until 1960 until he spent a season with the Toronto Argonauts in the Canadian Football League and a year later joined the Patriots as a punter and utility runner and receiver. In that one season of pro football, had thrown only eight passes, completed three for 25 yards, one touchdown and two interceptions.

* * * *

After throwing a 25-yard TD pass in the first quarter to tie the score, ex-Kentucky star George Blanda conneted on a 42 yarder to give the Oilers a 14-7 lead. Gino Cappelletti then kicked a 26-yard field goal to cut the Oilers' lead to 14-10 at the half.

Yewcic replaced Babe as the holder too, a responsibility he was much more accustomed to than passing. As a senior catcher at Michigan State, Yewcic had been named the most valuable player in the collegiate world series and had pursued a brief career in major league baseball.

In the third quarter, the Oilers scored again on a one-yard run to go ahead 21-10, but then Yewcic threw a 69-yard touchdown pass to halfback Ron Burton to narrow the lead to 21-17. But the Oilers held on through a scoreless fourth quarter to get the win.

* * * *

A week later, on Nov. 23, Yewcic threw three touchdown passes as the Patriots beat the Buffalo Bills 21-10 in Boston.

He completed 12 of 17 passes for 231 yards.

* * * *

On Nov. 30, after the New York Titans took a 10-3 halftime lead, Yewcic ran 27 yards to tie the score and in the fourth, scored again from the four and then hit halfback Ron Burton on a 75-yard pass play to give the Patriots a 24-17 victory.

Yewcic completed six of 20 passes for 195 yards and ran nine times for 90 more.

* * * *

On Dec. 9 in San Diego, Yewcic threw a 43-yard touchdown pass in the first quarter, a 12-yarder in the second and Gino Cappelletti kicked two field goals to beat the Chargers 20-14.

* * * *

In their final game of the season, the Patriots lost at Oakland 20-0 to a Raider team that had not won a game all season.

Boston managed only 82 yards rushing and Yewcic completed only 13 of 35 passes for 108 yards, was sacked five times and threw two interceptions. The Patriots also lost three fumbles.

* * * *

Despite Babe's injury and playing without him for 4 ½ games, the Patriots had managed to win three of their remaining four games to finish the season 9-4-1, third best in the league.

Over those 4 ½ games, Tom Yewcic had completed 49 of 118 passes for 842 yards with seven touchdowns and five interceptions and had rushed 33 times 215 yards for two more TDs.

Out of what could have been chaos and calamity, the Patriots had discovered a new strength.

Not only did they have a solid, experienced quarterback, but a surprisingly dependable backup as well.

* * * *

As they prepared for their fourth AFL season, the Patriots were becoming more settled rather than merely struggling to survive. They had come a long way. Although he was no longer part of the organization, perhaps no one knew how far as Lou Saban, their first coach.

In a *Boston Globe* interview, Saban recalled their hectic, patch-work, start-from-scratch beginning. Dozens, hundreds of men had tried out.

"We had tryouts in the city of Boston from one end to the other. We had bricklayers. We had carpenters. We had stoker men. You name it, we had it."

Before the 1961 regular season began, Babe had witnessed the continuing revolving-door search for players. Through tryouts, trades, the draft--it was a search that never seemed to end. Most were locals, but General Manager Ed McKeever, who lived in Louisiana, was partial to players from the South. Sometimes, the jarring combination of severely clipped New England accents and Deep South drawls seemed to suggest that the Patriots might have to hire an interpreter.

But there was at least one sign, concerning one key position, that seemed to be abating, at least at the time.

In the 1961 AFL draft, although 36-year-old starter Butch Songin was returning and having obtained Babe from the Oakland Raiders, the Patriots had chosen three more quarterback candidates for the upcoming season: But Fran Tarkenton, their first –round pick, signed with the NFL Minnesota Vikings and seventh-round selection Paul Teheres of Bucknell and Bryant Harvard of Auburn, chosen 280th in the 26th round, were not on the Boston roster when the season started.

But in choosing three more candidates that year, especially in spending their No. 1 draft pick in hopes of signing Tarkenton, the Patriots certainly had been considering options other than Songin and Babe.

Not in 1962. The only quarterback they had chosen was Jimmy Field, the 206th player selected, and even then, not until the 27th round.

In the 1963 draft, they did not choose a single quarterback.

* * * *

At long last, 10 years after he had begun his pro football career, Babe was beginning to settle in too.

In 1961, in 14 games, in his first full pro season of not having to share the job, he had completed 104 of 198 passes for 1,314 yards and 13 touchdowns with nine interceptions.

In 1962, in only 9 ½ games, he had thrown 140 of 253 passes for 1,988 yards and 18 touchdowns with eight interceptions

Over two seasons: 244 of 451 attempts for 3,302 yards and 31 touchdowns and 17 interceptions.

His contributions to back-to-back 9-4-1 seasons did not go unrewarded.

After playing two seasons at Green Bay, one in Canada, one in Oakland and two in Boston for the same amount of money, $12,500, the Patriots offered him a new contract.

They doubled his money to $25,000.

CHAPTER 18

In their season opener, after leading only 17-14 after three quarters, the Patriots scored 21 points in the final quarter to rout the New York Jets 38-14.

Babe ran 10 yards for the first fourth-quarter TD then threw a 33-yard touchdown pass to Art Graham, the speedy rookie receiver out of Boston College, for the second.

Babe completed 19 of 35 passes for 288 yards.

* * * *

In a sluggish game in San Diego that produced a lot of passes but not many completions, the Chargers edged the Patriots 17-13.

Babe completed only eight of 20 for 74 and Tom Yewcic seven of 14 for 59. Neither threw a touchdown pass.

Tobin Rote, with whom Babe had shared quarterbacking duties during his first two seasons with the Green Bay Packers, didn't do much better. Rote completed five of 12 for 97 yards and one touchdown.

* * * *

In a contest of run versus pass and ample resistance to both, Billy Lott hauled in a Babe pass for a 55-yard touchdown, Gino Cappelletti kicked a field goal, Larry Garron scored from the three and Cappelletti kicked another field goal to give the Patriots a 20-0 after three quarters.

Two touchdown passes in the fourth quarter by Tom Flores, with whom Babe had shared quarterbacking in Oakland in 1960, cut the lead to 20-14 but the Raiders got no closer.

Babe completed seven of 12 for 98 yards and his teammates ran 42 times for 160 yards.

* * * *

At Denver, on September 29, Gino Cappelletti kicked a field goal in the first quarter and caught a 31-yard Babe Parilli touchdown pass in the third to stake the Patriots to a 10-0 lead. But they never scored after that and a Bronco rushing touchdown in the third quarter and a 72-yard TD pass were enough to give Denver a 14-10 win.

For the third week in a row, the Patriots' passing offense was anemic, in part because of poor protection. Babe completed eight of 20 for 99 yards but lost 20 of it on a pair of sacks. He also threw three interceptions and the Patriots lost two fumbles.

Denver completed 11 of 25 passes for 232 yards but lost 79 of them on seven sacks.

* * * *

At the Polo Grounds, on Oct. 5, Babe got hurt again, this time suffering a bruised shoulder and missed nearly the whole game. Tom Yewcic took over and threw for three touchdowns and 338 yards with 18 completions in 38 attempts. He also was intercepted four times.

Coach Mike Holovak was not pleased about the interceptions---and let Yewcic know it.

To which Yewcic replied, "If you got somebody else to put in, put 'em in."

Knowing, of course that with Babe hurt, there was no one else.

Meanwhile, the Jets took a 14-0 lead in the first quarter, led 21-10 at the half and won 31-24.

* * * *

On Oct. 11, in Fenway Park, in a game defined more by miscues than highlights, the Patriots beat the Oakland Raiders 20-14.

After intercepting one of Babe's passes—he threw three—and returning it 47 yards for a touchdown in the first quarter and rushing for another from 11 yards out, the Raiders held a 14-3 lead.

Babe then threw a 56-yard touchdown and Gino Cappelletti kicked a field goal to cut the Raiders' lead to 14-13.

In the final quarter, Babe threw another touchdown pass, this one for 15 yards, for the winning score.

* * * *

On October 18, at Fenway Park, Gino Cappelletti kicked four field goals and Babe threw for two touchdowns as the Patriots beat the Denver Broncos 40-21

Babe completed 21 of 31 passes for 358 yards.

* * * *

A week later, with Buffalo leading 21-14 in the fourth quarter, Babe threw a 77-yard touchdown pass to former Boston College star Art Graham to tie the score. But Jack Kemp, who had already scored three touchdowns, all on one-yard quarterback sneaks, fired a 72-yard touchdown to give the Bills a 28-21 win.

Babe completed 12 of 31 for 217 yards; Kemp, 18 of 36 for 317.

* * * *

On Nov.1, Babe threw a 78-yard touchdown pass and ran for two in-close TDs and the Patriots (5-4) romped over the Houston Oilers 45-3.

Babe threw 21 passes and completed eight for 168 yards.

* * * *

The following week, in Fenway Park, Tobin Rote completed a 27-yard touchdown pass to put the San Diego Chargers out in front 7-0.

Gino Cappelletti kicked a field goal in the third quarter and another in the fourth but the Chargers' 7-6 lead held up as neither team scored again.

Babe completed 14 of 30 passes for 192 and was intercepted twice. The Patriots (5-5) also lost three fumbles.

* * * *

On Nov. 17, in a wild and wooly, up and down matchup in Boston that produced 804 yards of offense, but no winner, the Patriots and the Kansas City Chiefs played to a 24-24 tie.

A rare Gino Cappelletti miss on an extra point attempt and failure to score on a two-point conversion run proved costly.

Babe passed for one touchdown, ran for another and completed 25 of 47 for 354 yards.

* * * *

Against the Buffalo Bills in Boston, as in the Patriots' second game of the season against Oakland, there was an abundance of passes by both teams and a dearth of completions by either.

In the third quarter, after trailing 7-0 at the half, Babe threw a 44-yard touchdown pass to Larry Gannon and ran in front two yards out and Cappelletti kicked a fourth-quarter field goal to seal a 17-7 win.

Bills' Quarterback Jack Kemp passed 46 times and completed 19 for 191 yards and Babe, 12 of 31 for 195 yards.

* * * *

Houston quarterbacks George Blanda and Jacky Lee combined for 24 completions in 39 attempts for 314 yards and three touchdowns.

No matter.

After leading 14-10 in the second quarter, the Oilers self-destructed in a not-so-funny comedy of errors that helped enable the Patriots roll to a 46-28 victory.

A seven-yard touchdown return of a fumble, a 52-yard interception for another TD, two more interceptions, three lost fumbles, a safety—Houston committed them all.

The Oilers also rushed for only 60 yards in 18 attempts and gave up 100 yards on nine sacks.

Babe completed eight of 21 passes for 108 yards and a touchdown, Gino Cappelletti kicked three field goals

Tom Yewcic, who had appeared briefly in only two games and thrown only two passes, neither of them complete, since his three touchdown, 338-yard, four-interception, one- argument game on Oct. 5 against the San Diego Chargers, also passed for one TD.

* * * *

On Dec. 14, in their regular-season finale, the Patriots traveled to Kansas City where the temperature was nine degrees and the wind chill, minus 6.

The Patriots were colder than that, losing 35-3.

In his worst game of the season, and perhaps of his entire football career, Babe completed seven of 22 passes for 64 yards and threw five interceptions. Tom Yewcic completed two of five for 21 yards, but six sacks for 54 yards by the Chiefs' defense reduced the Patriots' total net yards passing from to 31.

The Patriots finished with 105 net yards; the Chiefs, 398.

The Patriots also were penalized 64 yards.

The good news though, was that even though their regular season record was only 7-6-1, no one in their division had fared any

better and only one, Buffalo, as well. The Bills also had finished
7-6-1.

That necessitated a playoff game in two weeks to determine
which would face the San Diego Chargers (10-3) in the championship game.

* * * *

BUFFALO, N.Y.
Dec. 28

This time, during the huddle, there would be no drawing up
plays in the dirt with his finger.

The temperature was 20 degrees; the wind chill, nine.

The ground was frozen.

The day and night before, throughout the stands, the moaning
arctic wind had piled up icy pyramids of snow that that looked like
miniature icebergs.

As the two not-so-warm teams warmed up, Babe was wearing
sneakers. He noticed that Bills' quarterback Jack Kemp was too.
He also noticed that Kemp was having difficulty keeping his footing.

Babe returned to the locker room and changed into football
shoes with short rubber cleats.

* * * *

When he returned to the field, four men in street clothes were
strolling toward him.

"BABE!" one shouted, rushing up and giving him a bear hug.

"Wha-what in the world are you doing?" Babe stammered.

It was his brother-in-law, George Edge. The others were friends
and relatives from back home too.

Babe knew that they and his father were coming to the game.

He didn't know though that after passing a flask around, they had decided to come out onto the field to say hello. His father remained in the stands.

* * * *

In the first quarter, Gino Cappelletti kicked a 28-yard field goal and Babe connected with Larry Gannon on a 59-yard touchdown pass and a 10-0 lead.

In the second quarter, Cappelletti kicked two more field goals and the Patriots headed to the locker room with a 16-0 lead.

In the third, former Notre Dame star Daryle Lamonica hit Elbert Dubenion, a swift, powerful running back out of tiny Bluffton (Ohio) College, for a 93-yard touchdown. A two-point conversion cut the Patriots' lead to 16-8.

But in the fourth, Babe threw a 17-yard touchdown pass to Larry Garron and Cappelletti kicked another field goal to give the Patriots a 26-8 and a ticket to the championship game.

The Patriots rushed 36 times for 83 yards; the Bills, 12 for seven.

Babe completed 14 of 35 passes for 300 yards and two touchdowns; the Bills' Lamonica, nine of 24 for 168 yards; and Kemp, 10 of 21 for 123 yards.

The Patriots' Larry Garron caught four passes for 120 yards, the longest 59; Cappelletti, four for 109, the longest 51; and the Bills' Dubenion, three for 115.

Babe was intercepted once; Lamonica three times; Kemp, once.

The officials stayed warm bending over picking up tossed flags.

The Patriots were penalized seven times for 65 yards; the Bills, nine times for 100 yards.

* * * *

The month before, on Nov. 30, when the AFL had held its annual college draft, the Patriots had had the first pick in the first round.

They chose Boston College quarterback/halfback Jack Concannon.

Signing Concannon was no sure thing, however. Two days later, the NFL Philadelphia Eagles had drafted him too.

For the Patriots, adding Concannon was more than just a matter of adding another quarterback to their roster. Because he had played at Boston College, Concannon would generate more fans in the stands and more headlines in the Boston and area newspapers.

If he played as well, or anywhere near as well, in the AFL as he had in college, Concannon also would be the key to the Patriots's long-range future. After all, Babe was 34; Yewcic, 32. How many more seasons did they—could they--have left?

Shortly after the draft, although nothing was said, Babe knew he would be expected to tutor Concannon, help develop him, prepare him to take over when Babe called it quits. He could not fault the logic, even though it meant tacitly agreeing to prepare Concannon to take over his job eventually, if not a whole lot sooner.

But Babe wasn't anywhere near ready to step aside. He believed his best playing days still lay ahead.

It all became academic, however, when the Eagles announced they had signed Concannon to a contract reportedly worth $50,000.
$50,000.

Twice what Babe was making.

* * * *

SAN DIEGO
Jan. 5, 1964

Tobin Rote, Babe's old teammate at Green Bay who had been traded to Detroit and led the Lions to the 1957 NFL championship, scored the first touchdown on the game from the two to give the Chargers a 7-0 lead. Keith Lincoln's 67-yard breakaway run made it 14-0.

After Larry Garron ran in from the seven to cut the lead to 14-7, the Chargers' Paul Lowe broke loose for a 57-yard touchdown and a two-touchdown lead.

By halftime, the Patriots trailed 31-7

Rote's third-quarter, 37-yard TD pass to Lance Alworth made it 38-7 and for the Patriots, bad only became worse.

The final score was 51-10.

Rote became the only quarterback to lead his team to a championship in both the NFL and the AFL.

Babe had thrown 37 passes and completed 15 for 228 yards with one interception, but was sacked six times, losing 42 yards. The Patriots had gained only 75 yards in 16 attempts for a combined net offensive output of 261 yards.

The Chargers had amassed 610 net yards, 318 rushing and 292 passing.

It was a dismal ending to an 8-7-1 season that could just as easily have been 11-4-1, of even 12-4-0. By a total of only nine points, the Patriots had lost three games, two to the Chargers (17- 13 and 7-6) and one to the Broncos (14-10). A missed extra point and/or a failed two-point conversion attempt had resulted in a tie with the Chiefs. They also had lost two other games by a single touchdown, one to the Jets (31-24) and the other to Bills (28-21).

In the two seasons Babe had served as their starting quarterback, the Patriots had won 17, lost 11 and tied one; in the three seasons he had been with the team, their record was 26-15-2.

Equally, if not more important, the Patriots were showing a profit for the first time.

CHAPTER 19

Before the season began, Babe received a surprising proposition.

Ten per cent ownership of the Patriots in lieu of his $25,000 salary for the 1964 season.

Given the continuing uncertain future of both the team and the league, he declined.

Little did he know that soon, behind the scenes, talks would begin that would result in the two leagues merging and pro football, richly fueled by huge television proceeds, blossoming into the biggest spectator sport in the country.

Or how much 10 per cent ownership in a franchise one day would be worth.

* * * *

In their season opener at Oakland, the Patriots fell behind 7-0 in the first quarter, but in the second, Babe connected with Art Graham for a 72-yard touchdown to tie the game at 7-7 at the half.

Babe struck again in the third quarter, this time on a 19-yard pass to end Tony Romeo and in the fourth, Gino Cappelletti kicked a field goal as the Patriots edged the Raiders 17-14.

Babe threw 21 passes and connected on nine for 166 yards with no interceptions.

Raider quarterback Dick Wood completed 18 of 41 passes for 183 yards. The Patriots picked off six interceptions, five thrown by Wood.

* * * *

On Sept. 20, the Patriots returned to San Diego, the all but obscene scene of their 51-10 thrashing at the hands of the Chargers in the 1963 AFL championship game.

In the first quarter, Babe completed a 17-yard touchdown pass to Gino Cappelletti who subsequently kicked a 41-yard field goal to put the Patriots in front 10-0.

After Lance Alworth caught an eight-yard touchdown pass from John Hadl, Cappelletti and the Raiders' George Blair exchanged field goals to end the half 13-10, Patriots.

In the third quarter, Cappelletti kicked another field goal and Babe threw a 27-yard TD pass to Art Graham and the Patriots held a 23-10 lead at the end of the third quarter.

In the fourth, after San Diego scored on a plunge from the one, Cappelletti kicked another field goal and Babe threw a 17-yard touchdown pass to Graham to increase the lead to 33-17. Hadl threw a 15-yard touchdown pass and Blair kicked an anti-climactic 12-yard field goal, to cut the final margin to 33-28.

In his second game without an interception, Babe completed 15 of 32 passes for 174 yards.

* * * *

A week later, in their home opener, Babe threw two 59-yard touchdown passes, one to Ron Burton, the other to Jim Colclough, and Gino Cappelletti kicked four field goals as Patriots beat the New York Jets, 26-10.

Babe completed 13 of 34 passes for 223 yards with two interceptions.

* * * *

On Oct. 4, in chilly 48-degree weather at Denver's Mile High Stadium, Gino Cappelletti kicked a record six field goals as the Patriots built a 19-0 halftime lead and won, 39-10.

Babe threw for one touchdown and completed 15 of 33 passes for 152 yards. The Patriots also rushed 32 times for 207 yards, giving them a 359-132 edge in net offense.

The Broncos were penalized eight times for nearly twice as many yards (101) than they gained rushing (53).

* * * *

On Oct. 9, San Diego quarterback John Hadl threw three touchdown passes and Babe was intercepted four times as the visiting defending champion Chargers dealt the Patriots their first loss of the season, 26-17.

Babe's touchdown pass to Larry Garron in the fourth quarter brought the Patriots to 23-17, but a Charger field goal sealed the win.

He completed 17 of 35 passes for 205 yards.

* * * *

A week later, at Fenway Park, on a day when both teams' defense might just as well have stayed home, or perhaps did, the 4-1 Patriots and the 0-5 Raiders played to a track meet 43-43 tie.

After trailing 3-0 at the end of the first quarter. The Patriots went ahead early in the second on Ron Burton's two-yard run. But then Raiders' quarterback Cotton Davidson threw two touchdown passes, one for 26 yards and the other for 50 to give his team a 17-7 lead.

Babe then threw a 36-yard touchdown pass to Jim Colclough to cut the lead to 17-14, but Davidson tossed another scoring pass, this one from 39 yards out, to increase the Oakland lead to 24-14 at the half.

Early in the third quarter, Billy Cannon, LSU's former Heisman trophy star, broke loose for a 34-yard touchdown and Mike Mercer kicked a 37-yard field goal and the Oakland lead swelled to34-14.

Then Babe came to the rescue.

Near the end of the third quarter, he passed to Larry Garron for a 10-yard touchdown to reduce the deficit to 34-21.

In the fourth, Garron ran in from the one and Babe threw an eight-yard TD pass to Art Graham and Gino Cappelletti's extra point kick put the Patriots ahead, 35-34.

Then Davidson threw his fourth touchdown pass of the day, from nine yards out, to put the Raiders back on top, 40-35. But Davidson's pass on a two-point conversion fell incomplete.

Back came Babe with his fourth TD pass of the day, this one to Larry Garron from 11 yards out. He also threw for a two-point conversion and the Patriots led 43-40.

But Mike Mercer's field goal tied the score again and that was how it ended, 43-43.

Davidson completed 16 of 34 passes for 337 yards with one interception; Babe, 25 of 47 for 422 yards and, playing catch up all day long, four interceptions.

Boston fans were not pleased with a tie. Not anymore. On the heels of their team's appearance in the championship game the season before and reinforced by the Patriots' winning four of their first five, their most vocal fans not only wanted to win, but fully expected to win not just the game of the moment but the league title as well.

Their displeasure would have been amusing if it hadn't been so serious.

That hadn't been the case that first season when the team was as green as empty seats at Boston University Stadium Field seats were plentiful... But before the 1963 season had begun, Patriots' owner Billy Sullivan had assured stockholders as well as their fans that there was every reason to be enthusiastic about the team's future.In 1962, home-game crowds, he pointed out, had averaged 16,500. Furthermore, the Patriots would play their home games at Fenway Park. When the Dallas Texans had come to town in 1962, not only was the Boston University Stadium full, another 10,000 fans had been turned away. That wouldn't happen at Fenway, which seated 38,000, offered better parking facilities and by playing there, would give Patriots big-time credibility.

All of which Babe did not necessarily know about in detail at the time, but, all it took was one glimpse at the packed stands in Fenway to know that money was rolling in. And, that it wasn't being lavished on the players or their practice facilities.

The Patriot team that had advanced to the 1963 championship game in San Diego was still practicing in a high school facility far older, smaller, darker, dirtier, than the one back home in Rochester, Pa. The dressing room was underneath the grandstand and as you walked from the back to the front you had to stoop lower and lower because each row bleachers was lower than the one above it. The shower had three sprinkle heads, two of which did not work. The drain clogged up.

And, worse of all, Athlete's Foot was rampant.

Babe ordered some medicinal jell and billed it to the team. When the invoice arrived a few days later, the business manager walked in, waving it like it was a federal indictment.

"Babe, what is this?" he demanded.

"It's medicine. For Athlete's Foot."

The business manager glared disdainfully at the bill again.

"We can't afford to pay this," he said.

Babe laughed.

"Give it me. I'll pay it."

The next week, Babe walked into the business manager's office and announced:

"I've got to have a $10,000 raise or I'm going to retire."

The startled business manager silently looked at him.

Then he said: Okay."

Babe was now making $35,000 a year—nearly as much as he had made the previous three years combined. In two seasons , he would receive nearly as much as he had in the *six* seasons since he had left the Cleveland Browns—two in Green Bay, one in Ottawa, one in Oakland and two in Boston.

The Bear would have been proud.

* * * *

On Oct. 23, in Fenway Park, having already beaten the San Diego Chargers, one of the two teams that had beaten them soundly the season before, the Patriots avenged a late-season 35-3 loss to the Kansas Chiefs too.

Babe threw two touchdown passes to Jim Colclough, one for 38 yards in the first quarter and the other for 11 yards in the third, to give the Patriots a 14-0 lead. Gino Cappelletti also kicked a third-quarter field goal and Ron Burton ran for another TD from the two for a commanding 24-0 lead after three quarters.

In the fourth, the Chiefs scored their first and only touchdown as the Patriots' defense, non-existent the week before against the Raiders, completed a magnificent performance. The Chiefs gained only 52 yards on 26 rushing attempts and completed only 12 of 28 passes for 137 yards – 170 net yards in all.

Babe completed 13 of 18 passes for 171 yards and the Patriots picked up 106 more on the ground in 35 attempts.

* * * *

Offense, defense—nothing went right the next week.

At home in Shea Stadium, the New York Jets, whom the Patriots had beaten 26-10 a month before, bolted out to a 21-0 lead in the first half and won going away, 35-14.

Babe passed for two touchdowns and completed 18 of 40 for 304 yards. But he threw five interceptions and the Patriots managed only 34 yards rushing on 17 carries and the defense gave up 464 net yards, 316 passing and 148 rushing.

Once again, as had been the case after the tie with Kansas City, there was no shortage of mumbling, muttering and salty swell words all over Boston.

How could a team look so good one week and so bad the next?

* * * *

By the end of the 1964 regular season, Gino Cappelletti would lead the league in scoring with a record 155 points, catch seven touchdown passes, kick a perfect 36 of 36 in extra point attempts, 26 of 39 field goal attempts and be voted the AFL Player of the Year.

In their Nov. 6 battle with the Houston Oilers in Fenway Park, Cappelletti demonstrated why he was worthy of the award.

After the Patriots fell behind 7-0 in the first quarter and Babe tied it with a one-yard run, Cappelletti kicked two field goals to give the Patriots a 13-7 halftime lead.

In the third quarter, after ageless George Blanda completed an 80-yard touchdown pass and kicked the extra point to move the Oilers back in front 14-13, Cappelletti kicked another one to put the Patriots back in front 16-14 after three quarters.

In the fourth quarter, Blanda threw a 37-yard TD pass and kicked the extra point to give his team a 21-16 lead. Boston again regained the lead at 22-21 when Babe scored on a five-yard, but his two-point pass was incomplete.

Blanda kicked another field goal and the Oilers reclaimed the lead 24-22.

Then Cappelletti, with the game on the line, calmly drilled another field goal, his third of the game, to give the Patriots a 25-24 win.

Babe completed 14 of 29 passes for 256 yards with one interception; Blanda, 21 of 45 for 329 yards, also with one interception.

The Patriots were 6-2-1 with five regular season games remaining.

Next up: the undefeated, high- scoring Buffalo Bills.

At Buffalo.

* * * *

After being fired as head coach of the Boston Patriots five games into the 1961 season, Lou Saban—Paul Brown with heart, one observer called him—had been hired to coach the Buffalo Bills the next season.

His was not an auspicious beginning. The Bills lost their first five games.

But then they won seven of their last nine games, losing one and tying one.

Their one loss during that turnaround stretch was the Patriots. The tie also was with the Patriots.

In 1963, the Bills once again had finished the regular season 7-6-1. Over that two year stretch, they had played the Patriots five times, including the 1963 playoff game. The Patriots had won three, the Bills one, and one had ended up in a tie.

Now, led by quarterback Jack Kemp who would finish the season 2,285 passing yards (13 touchdowns and 26 interceptions) and powerful fullback Cookie Gilchrist who would run for 981 yards, the Patriots had scored 278 points in nine games (27.8 per game) while allowing only 133 points (14.7 per game.)

Nor had the Bills forgotten that the last time the Patriots had come to Buffalo, they had deprived them of a spot in the championship game by losing the eastern division playoff matchup, 26-8.

The Bills began with a vengeance, going ahead 7-0 on Jack Kemp's 29-yard touchdown and then 10-0 when Pete Gogolak kicked a 41-yard field goal.

But in the second quarter, Babe threw two touchdown passes, one for 15 yards to Tony Romeo and the second to Gino Cappelletti for 35 to give the Patriots a 14-10 lead. Gogolak kicked a 33-yard field goal and the half ended 14-13, Boston.

In the third quarter, Kemp threw 22-yard touchdown pass and ran for a two-point conversion and the Bills led once again, 21-14. Then the Bills' Joe Auer picked up a fumble and rambled 18 yards to score and the Bills led 28-14.

It was the Babe Show after that.

Late in the third quarter, he tossed a five-yard pass to Cappelletti to bring the Patriots within seven, 28-21.

Then in the fourth quarter, he threw two more TD passes, one to Larry Garron from five yards out followed by a two-point pass conversion to put the Patriots up 29-28, and the second, a 35-yarder to Cappellitti.

Boston 36; Buffalo 28.

Kemp threw 41 passes and completed 16 for 295 and two touchdowns with two interceptions. The Patriots' defense held Gilchrist to 31 yards on 11 carries.

Babe attempted 35 passes and completed 18 for 242 yards and five touchdowns with one interception.

What could have been a knockout punch to the Patriots' hopes of playing in the championship game for a second straight time wasn't.

The race was far from over.

* * * *

On Oct. 4, in Denver, the Patriots had routed the Broncos 39-10. This time, in Boston, it wasn't so easy.

Boston scored first, in the first, when quarterback Jacky Lee was tackled in the end zone. Lee redeemed himself with an 11-yard touchdown pass to put the Broncos ahead 7-2.

In the second quarter, Babe completed a 25-yard touchdown pass to Gino Cappelletti to give the Patriots a 9-7 lead at the half.

The only score thereafter was Capelllettt's 51-yard field goal in the third quarter and the Patriots' sometimes erratic, but this day superb, defense did the rest, including picking off three interceptions to help offset the five Babe threw.

Denver completed 16 of 35 passes for 187 yards and only 70 rushing yards on 24 carries.

Babe attempted 33 passes and completed 13 for 222 yards.

In San Diego, the day before, the once-beaten Bills (10-1) beat the Chargers 27-24.

* * * *

On Nov. 29, in Houston, Patriots' defensive back Ross O'Hanley picked off a George Blanda pass and returned it 47 yards for a touchdown to give the Patriots a 7-0 first-quarter lead.

It didn't last long. The Oilers' Odie Burrell returned the ensuing kickoff 93 yards and Blanda kicked the extra point to knot the score at 7-7. Blanda kicked a field goal and the Oilers led 10-7.

But Babe threw a 26-yard TD pass to Larry Garron and Gino Cappelletti kicked a 28-yard field goal and Boston led 17-10 at the half.

In the third quarter, Babe connected with Art Graham for an 80-yard score to give the Patriots a 24-10 lead. But Blanda threw a 60-yard TD pass to cut the Patriots' to 24-17.

Babe threw another touchdown pass, though, this one a 20-yarder to Jim Colclough to increase the lead to 31-17 after three quarters. Cappelletti added a fourth quarter, 15-yard field goal and the Patriots left town with a 34-17 victory.

Blanda completed 27 of 48 passes for 379 yards, but was intercepted four times.

Babe completed 20 of 36 for 336 yards and one interception.

The Buffalo Bills were idle.

* * * *

The previous December 14, in their regular season finale, the Patriots had gone to Kansas City and come home a 35-3 loser, necessitating that brutally cold, frozen-field playoff game with the Bills in Buffalo. The week before the playoff game, the temperature had been frigid that dreadful day in Kansas City too: nine degrees with a wind chill factor of minus six.

This day, Dec. 6, the temperature was a balmy 24 with a wind chill of 17.

After Kansas City took a 7-0 lead on a one-yard Abner Hayes run, Babe fired a 58-yard touchdown pass to Gino Cappelletti and Cappelletti kicked a 12-yard field goal when a drive stalled to go ahead 10-7. The Chiefs' Tommy Brooker then kicked a 41-yard field go and the score was tied 10-10 at the half.

In the third quarter, Babe flipped a three-yard pass to Art Graham and then Chiefs' quarterback Lenny Dawson completed a touchdown pass from the nine and after three quarters, the score was again tied , 17-17.

But as had been the case of late, Babe again came through with a touchdown pass when the Patriots needed it most, this one for 39 yards, again to Graham.

With Boston leading 24-17, J.D. Garrett scored from the one giving the Patriots a two-touchdown lead. Kansas City scored on a run from the one to make the final score 31-24, Boston.

Babe had completed 20 of 41 passes for 300 yards with one interception ; Len Dawson, 22 of 42 for 258 yards with one interception .

Later, the Patriots were doubly cheered when they learned that the Bills, playing in Oakland, had lost to the Raiders, 16-13.

Buffalo was now 10-2 with two games to play; the Patriots: 10-2-1 with one game left.

* * * *

The following week, on Dec. 13, the Bills built a 23-3 halftime lead and beat the Broncos 30-19.

It all came down to one game now.

Boston versus Buffalo.

To the winner would go not only the right to play the western division champion San Diego Chargers (8-5-1), but do it on their own home field.

Patriots' owner Billy Sullivan was so sure that his team would win he ordered the printing of 40,000 tickets to the anticipated championship game against the Bills at Fenway Park.

* * * *

The temperature at Fenway Park was 28 degrees; the wind chill factor, 17.

The first score of the game came in the first quarter on a 57-yard touchdown pass from Jack Kemp to Elbert Dubenion. Babe countered with a 37-yard TD pass to Tony Romeo. Babe elected to throw for a two-point conversion but the pass was incomplete.

In the second quarter, Kemp sneaked across from the one an Pete Gogolak nailed a 12-yard field goal and the Bills led 17-6 at the half.

Following a scoreless third quarter, Kemp scored again on a sneak from the one and the Bills held a 24-6 lead. Babe threw a 15-yard TD pass to Romeo but that was the last of the scoring for either team.

The Bills had won the eastern division title with a 12-2 record and the Patriots closed out the season 10-3-1.

Babe threw 40 passes, completed 19 for 294 yards with two touchdowns and two interceptions; Kemp, 12 of 24 for 286 yards, one passing and two running touchdowns and three interceptions.

Not that any of that mattered to Boston fans. Once again, in their final game of the season, the Patriots had lost, both times with a shot at the championship. Nor did it help much that six days later, on Dec. 26, the Bills beat the Chargers 20-7 to win the title.

So close. So close. But again, no cigar.

* * * *

Not until later, much later, was it possible to appreciate fully how remarkable Babe's remarkable accomplishments had been during the 1964 season. He had thrown 31 touchdown passes, the most by any AFL passer in the league's five years of existence except George Blanda. In 1961, Blanda had thrown 36 while piling up 3,330 passing yards.

Babe also had eclipsed that passing yardage record for that season, amassing 3,465 yards.

His 31 touchdowns in one season also equaled his 1961 and 1962 totals (13 and 18) combined and set a team record that would stand, unbroken, for 43 years.

His 1964 season passing yardage also exceeded his 1961 and 1962 seasons combined (1,344 and 1,988).

And if anyone needed any more proof of his durability as well as his value to the team, there was this little-noticed statistical tidbit.

Tom Yewcic, the Patriots' backup quarterback, threw only one pass all season.

He completed it.

For two yards.

CHAPTER 20

If it was difficult for the Patriots and their frustrated fans to forget what might have been—and it was-- coping with what happened throughout the first half of the 1965 season certainly was no easier.

Management's failure, or inability, or unwillingness, to strengthen its team's roster before the season began did not help either.

The AFL draft, held on Nov. 28, 1964 prior to the Patriots' loss to Buffalo, inspired no runaway optimism in Boston. Only five players— Alabama quarterback Joe Namath, John Huarte, Notre Dame's Heisman Trophy winning quarterback, Kansas running back Gayle Sayers, Illinois linebacker Dick Butkus and Florida State receiver Fred Belitnikoff, were destined to have outstanding pro football careers.

None was drafted by the Patriots.

Namath, the first player chosen, and Huarte, the 12th, were selected by and signed with the Jets. Sayers was selected fifth by Kansas City but signed with the NFL Chicago Bears. So did No. 9 Butkus, chosen by Denver. Biletnikoff picked No. 11 by Oakland, signed with the Raiders.

Boston' No. 1 pick was Jerry Green, a tackle from Michigan State.

But the Patriots did land one valuable sleeper: Jim Nance, a bruising Syracuse fullback, the 151st player selected, in the 19th round.

Strong, agile, Nance also was an NCAA wrestling champion.

Nor did the Patriots make any significant pre-season trades. Holovak told reporters he liked the team he had. After all, it had been good enough to finish 10-3-1 and with a break here and there, might well have won the 1964 championship.

But during the first half of the season, the team he thought he had was not the same one that took the field. At one time or another, for one reason or another, the injury list included running back Ron Burton, kicker and primary receiver Gino Cappelletti, plus Babe's three other principal receivers: speedy Art Graham, running back Larry Garron and end Tony Romeo.

All of which contributed to a horrendous start to what would prove to be a long, long season.

* * * *

BUFFALO
Sept. 11

Following a scoreless first quarter, Babe got the Patriots on the scoreboard first with an 11-yard touchdown pass to Gino Cappelletti. Bills' quarterback Jack Kemp followed with a 26-yard TD pass and the half ended 7-7.

In the third quarter, the Bills scored on a 22-yard interception return and added a field goal to increase their lead to 17-7. They scored again in the final quarter and won 24-7.

Babe threw 35 mostly hurried passes, completed 10 for 151 and was intercepted five times. He also was sacked five times for 40 yards and scrambled, when his receivers were covered, seven times for 71 yards. The Patriots also were penalized seven times for 97 yards.

All in all, lack of pass protection was all too reminiscent of his early days with the Green Bay Packers and the infamous as well as inept "Look out!' blocks—"Look out!, here they come!"

The Patriots' defense gave up 348 net yards, 280 of it passing.

* * * *

HOUSTON
Sept. 19

Babe completed 20 of 50 passes for 201yards but again was intercepted five times as the Oilers rolled, 31-10.

He also was sacked six times for 51 yards.

In eight quarters, he had thrown only one touchdown, 10 interceptions and been sacked 11 times for 91 yards.

The Boston defense game was up 420 yards, 320 of them passing.

* * * *

BOSTON
Sept. 24

After the Denver Broncos recovered a Patriot fumble in the end zone, Babe threw a four-yard touchdown pass to Tony Romeo to tie the score at 7-7.

At the half, the score was 10-10.

The Patriots did not score again and lost 27-10.

The Broncos rushed 49 times for 220 yards; the Patriots, 19 for 34.

Babe completed nine of 23 passes for 111 yards with two more interceptions and was sacked twice more, for 20 yards.

The Patriots also lost two fumbles and gained only 120 yards of net offense.

* * * *

KANSAS CITY
Oct. 3

The Patriots lost 27-17, their fourth in a row; fifth, counting the playoff loss to Buffalo the season before.

Babe completed 16 of 36 for 219 with two more interceptions and no touchdowns. He also scrambled five times for 13 yards and was sacked five times for 45 yards.

The Patriots rushed 22 times for 32 yards and ended up with only 206 yards of net offense.

* * * *

BOSTON
Oct. 17

Babe threw a 73-yard touchdown pass to Ron Burton in the second quarter and two field goals by Gino Cappelletti, one in the third quarter and the other in the fourth, enabled the Patriots to tie the San Diego Chargers, 13-13.

Babe passed 31 times, completing seven for 152 yards with one interception. He was sacked once for 11 yards.

San Diego rushed 42 times for 116 yards; Boston, 21 times for 37 yards.

* * * *

OAKLAND
OCT. 24

The Patriots trailed 23-7 in the fourth quarter, then rallied for two touchdowns, one on Babe's 15-yard pass to Ron Burton and the other on a Burton run to trim the Raiders' lead to 23-21.

But a Raider interception and 36-yard return for a touchdown put the game out of reach, 30-21.

Babe completed 18 of 39 passes for 269 yards and two touchdowns and two interceptions. He also was sacked four times for 49 yards.

The Patriots rushed 23 times for 73 yards.

At the halfway point of the season, the Patriots were 0-6-1.

Babe had thrown five touchdowns, 18 interceptions and been sacked 26 times for 243 yards.

✳ ✳ ✳ ✳

SAN DIEGO
Oct. 31

Two weeks earlier, the Patriots and the undefeated San Diego Chargers (5-0-2) had tied 13-13 in Boston.

After the Patriots scored first on a safety, Babe threw a 29-yard touchdown pass to Gino Cappelletti to take a 9-0 lead at halftime.

In the third quarter, Cappelletti kicked a 30-yard field goal and in the fourth, caught a 46-yard touchdown and kicked a 33-yard field goal to give the Patriots a 22-0 lead.

The Patriots won, 22-6.

Babe completed seven of 21 passes for 148 yards, was sacked three more times for 28 yards and threw two more interceptions.

This time, the Patriots rushed 29 times for 133 yards and their defense held the Chargers to 80 yards on 25 carries.

Finally, Boston had won one.

✳ ✳ ✳ ✳

BOSTON
Nov. 7

The defending champion Buffalo Bills beat the Patriots 23-7.

Babe completed 18 of 39 passes for 245 yards. He also threw two more interceptions, was sacked only once, for nine yards, but was forced to run seven times for 16 yards.

The Patriots also lost two fumbles.

✳ ✳ ✳ ✳

BOSTON
Nov. 14

For Boston fans, it was their first opportunity to see New York Jets' rookie Joe Namath, who had spurned lucrative National Football League offers to sign with the Jets.

Although no figures were ever disclosed, Namath was said to have received a $427,000 contract spread over five years. Jets' owner Sonny Werblin did say, however, that Namath's was the highest salary ever paid to a professional athlete.

For Babe, it was a reunion of sorts. Both quarterbacks were from "The Valley," Beaver County, Pa., and both had played for Bear Bryant.

It also was a game in which they both threw two touchdown passes.

After the Jets jumped out to a 17-0 first-quarter lead, then extended it to 24-3 on Namath's second TD pass, Babe threw two to cut the lead to 24-17 at the half.

Three field goals, two by the Jets' Jim Turner and one by Gino Cappelletti, accounted for the only scoring in the second half, however, and the Jets (3-5-1) won, 30-20.

Namath completed 10 of 25 for 180 yards and no interceptions and was sacked three times for 25 yards. Babe, completed 22 of 50 for 275 yards and three interceptions. He was sacked once for 16 and was forced to run four times, losing two yards.

The Patriots (1-8-1) also lost three fumbles.

* * * *

A week later, at Fenway Park, with the Patriots trailing the Kansas City Chiefs (5-3-1) 10-3 in the final quarter, Babe threw a 10-yard touchdown pass to enable his team to gain a tie.

He completed 13 of 23 passes for 181 yards with one interception and was sacked twice for 13 yards.

* * * *

On Nov 24, after trailing 10-3 at the half, the Patriots scored 17 points in the third quarter and seven more in the fourth to beat the Jets 27-23 in New York.

The clincher, with the Jets leading 23-20, was Babe's two-yard pass to Tony Romeo.

Namath completed 16 of 30 passes for 284 yards and one touchdown with one interception; Babe, 10 of 33 for 183 yards, two touchdowns and one interception.

He was sacked twice for 26 yards.

* * * *

On Dec. 12, in Denver, Babe threw three touchdown passes, one to Larry Garron and two to Gino Cappelletti, to lead the Patriots to a 28-20 win over the Broncos.

He completed 11 of 21 passes for 201 yards with one interception.

* * * *

In the Patriots' seasonal finale at home, Babe threw three touchdown passes, two of them to Gino Cappelletti, who also kicked four field goals, to drub the Denver Broncos 42-14.

The win was the Patriots' third in a row, and after going a dismal 0-6-1 during the first half of the season, had compiled a respectable record of 4-2-1 in the second.

* * * *

On Dec. 26, the Buffalo Bills beat the San Diego Chargers 23-0 to win their second straight AFL title.

* * * *

For Babe, as for the Patriots, there had been, in effect, two 1965 seasons.

In the first seven games, he had thrown only five touchdown passes.

In the last seven games: 13.

In the first seven games, he had thrown 18 interceptions.

In the last seven: eight.

In the first seven games, he had passed for 1,121 yards.

In the last seven: 1,476.

Was Babe a better quarterback in the second half of the season, and therefore the Patriots, a better team? Or were the Patriots a better team, and therefore, Babe a better quarterback?

"Who's got the best offensive line? Who's got the best supporting cast?"

After he retired, that was always Babe's reply when asked who he thought was the best quarterback.

Clearly, Babe had had a better supporting cast the second half of the season than during the first.

In the first seven games, he was sacked 26 times for 243 yards.

In the second, 11 times for 104 yards.

In the first seven games, the Patriots' running attack produced 409 yards in 163 carries.

In the second, 705 yards in 201 carries.

And yet, even with fewer sacks and therefore more time to find his receivers, and a better, although not exactly overpowering, running attack to provide more offensive balance, Babe and the Patriots played both halves of the season without a full cast either passing or running.

Larry Garron, their leading rusher the year before, missed four games. So did Art Graham, one of the team's leading receivers the year before. Garron, who had rushed 183 times for 585 yards in 1964, finished the 1965 season with 74 carries and 259 yards.

But Garron's injuries alone did not account for the Patriots' anemic rushing attack. In 1960, their first AFL season, the Patriots had rushed for 1,479 yards; in 196, improved to 1,675; and in 1962, to 1,970.

But in 1963, production had dropped to 1,618; in 1964, to 1,361 and continuing downward in 1965 with 1,115.

Comparative team rushing statistics for the 1965 season revealed that the Chargers had led the league with 1,998 and the Broncos were second with 1,829. The Chiefs were third with 1,752; Raiders, 1,538; Jets, 1,476; Bills, 1,288; Oilers, 1,175 and the Patriots, 1,117.

Although Babe's total net passing yardage in 1965 was down from 3,166 the season before to 2,507, it fell within the 2,500 to 2,800 range compiled by six of the eight league teams. Only the Raiders had more (3,103) and only the Bills fewer (2,461).

And yet, despite his 26 interceptions, Babe's overall passing performance compared favorably with other starting AFL quarterbacks.

Babe finished the season with 2,597 yards, more than the Raiders' Tom Flores who started 11 games, and Dick Wood, who started three, combined (2,596); the Oilers' George Blanda (2,522); Bills' Jack Kemp (2,368); the Chiefs' Len Dawson (2,262); and the Jets' Joe Namath (2,220).

Only the Chargers' John Hadl (2,798) and the Broncos' three quarterbacks combined, John McCormick, who started six games, Mickey Slaughter , who started seven , and Jackie Lee, who started one-- (2,848) had more.

Babe's 18 touchdowns also compared favorably with Kemp (10), Namath (18), the McCormick, Slaughter, Lee combo (18), Flores and Wood (22), Hadl (20), Blanda (20) and Dawson (21).

His 26 interceptions also were fewer than Blanda (30) and the Denver combo of McCormick, Slaughter and Lee (29).

For all the aggregate facts and figures, however, the absence of halfback Ron Burton and Art Graham for all or most of several games deprived the Patriots of something they lacked overall even with them in the lineup.

Speed.

Often, what showed up in the game summaries as 50 and 60 and 70-yard touchdown passes actually were the result of Graham and Burton breaking free after catching a much shorter throw and blazing away from their defenders.

Graham had caught 45 passes for 720 yards and seven touchdowns in 1964 and 21 passes for 550 yards and five touchdowns in 1963. In 1965, he had only 25 and 316 yards and no touchdowns.

Also hobbled by injuries was end Tony Romeo, who in 1963 had caught 32 passes for 418 yards and three touchdowns and in 1964, a total of 26 passes for 445 yards and four touchdowns. In 1965, he caught only 15 for 203 yards and two touchdowns.

But after their team had lost a chance to play for the 1964 title and then free falling to 4-8-2, Boston fans didn't want to hear any of that.

A championship.

That's what they wanted.

And so far, the Patriots hadn't delivered one.

CHAPTER 21

Did the New York Jets *really* pay Joe Namath $427,000 to play in the AFL?

A year before, that was the question that had been asked all over the country. And, because no figures had ever been disclosed, it was still being asked, although some were convinced he had been paid ever more. The way some of the AFL and NFL teams were throwing money around, it seemed entirely possible.

Not only had the Jets made Joe Namath a rich man, they reportedly had shelled out an *additional* $200,000 to obtain their second pick, Notre Dame quarterback and Heisman Trophy winner John Huarte.

But that wasn't the question that had been asked, and was still being asked, in Boston. There, the question was:

Why are the Patriots spending so little?

After five seasons, they certainly weren't going broke. But they sure weren't going all out to sign the best available college seniors either.

Why?

Why were they so tight-fisted?

In some diners, taverns and barbershops around the city, they were being ridiculed as the "parsimonious Patriots."

Privately, the players themselves could not disagree. None of them certainly was getting rich, especially linemen short on glamour, glory and headlines and long on black eyes, broken noses and bruises.

And now, over in the haughty, mightier-than-thou National Football League, there was another hog snorting at the trough. The NFL had granted an expansion franchise to Atlanta, the first in the Deep South, and the new team, the Falcons, had been granted not only the first pick in the first round but the last in each of the first five rounds. Meanwhile, beginning in November, 1966, the two leagues would begin holding a joint draft instead of selecting players separately as they done since the AFL was formed. That meant more top-quality players likely would sign with the more established, and therefore more well heeled, NFL teams.

When was the Patriots' front office going to wake up and get in the game?

* * * *

If, when the AFL draft was held in November, 1965, Boston fans expected the Patriots to announce that they had pulled off a major coup or two—and few did—they were once again disappointed. Their draft selection list looked like the index to the latest edition of *Who's He In America?*

There were no stars; no big-name names. The first three and five of the first six picks were tackles. The first 10 included six tackles, two defensive backs and two linebackers. Of the 18 chosen, only five made the roster.

But before the season began, the Patriots did indeed do something that was hailed as a recruiting triumph.

In a trade with the Jets, they had obtained . . . drum roll . . . 1964 Heisman trophy winner John Huarte, whom the Jets had paid $200,000 to sign the year before.

Speculation then began circulating that Babe had agreed to groom Huarte as his successor. In exchange, the story went, Coach Mike Holovak had promised Babe a coaching spot on the Patriots' staff after he retired.

Not true. There was no promise of a coaching job. It was never mentioned. And yet, even though they were competing for the same playing time, Babe did help Huarte, just as he had always helped younger quarterbacks, including Tom Flores of the Raiders and Bart Starr of the Packers at the beginning of their careers.

But he had every intention not only of continuing to be the Patriots' starting quarterback, but having, and helping the Patriots have, a better season than they had the year before.

* * * *

Once again, neither Babe nor the Patriots got off to an illustrious start.

In San Diego on Sept., 10, they lost to the Chargers, 24-0.

Babe completed only 13 of 39 passes for 137 and threw four interceptions. Huarte completed one of two for 11 yards and ran once for 12 yards. The Chargers' defense recorded four sacks for 26 yards.

Unlike during the first half of the 1965 season, however, the Patriots exhibited an ability to run the ball. Fullback Jim Nance carried 12 times for 68 yards and Larry Garron, six times for 41 yards and the Patriots finished with 130 yards on 21 carries.

It was a good sign on a day when good signs were anything but easy to find.

* * * *

On Sept, 18, in Denver, fullback Jim Nance rushed 26 times for 124 yards, Gino Cappelletti kicked three field goals and the Patriots scored 15 points in the final quarter to beat the Broncos 24-10.

The Patriots' defense also caused four sacks for 48 yards and made three interceptions. Denver, the second-most prolific yardage passing team the season before, managed only 72 net yards through the air.

Babe completed nine of 23 passes for 133 yards with two interceptions.

The Patriots finished with 145 yards rushing on 33 carries, once again displaying the offensive balance they had lacked in 1965.

* * * *

The following week, Kansas City quarterback Len Dawson threw for 291 yards and five touchdowns as the Chiefs jumped out to a 17-0 lead in the first quarter and scored 21 more in the last to beat the Patriots 43-24.

Jim Nance rushed for 96 yards on 22 carries.

Babe completed 12 of 29 passes for 173 yards and one touchdown with three more interceptions.

* * * *

On Oct. 7, at Fenway Park, with their team trailing 24-7 going into the final quarter, Joe Namath threw two touchdown passes and Jim Turner kicked a field goal to give the New York Jets (3-0-1) a 24-24 tie with the Patriots.

Namath threw 56 passes and completed 28 for 338 yards with three interceptions; Babe, 14 of 29 for 152 yards and one interception.

Jim Nance carried 19 times for 59 yards and the Patriots (1-2-1) rushed 33 times for only 86 net yards.

* * * *

At Buffalo, on Oct. 8, the Patriots (2-2-1) beat the Bills 20-10.

The Patriots took a 10-0 lead in the first quarter on a Gino Cappelletti field goal and Jim Nance's 19-yard run. In the second quarter, another Cappelletti field goal extended the lead to 13-0 at the half.

After the Bills (3-3) kicked a field goal in the third quarter, Babe threw a 25-yard touchdown pass to former Navy star and Heisman Trophy winter Joe Bellino to put the game out of reach.

Bills' quarterback Jack Kemp completed 18 of 38 passes for 298 yards but Buffalo gained only 52 yards on 24 carries.

Babe completed 12 of 26 passes for 177 yards and no interceptions.

Jim Nance carried 23 times for 88 yards.

* * * *

Six weeks after they had lost to San Diego 24-0 in San Diego, Babe threw three touchdown s, two of them to Larry Garron for 53 yards each, to lead the Patriots to a 35-17 victory over the Chargers.

Babe completed 13 of 22 passes for 250 yards with one interception.

Jim Nance ran 25 times for 108 yards. The Patriots rushed 46 times for 172 yards; the Chargers, 21 times for 40 yards.

John Huarte, making his first appearance in several weeks, threw two passes, one of which was incomplete, the other, intercepted.

* * * *

On Oct. 24, at Oakland, Jim Nance rushed 38 times for 208 yards and two in-close touchdowns and Larry Garron 12 times for 73 more yards as the Patriots beat the Raiders 24-21.

Babe threw only 11 passes and completed four for 67 yards and a touchdown with one interception.

Trailing 24-7 after three quarters, the Raiders completed two touchdown passes to trim the final score to 24-21.

* * * *

At the halfway point of the 1965 season, the Raiders had been 0-6-1.

At the halfway point of this season, they were 4-2-1.

At the halfway point of the 1965 season, Babe had thrown five touchdowns and 18 interceptions and been sacked 26 times for 243 yards.

At the halfway point of this season, he had thrown eight touchdown and 13 interceptions and been sacked 13 times for 89 yards.

At the halfway point of the 1965 season, the Patriots had rushed 138 times for 337 yards.

At the halfway point of this season, the Patriots had rushed 253 times for 1,067 yards.

Of that total, Jim Nance had rushed 163 times for 753 yards.

* * * *

On Nov. 6, at Fenway Park, in a game during which the Patriots mustered only 43 net yards rushing in 28 attempts—28 yards in 10 tries by Nance—the Denver Broncos broke a 10-10 tie in the fourth quarter with a 64-yard touchdown pass to win 17-10.

Babe threw26 passes with 14 completions for 111 yards and had no interceptions, but was sacked four times for 44 yards. He also lost 14 more on five attempts to escape onrushing defenders.

Boston also lost five fumbles and managed only 110 total net yards.

* * * *

On Nov. 13, in Boston, Babe threw three touchdown passes and Jim Nance rushed 22 times for 104 yards as the Patriots beat the Houston Oilers 27-21.

Babe completed 12 of 30 attempts for 242 yards and the Patriots picked up 149 yards rushing on 37 carries.

Houston quarterback Don Trull completed 23 of 45 passes for 329 yards and three touchdowns, but the Oilers (3-7-0) had only 72 rushing yards on 30 carries.

* * * *

In Kansas City, on Nov, 20, Babe threw three more touchdown passes and Jim Nance picked up 107 yards on 22 carries as the Patriots (5-3-2) and the Chiefs (8-2-1)_ battled to a 27-27 tie.

Babe completed 19 of 34 for 252 yards and two interceptions. Art Graham caught 11 of them for 134 yards and two touchdowns.

The Chiefs' Len Dawson completed 25 of 38 for 324 yards and two touchdowns with one interception. Otis Taylor caught nine passes for 133 yards and two touchdowns.

* * * *

On Nov. 27, at the Orange Bowl in Miami, Babe threw a 22-yard touchdown pass to Art Graham, Gino Cappelletti kicked two field goals and Jim Nance ran 19 yards for a score to give the Patriots a 20-0 lead going into the final quarter.

The Dolphins (2-9-1) scored twice on passes by quarterback Dick Wood but the Patriots prevailed, 20-14.

Babe completed 14 of 32 passes for 273 yards and one touchdown with two interceptions. He completed three to end Jim Whalen for 76 yards, three to Gino Cappelletti for 76, three to Jim Colclough for 62 and four to Art Graham for 57.

Jim Nance rushed 23 times for 133 yards as the Patriots (6-3-2) picked up 159 yards on 27 carries.

Miami rushed 20 times for 68 yards.

Dolphins' quarterback Dick Woods completed 17 of 52 passes for 276 and was intercepted three times.

* * * *

On Dec.4, at Fenway Park, Jim Nance ran 65 yards for a first-quarter touchdown and Babe rolled out and ran in from the three in the fourth to provide all of the points the Patriots (7-3-2) needed to beat Buffalo (8-4-1), 14-3.

Nance rushed 24 times for 109 yards and Babe completed nine of 22 for 119 yards with one interception.

Bills' quarterback Jack Kemp threw 40 times, completed 19 for 274 yards with two interceptions and Buffalo ball carriers gained only 40 yards in 26 attempts.

Babe threw 27 times and completed 18 for 302 yards with no interceptions.

* * * *

At Rice Stadium in Houston, Babe turned a first-quarter 7-3 deficit into a 24-7 half-time lead by throwing three touchdown passes as the Patriots beat the (3-10) Oilers 38-14. In the third quarter, Jim Nance scored on a 57-yard run to up the lead to 31-.7.

Boston piled up 512 yards of offense, including 240 rushing on 46 carries and for the second game in a row, Nance carried 24 times for 109 yards.

Babe threw 27 times and completed 18 for 302 yards with no interceptions.

* * * *

In their final game of the season, Babe and Joe Namath each threw for three touchdowns as the Jets (6-6-2) beat the Patriots 38-28 at Shea Stadium.

Namath completed 14 of 21 passes for 287 yards and Babe, 21 of 38 for 379 yards.

The Jets rushed 45 times for 241 yards and two touchdowns and the Patriots, only 21 times for 82. Jim Nance ran for 78 of the 82 on 18 carries.

Once again, Babe went repeatedly to all four of his main receivers. Gino Cappelletti caught 11 for 111 yards; Art Graham, five for 94; Larry Garron, three for 86; and end Jim Whalen, three for 67.

For New York, Don Maynard had six catches for 129 yards.

* * * *

So now the season, Babe's fifth straight as the Patriots' starting quarterback, was over and despite a record that could have been better, he could look back on it with satisfaction and ahead to the next one with confidence.

His receivers were all healthy and had been nearly all season.

That sure helped.

He smiled when he thought about what Ohio State coach Woody Hayes had once said about the forward pass:

"Three things can happen—and two of them are bad."

Remembered too how, now that the game was becoming more wide open, Hayes' grind-it-out Buckeye offense was being referred to "Three yards and a cloud of dust."

During the 1965 season, critics might have labeled the Patriots' impotent rushing attack "Three clouds of dust and a yard."

But that hadn't been the case this time around. Whereas the Patriots had rushed for only 1135 yards in 1965 and the Patriots' defense had give up 1,531 yards, the '66 edition, primarily because of Jim Nance, had piled up 1,963 yards rushing and the Patriots' defense had given up only 1,135.

Nance alone had racked up 1,458 yards and 11 touchdowns on 299 carries and had been selected to play in the Pro Bowl and been named first team All Pro.

Besides his powerful running, Nance was a ferocious blocker, a comforting asset Babe had rarely enjoyed in all his years as a pro. Nance made Babe's job a whole lot easier.

Babe's figures had improved a little too. In 1965, he had thrown for 2,597 yards and 18 touchdowns with 26 interceptions. This season: 2,721 yards with 20 touchdowns and 20 interceptions.

The one change that was not so encouraging was pass defense. In 1965, the Patriots had given up 2891 yards, 37 more than the offense's total. This time, the defense had yielded 3,356 passing yards while the offense gained 2,784.

And as for next year, who knew? With a little luck and perhaps a little more help from the draft or via trades and a few timely breaks, there was no telling what might happen when the 1967 season rolled around. . . . .

CHAPTER 22

For decades, the faces of the rich and the famous along with world and national leaders had appeared on the cover of *Life* magazine. Winston Churchill, Charles de Gaulle, Nikita Khrushchev, Fidel Castro, Princess Margaret, Franklin Delano Roosevelt, Harry Truman. Dwight D. Eisenhower, Douglas MacArthur, John F. Kennedy, Robert F. Kennedy, Senator Barry Goldwater—all had appeared one time or another on the millions of copies delivered each week by the mailman and stacked on piled high newsstand shelves all over the country.

Movie stars and entertainers made the cover as well. Rudolph Valentino. Gretta Garbo. Hopalong Cassidy. Errol Flynn. Fred Astaire and Ginger Rodgers. Marilyn Monroe. Shirley Temple. Judy Garland. Gary Cooper. Sophia Loren. Frank Sinatra. Dorothy Dandridge. Spencer Tracy. Katherine Hepburn. Sophia Loren. Shelley Winters. Grace Kelly. Richard Burton and Elizabeth Taylor. The Beatles. Shirley McLaine. Steve McQueen.

So had authors, including Ernest Hemingway, William Faulkner and Carl Sandburg and TV personalities Jackie Gleason, Alfred Hitchcock. Lucille Ball and major league Joe DiMaggio, Ted Williams, Mickey Mantle, Roger Maris, Roy Campanella, Casey Stengel and Sandy Koufax. Now and then even a professional football star too, including quarterbacks Sid Luckman and Roger Staubach.

Even serial killer Charles Manson.

When the September 8, 1967 issue appeared, Babe's photograph was not on the cover, but it might just as well have been.

With a convict's prison number right below it.

For after hundreds of thousands, if not millions of readers had seen what appeared on page 93 and the ominous implications it suggested, many probably concluded that prison was where he was headed or deserved to be. For there was Babe's picture beneath a boldface headline stretching across two entire pages that said:

$7 Billion from illegal Bets and a Blight on Sports

The caption accompanying his photo and that of an older, somber-faced man wearing glasses and a hat said:

"To passersby in Revere, Mass. 'Arthur's Farm' appears no more sinister than any roadside store. But it is a gangster hangout, a thieves' market and sports betting center that has such diverse customers as Boston Patriots' quarterback Babe Parilli (*left*) and mobster Henry Tameleo (*below*).

At the bottom of the facing page were photos of two other men. The caption said:

"When police arrested big-time bookie Gil Beckley(*above*), they found in his notebook the name of Bob Cousy (*right*), former basketball great, now coach at Boston College. Cousy admitted his friendship with gamblers."

At first glance, the magazine cover, featuring Boston Red Sox star Carl Yastrzenski racing for first base after drilling a single, suggested the glamour, the excitement of a tight American League pennant race, a welcome diversion from the worsening war in Viet Nam and the turmoil of an increasingly tense civil rights movement. But above that momentary silver lining on the cover loomed a dark- cloud headline that said:

How The
Mob Muscles
Into Your Daily Life

To make matters worse, beginning on page 94 was a four-page spread about, and a photograph of, Carlos Marcello, identified as "King Thug of Louisiana."

On page 98, accompanied by a photo of the notorious Meyer Lansky, reputed to be the Mafia's financial "brains," was another article that continued several pages and was topped by a headline that said:

"Mobsters in the Marketplace: Money, Muscle, Murder

And with his picture prominently displayed in the eye of it, a dark cloud was pouring directly on the person and the reputation of Babe Parilli.

Here, verbatim, is what the article, beginning on page 92 and continuing on page 93 of the Sept 8. 1967 issue, said:

"More than from any other source, far more than from dope, prostitution and loan sharking combined, the Mob thrives by exploiting the almost universal human urge to gamble. Each year, it handles $20 billion in illegal bets, of which it keeps $7 billion profit. At least half of this is the takeoff from betting on sports events.

"Every day, in every city, by telephone and in person at outlaw betting centers like the roadside market at right, thousands of sports fans lay in wagers on the outcome of football, basketball and baseball games, horse races and boxing matches. On every bet made, be it $1 or $10,000, the Mob collects a cut of the action, called vigorish—usually 10 %,

"But the appetite of the Mob is boundless. Its involvement in sports has led to widespread attempts to corrupt—or at least to 'use'—individual athletes and coaches of high reputation. To the extent that such corruption succeeds, it threatens the fabric of spectator sport in the U.S., which depends for its existence on public confidence in the honesty of the game.

"Inside information is the life-blood of the bookie handicappers who run sports betting—a nationwide syndicate of big and small-time operators who are protected, partly staffed and almost totally controlled by Cosa Nostra. They need specific up-to-the-minute reports on the physical and mental conditions of the teams involved—the kind of information that goes deeper than that on the sports page. They use it to set the betting line—the odds or the number of points by which one team figures to beat the other. And, if they can get even more solid indications of the outcome of a sports contest—by fixing it—all the better.

"Accuracy in the assessment of a contest can pay princely dividends and mobsters are skilled at prying the information they need from the sources: the college and professional coaches and players themselves. They ingratiate themselves as friends and fellow sportsmen, doers of favors and, above all, good listeners. The success of their operation depends largely on how well the mobsters are able to build and maintain these pipelines to coaches and players who, either innocently or for their own advantage, feed them information.

"The biggest of the bookie handicappers—at least until his recent gambling conviction—is one Gilbert Beckley of Miami. When the FBI nabbed Beckley on Jan. 8, 1966, his records showed that on that day alone he had handled $250,000 in bets and turned a profit of $129,000.

"Top bookies are known among themselves by numbers—just like players on the gridiron. Beckley uses No. 1 or 111; Frank Rosenthal of Miami, 3; Eugene Nolan of Baton Rouge, La., 98. This allows for quick, nameless communication and also refers to the page number in the books in which the gamblers record business dealings among themselves.

"In Beckley's black book police last year found next a phone number the word 'Skiball,' the nickname for Francisco Scibelli. Scibelli, a member of the Genovese Family of Cosa Nostra, runs a gambling syndicate in Springfield, Mass. Scribbled next to 'Skiball' was the name of Bob Cousy, one of the half-dozen great players in basketball history. Before his retirement in 1963, Cousy helped the professional Boston Celtics to six world championships. Since then he has been a successful coach at Boston College.

"Questioned by *Life,* Cousy denied knowing Beckley but admitted that Scibelli was a friend whom he had met through an even closer friend, Andrew Pradella. Pradella, it turned out, is Scibelli's partner in bookmaking. Because they always have such excellent information, the Scibelli-Pradella ring is known as the 'Scholar Group.'

"Cousy admitted he knew the two were gamblers and that he often talked to them about both pro and college basketball teams and their chances of winning. 'I'd be having dinner with Pradella when Scibelli would come over,' said Cousy. 'They got together each night to balance the books or something.'

"Did Cousy realize his friends were using what he told them to fix betting lines and to make smart bets of their own?

"'No,' said Cousy.'I thought they figured the betting line with mathematics. But it doesn't surprise me. I'm pretty cynical. I think most people who approach me want to use me in some way.'

"Cousy conceded he had been warned about his associates by Boston police as long ago as 1963. But he refused to end his relationship, even after the experience that shook him up a bit. Pradella, he said, invited him to a banquet in Hartford that turned out to be a gangster enclave. 'Police were watching the place,' said Cousy, 'and the whole Mob was there.'

Cousy still defends his actions. 'In this hypocritical world we live in.' he said, 'I don't see why I should stop seeing my friends just because they are gamblers. How can I tell Andy when he calls and asks about a team that I won't talk to him about that?'

"The arrest of Beckley also led to the disclosure that as recently as last season he had been secretly feeding information about suspected fixing of pro football games and betting by players to the office of pro football commissioner Pete Rozelle. In return, Rozelle's chief investigator, William G. Hundley, (a former head of the Justice Department's Organized Crime Division) wrote a letter to the U.S. Probation Office seeking lenience for Beckley on grounds that he had 'cooperated' with the league 'on certain matters.'

"The 'certain matters' presumably included investigation of the relationship of a star American Football League quarterback and two bookies, Carmello Coco and Philip Cali. The inquiries were stepped up after the player's teammates were overheard in the locker room angrily accusing him of 'throwing' the game they had just lost. But no public accusation has been made yet.

"Another potentially explosive situation involves the strange affinity that several members of the Boston Patriots pro football team have for a ramshackle roadside store in Revere, Mass named Arthur's Farm. Behind its shabbily humdrum front, Arthur's Farm turns out to be a beehive of Mob activities. It does a fast business in sports betting and the exchange of stolen property and doubles as an informal conference hall where gangsters can get together with people who are of use to them.

"The proprietor is Arthur Ventola, a convicted felon. Among the regular habitués are Arthur's kinsmen—Nicholas (Junior) Ventola and Richard Castucci, both active bookies. Another is Henry Tameleo, a lieutenant of New England Cosa Nostra boss, Raymond Patriarca, who, with Tameleo, is now awaiting trial for an interstate gambling-and-murder conspiracy.

"Another regular at the farm, it turns out, is Babe Parilli, quarterback of the Boston Patriots. 'Half the team goes there,' Parilli told *Life*. 'One of our coaches, too. But we're not doing anything wrong.' Parilli admitted knowing Arthur and 'Junior' and to having met Tameleo. He insisted he did know they are mobsters, or that they used information garnered from Parilli and the other Patriots to make a killing on 'informed' bets.

"Why, then, do Parilli and his teammates visit Arthur's Farm so often? 'We stop on the way home from practice,' says Parilli, 'to buy toys, razor blades and things we get at wholesale prices.'"

* * * *

On page four of the same issue, *Life* published a lengthy editorial titled:

We Can Break the Grip of the Mob

Insofar as the spread on pages 92 and 93 focusing on Bob Cousy, Babe Parilli, sports betting and game fixing were concerned, no editorial was needed.

The story itself was an editorial.

It was an essay, as devoid of documentation as a term paper without footnotes, an indictment without evidence, a legal brief without supportive case law citations.

If intended to be, or to be perceived as being, an investigative expose, it lacked every element necessary to make its case.

It was nothing more than a recitation of conclusions and here-say, guilt by association if there indeed was any association, coated with innuendo, lacking in scope and context that raised more questions than it provided answers.

Among them:

If the threat, if not the practice, of corrupting coaches and players was so widespread, why did the story focus entirely on Cousy and Babe?

If the problem at both the collegiate and professional level was indeed nationwide, why did the magazine limit its investigation to one roadside stand in one small town in one state?

If Miami, more than any other, was such a hotbed of Mob-controlled sports betting, why didn't the story include, if not focus primarily, on schools and teams there?

Given the fact that the early 1950s college basketball scandal had occurred primarily in New York, home of the nation's five most powerful Mafia families, why wasn't it the focal point?

Then there was attribution.

Or lack of it.

Who said illegal betting was a $20 billion business, of which the Mafia pocketed $7 billion?

How did the source, if there was one, determine half of it was the result of sports betting?

Did Rozelle's chief investigator, William G. Hundley, (a former head of the Justice Department's Organized Crime Division) confirm that he "wrote a letter to the U.S. Probation Office seeking lenience for Beckley on grounds that he had 'cooperated' with the league 'on certain matters.'?

If so, why didn't the story say so?

As for the "certain matters' that ' presumably included investigation of the relationship of "a star American Football League quarterback and two bookies, Carmello Coco and Philip Cali"—*which* star American Football League quarterback?

Babe? Joe Namath of the New York Jets? Bob Griese of the Miami Dolphins? Steve Tensi of the Denver Broncos? Pete Beathard of the Houston Oilers? Len Dawson of the Kansas City Chiefs? Daryle Lamonica of the Oakland Raiders? Jack Kemp of the Buffalo Bills? John Hadl of the San Diego Chargers?

If there wasn't sufficient evidence to name the one who was under investigation—and reveal what that evidence was-- why make them all suspects?

Whoever the 'star AFL quarterback' was,' if in fact one was suspected of fixing games, which of his teammates, and when, and where, 'were overheard in the locker room angrily accusing him of 'throwing' the game they had just lost'?

Who overheard them "angrily accusing him"?

And if "no public accusation has been made yet," why not?

And if it would be, by whom?

As for the "strange affinity several members of the Boston Patriots have for a ramshackle roadside store in Revere, Mass. named Arthur's Farm"—which several?

Who said they did?

Why identify Babe and not the others?

Because he was Italian?

Why weren't those "several interviewed too?

Told that one of the Patriots' coaches went there too, why wasn't the coach identified and interviewed or at least an attempt made to obtain a statement from the Patriots' front office?

Then there was a little matter of the origin, motivation and timing of the story.

Who initiated it?

Life magazine?

The FBI?

The NFL?

Why?

And why did the story appear when it did: at the beginning of the 1967 AFL season?

But at the time, Babe was too stunned, too shocked to think about such matters. What bothered him more than anything else was the affect it might have on his family.

* * * *

Ten days after the Sept. 8 article appeared, *Sports Illustrated* reported that Patriot players --,although the story did not say which Patriot players or how many -- had heard about the impending story and that several would be mentioned, not just Babe.

They would deal with it, the magazine said, as a team.

At least 20 of the Patriots, a dozen of whom were still members of the team, had shopped at Arthur's Farm, it said. .

Citing an anonymous source, it also reported that 1) seven or eight players had been there before Babe ever did; 2) Hundley knew the story was about to appear; 3) had talked with Patriots' Coach Mike Holovak, Babe and another player; 4) told them that the NFL had investigated and cleared them; and 5) the league would issue a statement absolving them after the story appeared.

Hundley never told Babe in advance about the story.

There was no supportive statement from the league.

Babe found out about the article when Will McDonough, a *Boston Globe* reporter who covered the Patriots, brought a copy to Babe's room in San Diego.

His first reaction, even more than outrage:

What would his parents think?

His wife?

Babe tried to call home. The line was busy. And stayed busy for hours. When he finally got through, he learned that Priscilla had received so many crank calls, she had taken the phone off the hook.

At the Stardust Motor Hotel, where the Patriots were staying, Tom Addision, the Patriot's defensive captain, issued a written statement.

"We, the players," it said, "think that Babe has been dealt a serious blow to his character. We stand behind Babe 100 percent on and off the field because he is the type of person that is beyond reproach as a quarterback or as an individual. It is outrageous to think that Babe should be picked from so many of us—including myself—that have entered the doors of this so-called Arthur's Farm. If I had an Italian name, and was a quarterback, it could have been me. Why did they not use the name of an Irish or English player? Babe Parilli has done nothing wrong, nor have any of the other players who have shopped there. We want to drop the matter now and forget about it. It has not hurt our morale for this game with San Diego because we are a team and we will play like a team."

Addison, also said he had shopped for toys with his wife at Arthur's Farm for three or four years and that several of the Patriots had come to him and volunteered to be named as customers of the place.

"I don't think this has affected the team," Patriot's coach Mike Holovak told *Sports Illustrated*.."But what is all this supposed to prove? Who is being accused of what? How are you supposed to know if you are in a place that is run by gangsters? You know it could happen to anybody."

Billy Sullivan, president of the Patriots, said: "I would say our team tonight will play its best game in a long time. Babe is immensely popular with the players. I've been in professional sports for 32 years and I have never met a nicer man, a man with a better character than Babe. He'll sit for hours talking to little kids. I've never even heard him swear. In some ways he reminds me more of a violinist than of an athlete. He's a gentle person. Who can say how this will affect him? You can't put yourself into another person's mind. I've taken a lot of belts in this business. It's all part of the old ball game. But my wife has nearly had nervous breakdowns over some of the stuff written about me. Some guys on this team would have just laughed if they had been named in that story. But Babe is a very sensitive man. Nobody knows how this will affect him or his family."

* * * *

U.S. Senator Edward M. Kennedy called Babe in San Diego to express his outrage and to offer his support. But wherever Babe went in the days immediately after the article appeared, so did photographers and reporters.

While he was playing golf at a San Diego course, flashbulbs suddenly popped back in a grove of nearby trees.

When the Patriots' bus broke down, photographers following it attempted to take Babe's picture as he stepped off the bus. His teammates formed a human shield around him to block their view.

* * * *

Holovak and Sullivan were wrong. The controversy did affect the Patriots. Or something did. They did not play an inspired game. A bad pass from center resulted in a Charger touchdown. Babe's receivers dropped several passes. Babe was hit hard as he attempted to pass. The ball fell into the hands of a San Diego defender who ran for another touchdown.

The Patriots lost, 28-14.

* * * *

Babe told – ordered-- his teammates to forget it. If they wanted to help him, and themselves and the team, and their fans, play football. Good, solid, better-than-ever football. Go out there and do your job and forget about everything else.

That's what a leader was supposed to do and say. The Bear had taught him that. A good quarterback was more than a sure, deceptive ball handler, a pinpoint passer, a time-and-distance game manager. Through leadership, by example, he was responsible for maintaining poise in the face of mounting adversity, order amid impending chaos, confidence when others had lost, or were about to lose, theirs. As always, he did the talking in the huddle. They did the listening. He made the decisions. They carried them out. That's the way it was. Even in practice.

Lead.

The Bear had taught him that too.

Soon, the magazine story was rarely mentioned, at least not in his presence.

But he could not help but wonder: Had knowing about the impending story played a part—and if so, how big part?—in their season-opening loss to Denver, a team they should have beaten?

Had reading it, seeing Babe's picture juxtaposed with that of a man purported to be a known gangster, and knowing how much of a nationwide firestorm it all had created, been a factor in their loss to the Chargers too?

Like Coach Mike Holovak, Babe didn't think so. But he couldn't be sure.

The proof, or at least an indication, would emerge in the weeks to come.

But privately, he knew that the shock, the shame, the humiliation held him in their grip like a deadly paralyzing disease. Try though he might, he could not banish the anger, the outrage, the injustice and the helplessness he felt trying to deal with it.

Not for himself. He knew he had not done anything wrong.

For his family.

His wife, who could not go to the grocery without sensing the hard, cold stares, the accusing, hateful unspoken words directed toward her.

His mother and father back in Rochester, bewildered, feeling, no doubt, guilty and ashamed when there was nothing to feel guilty and ashamed about. They were good, honest, loving, hardworking people who treated life far better than it sometimes had treated them.

Put it out of your mind, he kept telling himself.

Remember?

Things always work out for the best.

But he couldn't.

Not this time.

* * * *

For Babe and the Patriots, things got no better the following week.

On Sept. 17, at Oakland, following a first quarter that ended 7-7, the Raiders erupted for two touchdowns in the second quarter and two more in the third to hammer the Patriots, 35-7.

The Patriots' only score came on Babe's 19-yard pass to Art Graham.

Babe completed 19 of 33 for 258 yards but was sacked eight times for 67 yards. He also threw three interceptions. The Patriots lost two fumbles.

Raiders' quarterback Daryle Lamonica completed 17 of 27 passes for 256 yards and three touchdowns.

Then in Buffalo, on Sept. 24, Gino Cappelletti kicked four field goals, Babe passed for one touchdown and Jim Nance rushed 34 times for 185 yards as the Patriots beat the Bills 23-0.

Former Raider quarterback Tom Flores completed 11 of 30 passes for 159 yards and was intercepted five times. Babe passed 24 times and completed nine for 94 yards with no interceptions. Boston had no turnovers.

Most important of all, The Patriots (1-3) had something to be confident about.

* * * *

SAN DIEGO
Oct. 8

Quarterback John Hadl threw two touchdown passes in the fourth quarter to erase a 31-17 Boston lead and enable the Chargers to salvage a 31-31 tie.

It was disheartening, not coming away with a win after leading a good, solid undefeated team by two touchdowns.

Offensively, the Patriots were cooking. Babe completed 17 of 34 passes for 264 yards and two touchdowns and one interception. Jim Nance carried 29 times for 127 yards.

But once again, pass defense, that was another matter.

* * * *

BOSTON
Oct. 15

Babe threw five touchdown passes, three of them to end Jim Whalen, as the Patriots clobbered the expansion Miami Dolphins 41-10.

He completed 16 of 21 passes for 281 yards with three interceptions. Jim Nance rushed 20 times for 131 yards.

Miami rushed 18 times for 29 yards and quarterback Rick Norton completed 19 of 46 passes for 216 yards with one interception. The Dolphins also lost four fumbles.

The Patriots might not be on a roll, but having won two and tied one in their last three games after losing three of their first four, they had reason to hope that they might on their way to one.

Then gloom set in again.

On Oct. 22, at Fenway Park, after leading 20-0 at the half, the Oakland Raiders scored again in the third quarter and three more times in the fourth to trounce the Patriots 48-14.

Babe completed 10 of 33 passes for 118 yards for one touchdown with no interceptions. He was sacked seven times for 78 yards.

The Raiders (5-1-0) completed 17 of 41 passes for 287 yards and five touchdowns, four of them by starter Daryle Lamonica and the other by George Blanda, who also kicked two field goals.

* * * *

At the halfway point of their season, the Patriots' record (2-4) was the exact reversal of what it had been the year before when they finished 8-4-1.

Babe had thrown for 14 touchdowns and 15 interceptions and in most games, Jim Nance not only was providing the rushing threat the Patriots had lacked in seasons past, but appeared to be on his way to a 1,000-yard year.

However, it was difficult to defend their defense, especially pass defense. While the offense had scored 14 or fewer points in three games, the defense had allowed more than 20 twice, more than 30 twice and more than 40 once.

While Babe was throwing 14 TD passes, the defense was giving up 16, many of them in the later stages with the game on the line.

* * * *

As disappointing as the first half of the season had been, the second was even worse. The Patriots won only one, lost six and finished 3-10-1.

Statistically, Babe had done well enough, completing 166 of 344 passes for 2,317 yards, and 19 touchdowns with 24 interceptions, six of which had occurred in the first game of the season and 11 in the first three games in the emotionally devastating wake of the *Life* magazine story.

Now, at last, the 1967 season, both on and off the field the worst of his entire pro career including that forgettable final year at Green Bay in 1958, was over. But not the specter of suspicion, the self-propelling winds of whispers and rumors and gossip that perhaps had played such a large, immeasurable role in making it so.

And try though he might, he could not make it go away.

CHAPTER 23

Perhaps it might have been fortuitous had Babe and his family spent the off season in Green Bay where they still owned the home they had purchased nearly a decade before. Under normal circumstances, a long, bleak winter in frigid, snowy Wisconsin would have constituted a four-month prescription for depression, not a relaxing, much-needed means to escape it. But because of the long, lingering dark shadow the *Life* magazine story had cast over their lives and the atrocious season the Patriots had just completed, circumstances were anything but normal.

They would remember him there, of course. But they would remember him frozen in time, the same way the folks still did back home in Rochester, Pa. and in Lexington, Ky. In Rochester, he remained, in the images that danced across their minds, and always would remain, the muscular, handsome single wing high school fullback who threw passes straight as a razor, accurate as a railroad watch. In Lexington, he remained, and always would remain, Kentucky Babe, the two-time, first-team All-American whose No. 10 they would never see again because it had been retired and no UK player would ever wear it again; the incomparable jump-passing, ball faking Houdini, the record-breaking passer who had led the Wildcats to heights they had never reached before, hadn't since, and likely never would again.

Yes, they would still remember him in Green Bay. He was the Packers' first-round, first pick back in – what year had that been?—and as a rookie he had alternated at quarterback with – who was it? Rote? Yes, that's right, Tobin Rote—for two seasons before he had to gone into the service.

Remember him in Cleveland too. Babe Parilli? Yeah, he was the one Paul Brown had anointed as Otto Graham's successor—their picture had even been in the newspaper together; Paul on one side, Otto on the other, Babe in the middle, Otto placing a helmet on Babe's head like it was a crown or something. But after a year he was gone. Got hurt, didn't he? Yeah, that's right, hurt his leg—no, it was his shoulder—couldn't even throw the ball after that. Traded him to Green Bay, wasn't it? Yeah, to the Packers . . .

Then, a few years later, he and Bart Starr had alternated at quarterback for a couple of years—"57 and '58, wasn't it, or was it '58 and 59?—well anyway, it's been awhile, you know. Let's see now, in 1955. that was the year when . . .

And so, yes, they would remember him and say "hello" and "how are you doing?" and he would have felt welcome, but all the while he would have known that what they really wanted to talk about was not those long-ago times when he was playing for the Packers but how the Packers were playing now.

In Green Bay, even during the numerous, most dismal years when they had lost far more games than they won, all anybody *ever* wanted to talk about was the Packers, one reason being, there really wasn't much else to talk about.

But this winter, long-suffering Packer fans were all but insufferable. And why not? Their beloved frozen-field heroes had warmed their hearts by winning the *Super Bowl.*

For the *second* time in a *row.*

In January, 1967 Bart Starr, Paul Hornung, Jim Taylor, Ray Nitschke, Jerry Kramer and company had finished the season 14 -2 by winning the big one, 35-10 over the Kansas City Chiefs in the Los Angeles Memorial Coliseum in front of 61,946 fans.

In Super Bowl II, just held at the Orange Bowl in Miami in front of 75,546, the '67 Packers had pounded the Oakland Raiders 33-14 to win it all again. Which meant that all of the breathless, red-nosed, rosy-cheeked regulars who hung out down at the neighborhood tavern, the hardware store, the car repair shop, the barbershop, the hotel lobby as well as everywhere else in town who still hadn't stopped raving about the first championship now had stored up enough wide-eyed joy and words and facts and figures to keep them all warm through another entire winter.

Life magazine?

Arthur's farm?

The Mafia?

The Patriots' miserable 3-10-1 season?

Nah. Nobody would want to talk—or even think-- about any of that.

And that would have suited Babe just fine.

He didn't want to talk – or even think—about any of that either.

But some did want to talk about it, if not in Green Bay, in DePere, two miles away, where Priscillia's parents lived and her father, Clarence Perkins, was a veterinarian. Especially, when they encountered Dr. Perkins at the store or walking down the street.

More times than he cared to remember, someone remarked, "Too bad about your son-in-law. Got himself into a little trouble, eh?"

Too bad about your son-in-law . . .

Such expressions of sympathy, if they were sympathy and not, as he sometimes suspected, perhaps gloating, thinly disguised sarcasm, were bad enough. He knew full well the allegations—no, insinuations— published in *Life* magazine were unfounded.

But every time he heard those words, *Too bad about your son-in-law,* Dr. Perkins felt like he had been stabbed with a double-edged sword. Once again he felt the cold-fear shock, the horror he had experienced the first time he had heard them.

One night, three years before, when the Patriots were preparing to play the Buffalo Bills in an AFL eastern division playoff game, a man trying to break up a fight had been shot to death in a Chicago bowling alley owned by Chicago Bears end Mike Ditka.

When he awoke the next morning, Babe heard the news on the radio. A Chicago radio station reported that the victim had been identified as Washington Redskins' linebacker John Parilli. But several hours later, a Wisconsin television station had erroneously reported that Babe had been killed and when Dr. Perkins heard the news, he was devastated. He and Babe were close friends.

"Too bad about your son-in-law," folks he met on the street had said.

Dr. Perkins had rushed home and told his wife.

"Wait a minute," she replied. "Let's call his apartment."

At that moment, Babe and teammate Bill Neighbors were about to leave to go to breakfast. As they closed the door and started to walk away, Babe heard the telephone ring. He went back inside.

"Hello?"

From the other end of the line, all he could hear was a deep sigh of relief.

And now there was this, this ugly, unsubstantiated, uncalled for attack on his son-in-law's reputation and all Dr. Perkins could do was say nothing and walk away.

It especially pained him to think what his daughter must be going through.

* * * *

Priscilla Perkins Parilli was a beautiful, vivacious woman who had adjusted well over the years to the demands of being the wife of a professional football player. Despite being a private person, reserved but not self-conscious, she enjoyed attending the games and the parties, banquets, private dinners and all the other social events that came with the territory.

She had frequently accompanied her husband to Arthur's Farm, where she had purchased fresh fruit and vegetables, perfume, toys at Christmas time and other items. She had even told her neighbors about the wide selection of merchandise and the cut-rate prices and occasionally invited them to go there with her.

Since the magazine article had appeared, she didn't go there anymore. Unless it was necessary, such as to the grocery, she didn't go anywhere much anymore. Even though only rarely, if ever, did anyone say anything about the story in *Life,* she could sense, or out of the corner of her eye, see customers and sometimes clerks staring at her when they thought she was not looking.

She felt humiliated, guilty, even though she knew neither she nor Babe had anything to feel guilty about. More than anything else, she felt angry. Outraged.

How could anyone, in good conscience, do such a thing?

Especially one of America's most widely read magazines?

* * * *

Meanwhile, if nothing much except back-to-back Super Bowl trophies had changed in Green Bay since his rookie season there in 1952, plenty had everywhere else. Socially, politically, culturally, technologically, America was a dramatically different place. Even within the relatively tiny and comparatively insignificant world of sports, it boggled the mind to consider how much. Over the airways, as well as along the highways, what once had seemed a slow-paced, single-wing way of life was now a hurry-up, fast-paced, run-and-gun T formation world.

In 1948, when Babe had enrolled in college, fans all over America had sat on the edge of their seats as they gathered around the radio to listen to Bill Stern, Mel Allen, Red Barber and others paint vivid word pictures that brought the tension, the thrills, the flavor, right into the living room as they broadcast, coast to coast, the gripping, unforgettable drama and excitement of the World Series, the Army-Navy and Notre Dame football games and blow-by-blow accounts of every world heavyweight championship fight featuring the great Joe Louis and his swift destruction of the latest member of what was commonly, if not affectionately, known as The Bum of the Month Club.

One of the most popular movie- theater attractions, along with the cartoons and weekly serial adventure, was the newsreel which each fall enabled patrons to actually *see* highlights of the most important college football games each week.

Television had changed all that.

When he had played in the 1951 Sugar Bowl and the 1952 Cotton Bowl, the folks back home as well as fans all over the country could see him in action, for the entire game, rather than just listen to and read all those glowing reports in the newspapers.

His name had been headlined on the local sports page along with the likes of major league baseball stars Joe DiMaggio, Ted Williams, Stan Musial, Jackie Robinson, Bob Feller, Mickey Mantle and Willie Mays; boxing champions Sugar Ray Robinson, Ezzard Charles, Jersey Joe Walcott, former champion Joe Louis and soon-to-be champ Rocky Marciano; Heisman Trophy winners Leon Hart, Doak Walker, Vic Janowicz and Dick Kazmaier; college basketball All-Americans Bob Cousy, Bill Sharman and Bill Spivey.

All were gone now. Off the field. The diamond. The court. No longer in the spotlight.

In 1952, more than 350 college seniors had been selected in the NFL draft. Many never played a down, others only a year or two and most not much longer.

Now, 15 years later, only Babe and a handful of others were still playing.

At mid century, with few exceptions, the rosters of America's pro football as well as pro baseball teams looked like the all-white pages of a telephone directory. Other than the Harlem Globetrotters, and the New York Rens, there were no black pro basketball players. But then, beginning with Chuck Cooper and Nat "Sweetwater" Clifton and soon followed by the rest of the best of America's best black basketball players, the NBA had become integrated, even if the rest of the country had not.

Several long-entrenched, famous -name major professional sports teams had vanished too. In 1953, the Boston Braves had become the Milwaukee Braves. In 1955, the Athletics, after having played in Philadelphia since 1901, had moved to Kansas City. Come 1958, they would move again, this time to Oakland. Following the 1957 season, the Brooklyn Dodgers had forsaken Flatbush and Ebbets Field to become the Los Angeles Dodgers. The Polo Grounds also stood silent and empty. The New York Giants had packed their bags for San Francisco.

That same year, the charter-member NBA Fort Wayne Zollner Pistons had pulled up stakes and moved to Detroit. Three years later, the Minneapolis Lakers, another original member of the NBA, had become the Los Angeles Lakers.

Beginning during the early and mid 1950s, far from the roaring crowds, the blaring of the bands, America also had been in the process of being bisected by interstate highways; deafened by rock 'roll music; sombered and saddened by a "police action" war in Korea. Air conditioned. Hoola hooped. Duck-tailed and flat-topped at the barbershop. Pizza-addicted. Three-D'd at the movies. Burgered and French fried in their drive-in automobiles. Fascinated, however briefly, by such passing fancies as pants stretchers, curb feelers and an oddball, ill-fated new automobile called the Edsel.

In the early 1960s, along with the newly formed American Football League, had come another war, this one in Viet Nam as well as anti-war protests, Civil Rights demonstrations complete with attack dogs and fire hoses and traumatic political assassinations.

And, through it all, Babe had been able to continue doing the one thing –the only thing-- he had ever truly wanted to do: play football.

In the meantime, at the age of 38, he would continue to work out, stay in shape and, come fall, be ready to go again.

And then the telephone rang.

* * * *

The caller was Pete Rozelle, commissioner of the National Football League.

"Babe," he said, "would you be willing to come down to New York and take a polygraph examination? We'd like to ask you a few questions."

Babe didn't have to ask what about.

Here it came all over again. Arthur's Farm. Gangsters. Gambling. Guilt by association.

"Sure," he replied. "I would be glad to."

Later that week, he drove down to Manhattan.

* * * *

The narrow hallway that led up the back stairs was dark and gloomy. When he opened the door and stepped inside, the office was no better. Cluttered, shabbily furnished, it looked like a movie - scene office of a coat hanger abortionist. If anyone ever looked like he needed to submit to a lie detector test, it was the man, unshaven, a soggy cigar drooping from the corner of his mouth, who was about to administer it.

Beneath the dim glow of a single bare light bulb, Babe settled into an uncomfortable wooden chair as the operator fidgeted with the equipment.

Then the questions began. Broad, general, ambiguous questions. And with each of them, an uneasy feeling, a disturbing uncertainty about how to answer.

_____

Question: *Have you ever associated with a known gambler?*
Answer: *No.*
Hesitant thought: *Well, my Uncle Frank liked to gamble on sports events and when I was a senior in high school and we played Ambridge, he came to the game with $600 in his pockets and made a lot of bets and he told me later after we won that he had doubled his money. Did that count?*

But the guy didn't want to hear any of that.

Yes or no.

No elaboration allowed.

–––––––––

Question: *Have you ever bet on a sporting event in which you partici-pated?*

Answer: *No.*

Hesitant thought: *Well, there was that time the day after the 1952 College All-Star game when I was a rookie with the Packers and Frank Gif-ford a rookie with the Giants and we played against each other, although we played very little because we didn't know the offensive systems, and I said to Frank before the game, "I betcha a dollar we beat you" and Frank laughed and said," Okay, you're on" and the Giants won and later, in the regular season, when the Packers and Giants played again, we did it again and this time, we won so the two of us broke even, and besides no money ever changed hands.*

Should I tell the guy about that? No, remember, he said he wanted only yes or no answers. So which was the right answer: yes, or no?

–––––––––

Question: *Have you ever received any benefits of any kind from money you knew to have been the result of gambling on a game in which you par-ticipated?*

Answer: *No.*

Hesitant thought: *About that $600 my Uncle Frank bet on the Rochester-Ambridge and doubled his money: The next fall, right before I left to enroll at the University of Kentucky, he gave me $15 so I could buy a new coat. He said that was for winning the Ambridge game, but I don't know if that was from the same money he won or if it was different money.*

–––––––––

Question: *Have you ever been introduced to and had conversations with known gangsters or gamblers when you visited Arthur's Farm in Revere Mass or anywhere else?*

Answer: *No.*

Hesitant thought: *I met so many people, you know, was introduced to them-- you know, shook their hand, Hey, how you doin', but I didn't pay any attention. Maybe they were, but I didn't know it if they were. My wife and I would go there, look around, maybe buy some toys or something, but that was about it. I never hung around there.*

––––––––––

Question: *Did anyone on another team ever ask you, or did you ever agree, to do anything that would alter the outcome of a game or give the other team an advantage?*

Answer: *No.*

Hesitant thought: *What about that time Skippy Doyle asked me to let him intercept a pass and run for a touchdown when we played the Broncos and I laughed and then during the game, when I saw him streak in for what he thought was a sure touchdown, I pump faked and our receiver raced past him like he was standing still and was 15 yards in the clear and I lobbed a perfect pass for a touchdown and I grinned as I trotted down the field to hold the extra point snap and said to myself, "Finally gotcha. That one's for Barbara and Eleanor?"*

––––––––––

And so it went. Seemingly simple questions that, truth be known, required complex, sometimes contradictory answers.

At last it was over. Babe headed down the dark stairway into the bright, chilly sunlight. Now, maybe Rozelle would be satisfied.

* * * *

A couple of weeks later, Babe and his family headed for a badly needed vacation in Hawaii.

The telephone rang again.

Rozelle again.

"Babe," he said, "Would you be willing to take another polygraph test? The results on the first one weren't so good."

"Of course, I would," Babe replied. "In fact, I already have. I went to the second-best man in the country and I have the results back. Why don't I just send them to you?"

"How would you feel about going to the *best* polygraph man in the country?" Rozelle asked, summarily and simultaneously dismissing and discounting the results Babe had offered to provide.

"Certainly. I would be more than glad to. I'll do it as soon as I get back."

He smiled as he hung up. He knew he had nothing to worry about.

* * * *

During the second test, held in Providence, R. I., the man who administered it not only had reviled the league-appointed first examiner as incompetent, but declared that the questions he had asked were too numerous as well as too vague.

This time, he explained, Instead of 30 questions, there would only be 10. This time, they would be very specific.

"Babe," the examiner said when he finished, "you got nothing to worry about. You're clean."

* * * *

The third polygraph examination was held at the Hilton, adjacent to Boston's Logan Airport.

This time, William G. Hundley was present.

If Babe had anything to hide, he could not have faced a tougher, more experienced, more knowledgeable interrogator than Huntley.

If he hoped to be exonerated, he could not have received a more convincing endorsement than one from Hundley.

Hundley was Rozelle's special assistant "whose Brooklyn street smarts made him a leader in the Eisenhower and Kennedy administrations' fight against organized crime," *The New York Times* reported when it published his obituary on July 7, 2006.

After graduating from the Fordham Law School in 1950, Hundley had worked a year for a Wall Street firm, then joined the U.S. Department of Justice. During the witch-hunting McCarthy era when so many lives and careers and reputations had been ruined, so many innocent people smeared, Hundley had investigated those suspected of being communists or communist sympathizers.

Seven years later, he was named head of the department's Organized Crime Division. In 1964, Hundley had supervised the interrogation of Joseph Valachi, the first-ever mob member to confirm that the Mafia did indeed exist despite J. Edgar Hoover's long-standing insistence that it didn't.

He later would become a prominent defense attorney whose clients included former Attorney General John Mitchell, was convicted of conspiracy, obstruction of justice and perjury in the Nixon administration Watergate scandal.

After an intense grilling that lasted eight hours, or at least seemed like it did,

Hundley stood up and walked over to Babe.

Then shook his hand.

"You're clean," he told Babe."You're a class guy."

And then he added, "I'm quitting my job."

Babe never did learn whether Hundley's resignation had anything to do with their polygraph-exam meeting at the Hilton or whether it was merely coincidental. But he never was asked to take another one.

Rozelle did call one more time, however. This time he offered a suggestion.

"Babe, why don't you retire."

It was a statement, not a question.

Babe refused.

"Why should I?" he replied. "I haven't done anything wrong."

So now it was over. But he would never get over it.

Nor would he ever understand what *it* was.

What had caused *it*?

Who had initiated *it*?

Why had *it* been focused on him?

He knew who had been damaged by *it*. He had. Even more so, his wife. His parents. Her parents. Other family members.

But who had profited the most from *it*?

Life magazine, suffering from dwindling circulation, rapidly diminishing cash flow and spiraling costs? *Life* magazine, struggling for its very survival, and as a result, destined, on Dec. 8, 1972 to cease to exist as a regular weekly magazine?

Rozelle, like Senator Joe McCarthy, obsessing over what he perceived to be a pervasive threat, but in the process, convicting innocent people of guilt by association or even suspicion of association?

The FBI, at long, long last turning the spotlight on Organized Crime-- La Cosa Nostra-- the Mafia—whose very existence J. Edgar Hoover so vehemently, for so long had had refused to admit?

Babe was innocent. He had said that all along. And, he was. But that was the problem. He wasn't merely not guilty, he was innocent in the true naïve sense of the word—and had been his entire life. As a child, as a teenager, he had been raised in an innocent home where old-fashioned values were not only preached but practiced. He had been taught to tell the truth by parents who themselves were truthful. To be generous by parents were generous. To be trusting as they themselves were trusting.

At Kentucky, the Bear had taught him to trust his own judgment; to listen to his own instincts. To take responsibility for his own actions. To be true to his word. Above all, to play to win and win fairly because no victory was a victory unless it was won fairly.

Little wonder then that during months, the years, the decades to come, although he knew all too well what had happened to him, he still did not know why or how it had happened.

Michael E. Lomax could have told him though.

The two men never met, but in the summer of 2002, Lomax, a respected sports historian, researcher and faculty member of the University of Georgia's Department of Physical Education and Sports Studies, wrote an article that was published in Volume 29, No.2 issue of the *Journal of Sport History*.

Although it did not mention Babe or the story in *Life*, Lomax's article left no doubt that what had happened to him in September, 1967 was but yet another chapter in a long-running story, a perpetual policy, a process, an uneven-handed punitive action, that sometimes selectively overlooked evil practiced by some in order to quash or prevent the appearance of evil maybe—maybe--, involving others.

* * * *

The NFL did not hold a patent on investigating allegations of point-shaving and game fixing involving gamblers, gangsters and star players. Nor had it begun in the 1960s.

In 1919, major league baseball had been rocked to its foundation by the Chicago White Sox' Black Sox Scandal. Seven years later, two of the American League's biggest stars, Tris Speaker and Ty Cobb, were accused of having fixed a game in 1919 too.

In 1951, the integrity of college basketball had been devastated when a point-sharing scandal errupted involving Manhattan, City College of New York, Long Island University, Kentucky and Bradley

Pro basketball had seen its reputation tarnished as well. The 1953-54 and 1954-55 Fort Wayne Zollner Pistons were suspected of having shaved points and thrown games, including the deciding seventh game of the 1955 NBA finals.

Pro football's first public embarrassment came even earlier. In 1946, rumors began circulating that the NFL championship game pitting the Chicago Bears against the New York Giants was fixed. It was on that event that Michael Lomax's article, titled *"Detrimental to the League": Gambling and the Governance of Professional Football, 1946-1963*, focused.

_____

Documented by dozens of footnotes—nothing in the *Life* magazine article had been attributed to a readily verifiable source-- the scenario Lomax chronicled revealed not only how the NFL had responded to reports that the 1946 NFL championship game was fixed, but how that response set in motion the preventative and punitive machinery that would remain in effect for decades to come.

Here, verbatim, is what Michael Lomax wrote:

"In 1963, National Football League (NFL) Commisioner Pete Rozelle suspended Green Bay Packers running back Paul Hornung and Detroit Lions defensive tackle Alex Karras for betting on professional football games. Although he found no evidence that either player attempted to influence the outcome of a game, Rozelle suspended both players indefinitely, reinstating them after eleven months. Several players on the Detroit Lions were also fined for betting on the 1962 NFL Championship game. At the same time, Baltimore Colts owner Carroll Rosenbloom was also under investigation for allegedly betting on football games. After a full investigation no evidence was found to incriminate Rosenbloom.

"Scholarly research regarding the link between professional football and gambling has been minimal. Scholars have virtually ignored the NFL's first gambling scandal, the 1946 championship game. A few popular sources highlight events leading up to

Hornung's and Karras' suspensions. In addition, scholars have yet to examine how the NFL's response to gambling influenced the development of its governance structure. This paper analyzes the forces that led to the proposed fix of the 1946 NFL Championship game, examines Carroll Rosenbloom's association with gamblers, and investigates the events that led to Hornung's and Karras' suspensions. Three questions will serve to guide the narrative: how did the proposed fix of the 1946 championship game shape the NFL's policy on gambling; what were the forces that resulted in Hornung's and Karras' suspensions and Rosenbloom's pardon; and how did the NFL's response to these gambling occurrences influence the development of the sport's governance structure in terms of conduct detrimental to the league.

"The National Football League's response to gambling was instrumental in shaping the sport's governance structure to deal with league misconduct. The gambling scandals of 1946 and 1963 occurred at a time when the NFL's popularity rose dramatically. The effort to fix the 1946 championship game marked the beginning of the NFL owners granting Commissioner Bert Bell control of the decision-making process. The gambling scandal was one of many ways Bell centralized power within the commissioner's office. This centralized power allowed him to develop an investigative staff, create what can best be described as an information bureau, and devise a more structured set of penalties and fines to prevent players, owners, and officials from associating with gamblers. Furthermore, Bell sought to quell rumors that could cast doubt upon whether a game was played on the level. Bell recognized that he could not stop people from betting on league games. Therefore, his major concern was to maintain the sport's integrity in times of increased popularity.

"Unlike the 1946 scandal, the Hornung and Karras incident involved two high profile players and a NFL owner. Like Bell, Rozelle utilized the gambling scandal to further centralize power within the commissioner's office. The owners increased his authority to impose sanctions that included a raised ceiling on fines, and he increased the investigative staff to gather evidence of wrongdoing. Rozelle's suspension of Hornung and Karras served to sustain the league's integrity before the public and sent a strong message to the other players regarding the consequences of betting on games. His exoneration of Rosenbloom, however, established a double standard regarding the administration of fines or suspensions.

"Neither Bert Bell nor Pete Rozelle deluded themselves into thinking their efforts would eliminate gambling from their growing sport. Both of their responses to the scandals led to formalizing the NFL's governance regarding league misconduct. However, both commissioners focused primarily on constructing a public relations campaign designed to sustain the NFL's image and integrity. The NFL benefited from an informal alliance with the bookmakers themselves.

"Bookmakers also had a vested interest in professional football remaining honest or face possible ruin. More important, public relations served as the fundamental underpinning of the NFL's governance structure. Bell and Rozelle sought to create the perception that the commissioner safeguarded the game's image and integrity.

"In other words, a change in image more than the rules against gambling proved every bit as powerful and effective.

"Professional football's early history can best be described as a quest for respectability and stability. During the 1920s, NFL franchises were cheap and almost always unprofitable as the professional game was neither very popular nor respected. All teams had a hard time surviving, especially clubs in minor towns that had a smaller potential audience.

"Although the majority of their clubs were located in large urban centers, professional football remained a minor sport in the 1930s. The early owners had survived through their business acumen, political associations, underworld connections, and even by gambling. Tim Mara, a bookmaker and member of Tammany Hall, formed the New York Giants in 1925 and conducted business under the striped umbrella at New York State racetracks when bookmaking was still legal. Arthur Rooney, a gambler involved in local politics, won $256,000 at the Saratoga Race Track in 1927 and bought the Pittsburgh Steelers franchise for $2,500. The Steelers were established in 1933 in anticipation of the passage of laws permitting Sunday sports. Rooney also allegedly hired Joe Bach as his head coach in order for the Steelers coach to pay back a gambling debt. Charles Bidwell, owner of the Chicago Cardinals and Sportsman Park racetrack, was the third NFL patriarch with questionable associations, while Eddie O'Hare, a Bidwell partner and director of the Cardinals, had fronted for Al Capone at the Hawthorne Dog Track.

"In 1941, the NFL established the commissioner's office. Elmer Layden, head football coach and athletic director at Notre Dame, was named the league's first commissioner.

"The move was in part a response to League President Joe Carr's death in 1939 and the magnates' dislike of his successor, Carl L. Storck, the league's secretary-treasurer. In addition, the owners had the lofty aspiration of forming an umbrella organization patterned after Organized Baseball with a commissioner at the helm. The sport's growth facilitated the need for an executive with the authority to settle disputes, impose sanctions, and negotiate contracts with radio. According to *Chicago Tribune* sports editor Arch Ward, the NFL owners were prepared to grant Layden the authority to handle these duties. Whatever ambitions they may have had about developing this organizational structure was thwarted by U.S. entry into World War II.

"In 1943, Layden investigated rumors regarding professional football players associating with gamblers. The *Washington Evening Star* reported that rumors circulated linking several Washington Redskins players with a "gambling coup or a series of them." Several games toward the end of the season ended with questionable outcomes, but when Layden released the results of his investigation he did not find "the slightest bit of factual evidence of collusion between anyone in the league and gamblers."

"Rumors linking the Washington Redskins to local gamblers marked the first time allegations of possible game fixing appeared in print. According to *Washington Evening Star* journalist Walter McCallum, rumors regarding professional football's association with gamblers had been heard for years but seldom appeared in print. Given that several NFL owners had connections with the gambling underworld, a gambling subculture undoubtedly existed among the players. McCallum concluded that the potential gambling coup regarding the Washington Redskins had "gone too far beyond the rumor stage to brush off in a city where on six Sundays more than 35,500 people . . . watched the pros play football."

"Despite these rumors, by the end of World War II, the NFL appeared to be on the brink of stability. According to the *Chicago Tribune,* in 1945 the NFL's attendance reached 1,918,000 spectators for fifty league and seventeen exhibition games. The following year the NFL's attendance leaped to 2,600,000. This increased spectatorship was an unparalleled achievement in professional sports. It was within this context that the NFL experienced its first gambling scandal. On the morning of the 1946 NFL Championship game between the Chicago Bears and the New York Giants, Commissioner Bert Bell learned that Giants players Frank Filchock and Merle Hapes had been offered bribes to throw the game. Filchock was the Giants starting quarterback and enjoyed his best year as a pro, finishing seventh in the league in passing and tenth in rushing. Hapes was a reserve fullback who signed with the Giants after spending three years in the U. S. Army. He was expected to see plenty of action due to the injury to the Giants leading ball carrier, Bill Paschal. Alvin Paris, a novelty storeowner, offered Hapes and Filchock $2,500 and a $1,000 bet each on the Bears provided they "lay down" in the championship game. The players refused the offer. New York police had Paris under close surveillance as part of a citywide crackdown on gambling. Detectives learned of the attempted fix as a result of tapping Paris' phone.

In addition to the police investigation, rumors of the prospective fix occurred the day before the game. The Bears were favored by ten points the entire week. Suddenly the spread dropped to 7½ points after some heavy betting took place at the ten-point price.

"*Washington Post* sportswriter Shirley Povich reported that 'word of the attempted 'fix' spread rapidly across the nation via the bookies' underground, and hit them during the business peak in the two hours before the game.' Prior to kickoff, the point spread rose to thirteen points when the bookmakers learned that Hapes and Paschal would be missing from the Giants' lineup. According to the *Chicago Times*, the 'bookies took a sound beating' when the Bears won 24-14.

"The police investigation led New York Mayor William O'Dwyer and Police Commissioner Arthur Wallender to summon Bell, Giants owner Tim Mara, head coach Steve Owen, and Filchock and Hapes to the mayor's home. After an intense interrogation that lasted the entire night, Hapes admitted that he had received a bribe offer but refused Paris' bid. On the other hand, Filchock denied any knowledge of the affair. Evidently, O'Dwyer was convinced that Filchock was telling the truth and recommended that he play in the championship game. Based upon the mayor's recommendation, Bell allowed Filchock to play but suspended Hapes pending further investigation.

"The police's preliminary investigation revealed that Hapes and Filchock had met Paris on several occasions throughout the season. On November 23, Paris met Hapes at a cocktail party, and Filchock's name came up during the course of their conversation. On December 8, Paris took Hapes and his wife to dinner after the Giants clinched the Eastern Division title. After dinner Paris supposedly told Hapes it would be a good idea to 'fix' the championship game. When Hapes indicated how problematic that would be, the issue was dropped. Two days later, Paris telephoned Filchock and invited him to his novelty store. At this time Paris offered both players a bribe to throw the championship game, but they declined.

"On January 7, 1947, the trial reinforced the police's preliminary investigation. The *Chicago Times* reported that the district attorney's office had evidence eight hours before the game that

Filchock had received a bribe offer prior to the contest. Assistant District Attorney George Monaghan read into the record Paris' sworn statement, revealing his bribe offer to Hapes and Filchock five days before the game. On the witness stand, Filchock admitted lying to Mayor O'Dwyer about receiving a bribe offer because he had rejected it. Filchock admitted he was aware that the NFL rules required a player to report such offers. Hapes's rationale for not reporting the bribe was due to Paris' promise of a job in his novelty store during the off-season. The trial revealed both players' associations with Paris throughout the regular season.

"During the course of the trial, Bell took initial steps to prevent the possible reoccurrence of fixing a NFL game. Responding to Paris' swift conviction, Bell suspended both players and then granted them hearings. After the hearings, Bell stated that he would not render a final decision until he gathered more evidence from the district attorney's office.

"Next, he contacted officials of all NFL clubs urging them to push for anti-bribe legislation in their respective states, to make it a crime to engage in such action. Bell asked his brother, Pennsylvania Governor John Bell, to secure appropriate legislation. Since the 1919 Chicago Black Sox scandal, New York State had anti-bribe legislation, which led to Paris' conviction.

"Bell proposed three resolutions at the NFL owners' winter meeting to amend the leagues bylaws. On January 22, 1947, the ten club owners gave Bell the power to suspend for life anyone connected with the league involved in crooked operations. Failure to report a bribe could result in one of three penalties: definite suspension, indefinite suspension, or a lifetime ban. This decision rested solely in the commissioner's hands. Players were directed to make reports of bribe attempts to their coach, owner, or immediate supervisor. All others involved in the game must bring that information to the commissioner's attention.

"On April 3, 1947, Bert Bell suspended Filchock and Hapes indefinitely from the NFL. According to Bell, both players were "guilty of actions detrimental to the welfare of the National League and of professional football." The penalty was the severest Bell could administer, since the bylaws were amended only after the attempted fix occurred. The suspension ended Hapes's NFL career, and he accepted a coaching position at the Bryan Consolidated School near Jackson, Mississippi.

"Hapes felt that Bell's action 'was a little bit stiff.' 'It's a bunch of baloney about hurting the league,' he added. Hapes continued, 'All they got against us is just not reporting the attempt.' What the Giants fullback failed to recognize was that his association with Paris throughout the season also influenced Bell's decision. On the other hand, Filchock held aspirations that he would play again in the NFL. During his banishment from 1947 to 1949, Filchock played with the Hamilton Tiger-Cats of the Canadian Football League. In 1950, Filchock was reinstated, finishing his professional career with the Baltimore Colts.

"Press reaction reinforced Bell's suspension of the two Giants players. From the beginning, several sportswriters stressed the need for NFL officials to take stern measures to protect the sport's image. *Chicago Times* sportswriter Gene Kessler argued that it was in pro football's best interests 'to discipline any player who even associates with known professional gamblers.' Paul Zimmerman of the *Los Angeles Times* suggested the best way to handle this problem was to 'cease disclaiming knowledge of gambling; admit the presence of this octopus and take necessary steps to cut off its tentacles.' After Bell suspended Hapes and Filchock, Arthur Daley of the *New York Times* declared that pro football 'must' be like Caesar's wife— 'above suspicion.' He added if Hapes and Filchock's actions were not detrimental to football then there was no true definition of the term. *Washington Evening Star* journalist Francis Stann asserted Bell protected professional football's good name 'without further damage to the reputations of the young men whom the gamblers hoped to use.'

"Bell continued to bolster the NFL's defenses against the reoccurrence of another gambling scandal. He compiled a list of all the big gamblers in the country and hired an ex-Federal Bureau of

Investigation man, Austin Gunsel, to work out of the league office in Philadelphia. Bell also employed at least one former FBI investigator in each league city on a retainer-fee basis. The commissioner hired the ex-FBI men to watch the gamblers and check the backgrounds of new owners, officials, or broadcasters. Bell established what could best be described as 'a system of listening posts,' informing him of substantial bets placed on any one team or any particular game. Each week during the season he received the betting prices and point spreads on Monday, Wednesday, Thursday, and Friday nights, Saturday morning and Saturday night. Bell also wrote an article in the *Saturday Evening Post* to educate the public about 'rumor mongers' who cast doubt about the game's integrity.

"Finally, before the start of the season Bell talked to every squad in the league, stressing the need for players to exhibit the 'proper conduct' on and off the field.

"The foundation of the NFL's policy on gambling was to minimize the contacts between gamblers and players or league officials and simultaneously marginalize rumors that cast doubt on the game's image. The amendments to the bylaws served as a strong deterrent against the association of players and officials with known gamblers and standardized the league's policy on conduct detrimental to the league. In addition, by amending the bylaws, compiling a list of known gamblers, hiring former FBI investigators, and devising a system of 'listening posts,' Bert Bell shaped the NFL's governance structure dealing with league misconduct. The NFL's gambling policy was also a public relations campaign designed to insure the public that the league was taking initial steps to ensure their sport was honest.

"Bert Bell, however, did not delude himself into thinking that his efforts would eliminate gambling occurrences from his growing sport. 'I don't care if people bet, because people are [going to] bet,'Bell told *Saturday Evening Post* writer W. C. Heinz. 'I just want to be sure they stay away from our ballplayers and don't spread rumors.'

"The attempt to fix the 1946 championship game occurred after a very successful year. Attendance reached new heights, the sport's popularity increased significantly, and the NFL met the challenge of a rival league, the All-America Football Conference (AAFC), even though costs rose dramatically. The fix attempt highlighted professional football's increased popularity, but it also attracted the gambling element to the sport. *Los Angeles Times* sportswriter Paul Zimmerman argued that an increase in gambling and a greater effort on the part of 'sharpsters to put over 'deals' come with any boom, whether it be in sports or any other field.' In essence, the fix attempt reflected the kinds of growing pains professional football endured to achieve a sense of stability.

"As football's popularity increased, NFL officials had to be concerned with the sport's image and maintaining a sense of integrity. Thus it was imperative to structure their governance in a way to achieve these ideals. Certainly Bell was responding to the Landis precedence in the 1919 Black Sox scandal. No doubt the personalities of the two commissioners contrasted in the way each man handled their gambling scandals. Unlike the moralistic Landis, Bell was comfortable in the gambler's world despite his upper-class upbringing. More important, the effort to fix the 1946 championship game marked the start of the owners granting Bert Bell control of the decision-making process. The scandal was one of many ways Bell centralized power within the commissioner's office. This centralized power allowed him to develop an investigative staff, create what can best be described as an information bureau, and devised a more structured set of penalties and fines to deter players, owners, and officials from associating with gamblers.

"Public relations, however, served as the cornerstone of Bell's governance structure. Bell sought to create the perception that the commissioner safeguarded the game's image and integrity.

"In other words, a change in image more than the rules against gambling was every bit as powerful and effective.

"Bert Bell had formalized the NFL's governance structure regarding league misconduct.

"But how effective would the NFL's policy on gambling be? Were the penalties severe enough to deter players and officials from betting on NFL games? Moreover, if one of the owners were implicated, would a standing commissioner be willing to impose sanctions?

"In the 1950s, the National Football League achieved economic stability. This achievement, in conjunction with the development of the NFL's symbiotic business relationship with television, resulted in a dramatic increase in betting on NFL games. The culmination of the point spread and television established the pattern for modern sports betting and bookmaking.

"An NFL owner, Carroll Rosenbloom, was implicated in gambling activities because of his business interests outside the NFL. These charges were brought to the owners' attention at their 1963 league meeting because Commissioner Pete Rozelle failed to investigate them. Rosenbloom's indiscretions, however, were overshadowed by allegations of players betting on NFL games and associating with known gamblers.

"Several factors contributed to placing the league on sound economic ground. First, in 1949 the AAFC collapsed with three franchises—Baltimore, Cleveland, and San Francisco—absorbed into the NFL. With the move of the Rams to Los Angeles in 1946 and the San Francisco 49ers incorporated into the league, the NFL expanded its structure to the West Coast, thus making it a national league. Since none of the AAFC franchises absorbed in the NFL competed in an existing league market, the 'merger' restored the NFL's monopoly.

"Bert Bell's efforts to establish a symbiotic business relationship with television represented the second factor that placed the sport on sound economic ground. At first the television industry approached pro football cautiously, particularly NBC and CBS who virtually ignored the NFL. In 1954, the DuMont network increased its regular season coverage to twelve games. When DuMont's average audience rating rose to nearly 37 percent of all households that had sets turned on, major advertisers and big networks began taking notice of the NFL. Sport historian Ben Rader points out that television was carrying the sport far beyond the franchise cities, to such remote outposts as Bippus, Indiana and Bangor, Maine.

"In 1956, NBC seized the rights to televise the NFL title game from DuMont, while CBS began to air regular season games. For their rights, CBS paid slightly over a million dollars annually.

"The NFL's business relationship with television coincided with what gambling scholar Richard Sasuly referred to as a new style of bookmaking. Television set the pattern for modern sports betting and bookmaking. Sports betting was simply the unrecorded part of the flood of money set loose by TV broadcasts. On Saturdays, Sundays, and Monday evenings during the football season numerous bars and taverns nationwide had its own wire service hanging on the wall. It was free too, courtesy of advertisers, and it would later come complete with instant replay and in color. The increase in gambling on professional football paralleled its increase in popularity, spurred by the sport's business relationship with television.

"From the outset, gamblers would simply get odds on a game. For example, if a team were an eight-to-five favorite, a gambler would wager eight dollars to win five betting the favorite, or five to win eight betting the underdog. Obviously few gamblers were willing to risk money on a game between two mismatched teams.

"To minimize their losses and facilitate betting on professional and collegiate sports, bookmakers invented a point spread covering a three-point range. A team might be quoted as a six-eight favorite; in other words, the bettor collected if the favorite won by eight or more, while a bet on the underdog paid off if the game was lost by six or fewer. Bettors soon recognized the pitfalls to this system as an unusually large number of games seemed to hit the middle and nobody won except the bookie. An adjustment was made where only one point line was given, usually a half-point added to avert a tie. Therefore, if a team were a seven-and-a-half favorite, it would have to win by eight for its backers to win. If the team won by seven or fewer points, the underdog won. Theoretically, the point spread made every game even. The new medium, in conjunction with the point spread, resulted in a dramatic increase in betting on NFL games.

"Yet the symbiotic business relationship between the NFL and television was instrumental in the sport challenging major league baseball's preeminent position in U.S. society. Undoubtedly, the sport's meteoric rise in the 1950s marginalized any concerns regarding the increase in betting on NFL games.

"It is somewhat problematic to place a dollar amount on the increased wagering on NFL games. However, there is evidence to show a substantial increase in sports betting in the late 1940s and 1950s. The *Washington Post* reported that roughly 30 million Americans bet on horse racing, wagering approximately $3.5 billion a year legally at the racetrack and another $50 billion with bookies.

"The Special Committee to Investigate Organized Crime, headed by Senator Estes Kefauver, reported that the gambling syndicate of Frank Costello and Joe Adonis dominated every form of gambling in Bergen County, New Jersey. Adonis' Gambling casinos alone grossed a reported $1 million a month. Subsequent investigations revealed bookmaking earned more than $4 million a year, with profits to the underworld so enormous they were difficult to estimate. Undoubtedly the NFL was caught in this web of increased gambling.

"A final factor that led to the NFL being placed on a sound economic footing dealt with the disposition of the league's weak franchises. In 1952, New York Yanks owner Ted Collins exhibited a willingness to sell his club to Baltimore interests after the latter lost their NFL franchise the previous year. Instead, Collins sold the Yanks to businessmen in Dallas, Texas. The sale proved ill advised, and the Dallas franchise collapsed before the end of the season. The league took over the club, and the Texans operated as a road club in Hershey, Pennsylvania. Facing a lawsuit by the Baltimore stockholders for reinstatement of their franchise, Bert Bell turned the Dallas club over to Baltimore in 1953, but the move was contingent upon the stockholders selling 15,000 season tickets. This was a monumental task since, according to the *Washington Post,* only two of twelve clubs sold 15,000 or more tickets for the upcoming season. The undertaking was further complicated by the fact that Baltimore would inherit a franchise that won only one game the previous season.

"In any event, Baltimore accomplished this during the 1952 Christmas season. By the time the campaign ended, $300,000 was in the bank awaiting an owner.

"It was within this context that Carroll Rosenbloom became the owner of the Baltimore Colts. Born on March 7, 1907, Rosenbloom inherited a clothing manufacturing business from his father and later expanded into other business ventures. His firm manufactured work clothes, including most of the battle fatigues the U. S. armed forces wore in World War II. While attending college at the University of Pennsylvania, Rosenbloom played under Coach Bert Bell.

"At first, Rosenbloom was reluctant to become the Colts new owner. According to the *Washington Evening Star,* Rosenbloom was not happy about the personal publicity the job might entail and contemplated withdrawing from consideration. However, Bell proposed that the prospective owner take over the Colts on a promise that the league would underwrite his losses. Rosenbloom accepted, and in later years he would be fond of saying, 'the investment never cost me a dollar.'

"From the beginning, Rosenbloom attempted to remain aloof from the club's day-to-day operations. He delegated that responsibility to Don Kellett, the Colts general manager and former television executive. When the Colts defeated the Chicago Bears in the 1953 league opener, sportswriter Tex Maule reported that Rosenbloom retained an active role in the club's affairs.

"In 1954, he hired Weeb Ewbank as the team's head coach. Ewbank replaced Ted Molesworth who became the Colts chief talent scout. The management team of Rosenbloom, Kellett, Ewbank, and Molesworth transformed the Colts into one of the NFL's most successful franchises by the end of the decade.

"Carroll Rosenbloom's alleged gambling activities surfaced when the NFL underwent a transition in leadership. On October 11, 1959, Bell died and Alvin "Pete" Rozelle replaced him the following year. Born on March 1, 1926, in South Gate, California, Rozelle began his career as an assistant athletic director at the University of San Francisco in 1950. In 1952, he left that job and became publicity director for the Los Angeles Rams.

"Four years later Rozelle left the Rams to work for a public relations firm. In 1957, Rozelle returned to the Rams as general manager at Bell's behest. The commissioner felt that Rozelle could bring harmony to a club divided by warring factions. When Bell died, a deadlock developed in the choice of a new commissioner, and Rozelle was chosen as a compromise candidate.

"Wellington Mara and Paul Brown put Rozelle's name forward, and Rosenbloom recommended him for the job.

"To understand the controversy surrounding Carroll Rosenbloom, it is necessary to describe his relationship with Louis A. Chesler. Chesler was one of Rosenbloom's close friends, and they were involved in several business deals. In 1962, Chesler controlled three large companies—Universal Controls, General Development, and Seven Arts, Ltd. Other corporate officers involved in this sophisticated acquisition of these three companies included Morris M. Schweble, a New York attorney; Max Orovitz, an associate of gangster Meyer Lansky; and Carroll Rosenbloom. According to author Robert Pack, Chesler was instrumental in bringing gambling to Freeport in the Bahamas in 1963. When Chesler needed advice on staffing the Monte Carlo Casino at Freeport, he turned to Meyer Lansky, a renowned mob boss and reputed controller of gambling in the Caribbean. Acting on Lansky's advice, Chesler chose Frank Ritter, Max Courtney, and Charles Brudner—all New York bookmakers with large clienteles—to run the casino.

"In addition to being business associates, Rosenbloom and Chesler were betting partners. Chesler was known as a "compulsive gambler," and he reportedly wagered as much as $500,000 on a horse race.

"Reportedly, Rosenbloom and Chesler wagered a "bundle" on the 1958 championship game between the Baltimore Colts and the New York Giants. This contest that went into sudden death overtime has been touted as the game that established the NFL as a television attraction with enormous audience potential.

"Both men supposedly bet on the Colts to win by four or more points. On their way down the field to ultimate victory, the Colts surprised everyone by passing up an opportunity to kick a field goal and win by three points. Instead, the Colts risked losing it all, scored a touchdown, and won by six points.

"The decision to go for the touchdown instead of a field goal was a source of controversy. Rosenbloom allegedly got on the press phone and ordered his team to go for a touchdown, but no evidence exists to determine whether this call was made. In any event, the Colts won by six points, and Rosenbloom and Chesler were ecstatic.

"In 1958, Rosenbloom and Chesler advanced the initial start-up capital to Mike McLaney, a professional gambler, to purchase the Hotel Nacional with its casino in Havana, Cuba. Rosenbloom loaned McLaney a reported $200,000 to buy the hotel. This venture, however, coincided with Fidel Castro's takeover of Cuba, forcing McLaney to flee the country, leaving Rosenbloom and Chesler's money behind. McLaney then filed a $4.2 million lawsuit against Rosenbloom, claiming he had been cut out of a share in the American Totalizer Company takeover, engineered by the Baltimore owner and Chesler. McLaney argued that he had introduced the two men and was entitled to a finder's fee. On September 2, 1960, McLaney filed his suit in federal court in Miami, Florida, to recover the fee in either money or stock.

"The trial's bizarre testimony resulted in revealing Rosenbloom's prior gambling activities.

"Four principals who claimed Rosenbloom bet on or against the Baltimore Colts produced two sets of affidavits. Robert J. McGarvey, a former Philadelphia detective and onetime Rosenbloom employee, stated that he placed bets for the Baltimore owner on professional football games. The former detective pointed to the last game of the 1953 season, between the San Francisco 49ers and the Colts, when Rosenbloom bet against his club and won a substantial amount of money.

"Larry E. Murphy, McLaney's chauffeur and Rosenbloom's golf caddy, asserted, 'I particularly remember that in 1953 when his team, the Colts, was playing against the 49ers out on the coast, Rosenbloom bet a large amount of money against his own team, and because of the point spread, won the bet.'

"Richard Melvin, an investor married to Tommy Dorsey's widow, claimed: 'I distinctly remember that during one professional football season he made nine straight winning bets on professional football games.'

"McLaney also pointed to the final game of the 1953 season. Although he erroneously stated the Colts played the Pittsburgh Steelers instead of the 49ers, McLaney declared that Rosenbloom wagered $55,000 against his own team. McLaney also alleged that the Baltimore owner left several of his best players at home for that game.

"Despite this damaging testimony, Federal Judge Joseph P. Lieb dismissed the suit and ordered the records sealed, on the grounds that revealing the contents of the depositions would humiliate and embarrass Rosenbloom.

"In 1961, ten months after the depositions were sealed, Sam Benton, a Miami Beach private investigator, delivered new affidavits from McLaney, McGarvey, Melvin, and Murphy to Commissioner Pete Rozelle. Evidently these men used the same information in the construction of four new affidavits. Benton became involved in the Rosenbloom affair because of his investigation of an insurance fraud case against the Baltimore owner. According to the Miami *Herald,* four insurance companies sued Rosenbloom over a 1950 fire, alleging that he had made false claims to collect $130,000.

"In any event, Benton admitted that his interest in taking the affidavits to Rozelle was to "'remove the halo from Rosenbloom and reveal his true character.'"

"According to the private detective, Rozelle received him 'coldly.' When Rozelle failed to investigate these charges, Benton delivered forty copies of the affidavits to the NFL owners at their 1963 league meeting.

"While Benton delivered the affidavits to the NFL owners, McLaney continued his court battle with Rosenbloom. For the first time, the press reported Rosenbloom's alleged gambling activities. According to *Baltimore Sun* sportswriter Bob Maisel, these affidavits were essentially given to the Miami *Herald for* publication.

"Rosenbloom's attorney Jerome Doyle argued that the new affidavits were in violation of the court order when the four men used the same information in the sealed depositions. However, Judge George C. Young threw out the motion, carefully emphasizing that he was not ruling on the truth or falsity of the accusations. Judge Young added that he was 'of the opinion that the facts of the evidence do not constitute cause for contempt.' Moreover, the sealing order applied only to the first McLaney-Rosenbloom lawsuit three years earlier.

"Rosenbloom's alleged gambling activities placed Pete Rozelle in an awkward situation. Rozelle's selection as a compromise candidate to succeed Bell was due, in part, because he had no enemies among the owners. From the outset, Rozelle began his tenure by focusing primarily on maximizing the magnates' profits. He devised 'League Think,' an organizational concept designed to sell the league's collective television rights as a single package, centralize its video marketing, and share its broadcast revenues equally among all franchises.

"'League Think' would never have gotten off the ground without the passage of the Sports Broadcasting Act of 1961. Rozelle's initial effort to get legal sanction for 'League Think' was struck down in a court decision, leading the commissioner along with major league baseball to turn to Congress to push through the federal legislation.

"Simultaneously, Rozelle had to convince the owners in the three largest markets—the Maras in New York, George Halas in Chicago, and Dan Reeves in Los Angeles—to agree to share equally the revenues generated by television. Rozelle successfully lobbied Congress for passage of the Sport Broadcasting Act and convinced the aforementioned owners to go along with the plan.

"In 1962, he negotiated the first of several contracts with CBS that marked the start of the NFL's unprecedented prosperity.

"Rozelle was now placed in the unenviable position of investigating one of his employers. The situation was further complicated by Rozelle's need to probe an owner who had endorsed him for the job. Therefore, it was somewhat predictable when he stonewalled any inquiry into these alleged gambling activities.

"Since the affidavits were delivered to the owners, Rozelle had to take some action. However, allegations of players betting on NFL games and associating with gamblers overshadowed Rosenbloom's questionable activities.

"On January 5, 1963, the *New York Herald Tribune* reported that Pete Rozelle had been investigating rumors of a possible pro football scandal. The probe was in response to Chicago Bears owner George Halas' request to determine whether any members of his club were involved.

"Chicago Bears fullback Rick Casares voluntarily took a lie detector test and was asked if he had thrown games or tried to reduce the margin of victory.

"Although Casares passed both tests, the episode served to cast doubt upon his integrity.

"According to the *Milwaukee Journal*, the test revealed that Casares associated with known gambler and businessman Abe Samuels, and he also frequented 'hoodlum hangouts.'

"Rozelle admitted that he had been investigating rumors of 'unusual activity' for the past two years and, in addition to the Bears, had probed 'three or four other clubs.'

"Two other teams under investigation were the Detroit Lions and the Green Bay Packers. Reports of unusual betting activity involved two games with the Packers during the 1962 season. According to the *New York Times,* in both cases the reports said money from the same source had wagered correctly. As a result, bookmakers in Boston and New York refused to accept subsequent Packers games.

"On January 31, the *Detroit Free Press* reported that Rozelle had extended his probe to include the Baltimore Colts and the Pittsburgh Steelers. Although he found nothing criminal in nature, Rozelle added that a number of players from these various clubs were found to be 'associating with undesirable types'.

"Green Bay Packers halfback Paul Hornung and Detroit Lions defensive tackle Alex Karras were two of those players under suspicion. Nicknamed the 'Golden Boy' at Notre Dame where he won the Heisman Trophy, Hornung was the Packers' first round draft pick in 1957. In 1959, he had developed into an all-purpose halfback and led the NFL in scoring with 94 points.

"The following year Hornung set a single season record, scoring 176 points and, by 1961, was named the NFL's most valuable player.

"Early indications of Hornung's betting habits had surfaced during his senior year at Notre Dame. At the end of the season, Hornung played in the East-West Shrine game in San Francisco. At dinner one night on the coast he met Barnard 'Barney' Shapiro, a big, suave man in his early thirties. Shapiro, a Nevada businessman, owned the United Coin Machine, a pinball and slot company, and also had a stake in the Royal Nevada Hotel, which included a gambling casino. Hornung and Shapiro became friends, and the latter called the Packers halfback once or twice a week during the football season.

"One of his questions was always the same:

"'How do you think the Packers will do this week?' According to Lombardi biographer David Maraniss, by 1959 the nature of the telephone conversations changed. Along with making recommendations to Shapiro, Hornung began asking the gambler to place bets for him.

"Hornung reportedly made bets of $100 to $200 with some as high as $500.

"Hornung ceased placing bets by the 1962 preseason, except for one occasion where he won $1,500.

"After the 1962 championship game, Rozelle summoned Hornung to New York. From the outset, it appeared obvious to him that Rozelle was aware of his betting activities. According to Maraniss, Hornung suspected they had tapped his phone in the apartment he shared with teammates Max McGee and Ron Kramer. Rozelle wanted Hornung to take a lie detector test, but he refused. Instead, Hornung threatened to appear before Arkansas Senator John L. McClellan's Investigation Committee on gambling and expose the NFL's gambling subculture. "Rozelle admitted he did not want that to happen and urged Hornung to keep their meeting confidential.

"Alex Karras was an All-American from the University of Iowa. In 1957, Karras won the Outland Trophy, an award given to the best offensive or defensive lineman in college football. The following year he joined the Detroit Lions and was one of the premier defensive linemen in the NFL for twelve years.

"Karras' involvement in gambling surfaced as the result of a joint investigation by the FBI, the NFL, and Senator McClellan's Investigation Committee. Karras reportedly made six bets on NFL games in 1958, his first year in the league. In 1962 Karras wagered $100 on his own team against Green Bay.

"That same year, he bet $100 on the Packers in the championship game against the New York Giants.

"Karras was the co-owner of the Lindell A. C. Cocktail Lounge with Jim and John Butsicaris. The FBI had the Butsicaris brothers under surveillance because of their connections with gamblers and bookmakers. Because of their association with gamblers, Detroit Lions officials exerted pressure on him to sell his interests in the Lindell Bar.

"Edwin J. Anderson, the Lions general manager, reportedly said, "I don't like the idea of a player owning a part of a bar where he might run into undesirable people."

"In response, Karras stated he would not give up his $45,000 investment without a fight.

"On January 9, 1963, the Detroit Police Department had reportedly observed Detroit Lions players in the company of "known hoodlums" and notified the NFL authorities.

"Police Commissioner George Edwards reported that he notified the Lions ten days earlier regarding the players' associations with notorious gamblers. According to Edwards, two gamblers, Vito and Anthony Gicalone, continually associated with the same Lions players.

"While no evidence of anything involving criminal activity was found on any of the Lions players, the extensive media coverage had the makings of a public relations nightmare.

"On January 17, Rozelle summoned Detroit Lions head coach George Wilson and Karras to New York for questioning. The summons was sparked by Karras' confession on the television show the 'Brinkley Journal' that he bet on NFL games. Karras' admission placed him in violation of the NFL rules forbidding gambling, further casting doubt upon his integrity.

"The following day Karras and Lions linebacker Wayne Walker had a private conference with Rozelle in New York regarding betting on league games. After the meeting, Rozelle refused to comment and the players were 'unavailable.' Not until mid-April did news of the breaking scandal hit the sport pages and capture the nation's attention.

"Clearly Pete Rozelle was aware of the players and owners gambling activities and associations. He had inherited Bert Bell's infrastructure that kept tabs on known gamblers, the point spread on NFL games, and the cadre of ex-FBI men in league cities to investigate league misconduct. Rozelle expanded Bell's infrastructure to include the constant counseling of players and club officials regarding the importance of maintaining high standards of conduct.

"Yet the majority of the information on Rosenbloom and the players came from sources outside the NFL's governance structure, casting doubt upon its effectiveness. By the 1960s, the NFL was on the verge of becoming a booming industry, and the issues of image and integrity were critical elements in sustaining the league's popularity and prosperity. Furthermore, the sport's unpredicted outcome had always been its most appealing characteristic. Any indication that this outcome was pre-determined, or the insinuation that the outcome was pre-arranged, could prove catastrophic.

"Rozelle responded slowly to the gambling allegations. Several factors contributed to his pace and somewhat indecisive actions. External pressure from various civil rights groups and low-level members of the Kennedy Administration against George Preston Marshall's refusal to sign black players constituted the first factor. As early as 1957, several civil rights groups and labor organizations picketed Washington Redskins home games in order to pressure Marshall to sign black players.

"In 1961, the Redskins owner signed a thirty-year lease to play all home games in D.C. Stadium. As the 'residential landlord' of the parks area, the Interior Department could deny the use of the stadium to any party practicing discriminatory hiring policies. Signing the lease led Secretary of the Interior Stewart Udall to pressure Marshall into signing black players.

"Simultaneously, several local NAACP chapters threatened to boycott NFL exhibition games because of the segregated seating policies of several Southern cities. For example, on August 10, 1961, the NAACP's local chapter in Roanoke, Virginia, sent telegrams to six black players on both the Pittsburgh Steelers and Baltimore Colts, urging them to boycott the game on August 17. The Association charged the local chamber of commerce with selling tickets on a segregated basis. A suit was filed in federal district court charging the promoters with using a municipal property for the promotion of discrimination. The NAACP also stated that picket lines would have to be crossed by fans and players. The Roanoke situation required Rozelle to mediate the conflict. The Association withdrew its picket lines after the commissioner promised there would be no segregated seating.

"The judge's ruling in the American Football League's antitrust suit against the NFL represented the second factor contributing to Rozelle's slow response to the gambling allegations. The suit was in response to the NFL placing franchises in Dallas and Minneapolis to drive the rival league out of business. Concurrently, AFL owners sought to loosen the NFL's hegemony over its player force. *Sports Illustrated* journalist Kenneth Rudeen reported that Rozelle spent a great deal of time exploring whether the government might prosecute the NFL for barging into the AFL's territory. He researched antitrust litigation and hired a Washington lawyer to defend the NFL.

"Rozelle's efforts paid dividends when Judge Rozel Thomson of the United States District of Maryland ruled that the AFL had no monopoly case against the NFL.

"Rozelle's choice as a compromise candidate formed the final factor influencing his slow response to the gambling allegations. According to David Harris, several NFL observers gave odds that Rozelle would not last more than three or four years before the owners devoured him and found someone more seasoned. It was problematic to suggest that the amiable Rozelle would be able to handle the notoriously carnivorous egos of his employers.

"For a little over two years Rozelle had information from outside sources pointing to Rosenbloom and the players' gambling activities and associations. But the commissioner preoccupied himself with maximizing his employers' profits and simultaneously dealt with a potential NAACP boycott of exhibition games and the AFL's antitrust suit.

"However, the media storm in early January placed Rozelle in a position where he had to act. His response to these gambling allegations could make or break his commissionership.

"On April 17, 1963, Rozelle made public the results of his investigation. He began his official report by stating there was 'no evidence that any player has given less than his best in playing any game.' No evidence was uncovered that any player wagered against his own team, but there was 'clear evidence' some NFL players knowingly carried on undesirable associations, which, in some instances, led to their betting on their team.

"Based on this premise Rozelle suspended Hornung and Karras indefinitely for betting on league games and associating with gamblers or 'known hoodlums.'

"Five Detroit Lions players—John Gordy, Gary Lowe, Joe Schmidt, Wayne Walker, and Sam Williams—were fined $2,000 each for betting on the 1962 NFL Championship game. Rozelle pointed out that neither Hornung nor Karras bet against their own team, sold information for betting purposes, or performed less than their best in any game. Their pattern of betting and transmission of specific information regarding NFL games for betting purposes, however, constituted serious breaches of their player contracts and the league's constitution and bylaws.

"In regards to the five Lions players, Rozelle concluded that their actions were 'abnormal.'

"He added:

'This single violation of the constitution and bylaws should be placed in its proper perspective as an act that cannot be condoned because of the strict rules of the NFL, but one that should in no way adversely affect the reputation of those involved.'"

"Several sports writers across the country praised Rozelle's actions. Morris Siegel of the *Washington Evening Star* stated Rozelle's actions was the only course and the 'guilty parties had to be punished to satisfy the public's rightful demand to know what the sports world was doing about cleaning up its house.'

"Miami *Herald* sportswriter Jimmy Burns argued that Rozelle pursued his probe diligently and 'right-thinking' people would applaud his judgments.

"Oliver Kuechle of the *Milwaukee Journal* declared that Rozelle should be commended for his actions.

"Arthur Daley of the *New York Times* acknowledged that Hornung's and Karras' suspensions were harsh penalties, but the sanctions were justified because it involved the 'honor' of the NFL

"*Detroit Free Press* journalist Lyall Smith stated that the commissioner 'not only stifled the snickers but jammed them down the throats of those who claimed he was too young, too mild, too meek, and too inexperienced.'

"Rozelle received high marks from several NFL owners, officials, and Senator John L. McClellan. George Marshall claimed the penalties were 'just and gentle' and praised Rozelle for a job well done.

"Cleveland Browns owner Art Modell declared that the NFL-would be stronger than ever, and the suspensions and fines served as a 'strong deterrent in the future.'

"Dallas Cowboys General Manager Tex Schramm pointed out that Rozelle's handling of the scandal 'made everybody accept him as commissioner and no longer as a boy playing the part. He gained once and for all everybody's complete respect.' Schramm added that Rozelle's handling of the scandal was a skillful display of crisis management requiring 'fortitude under extraordinary pressure.'

Senator McClellan commended the NFL for taking "'affirmative action to clean up conditions in professional football.'

"Detroit Lions owner William Clay Ford was the lone dissenter among the NFL elite. The Lions' owner recognized that the punishment Rozelle administered would be rough, 'but not as rough as this.'

"Ford added that he did not feel the Lions' organization was derelict in the supervision of its affairs or its personnel. He was quick to assert that the Lions did not condone actions in violation of league rules. Since Rozelle levied a $4,000 fine against the

Lions' organization, fined five of their players, and suspended their All-Pro defensive tackle indefinitely, Ford's grudging remarks were predictable.

"Virtually overlooked, and underreported, was the ongoing investigation of Carroll Rosenbloom. From the outset, the press focused primarily on the players' indiscretions and marginalized the Rosenbloom investigation.

"*Baltimore Sun* journalist Cameron Snyder reported that Rozelle said Rosenbloom's accusers withdrew their charges. Tex Maule and Shirley Povich raised some doubts about the way Rozelle handled the investigation. Maule pointed to the commissioner withholding the name of Hornung's associate, Barney Shapiro, until the day he announced the suspensions.

"Povich focused on Rosenbloom's on-going investigation citing Rozelle's critics and admirers would anticipate his judgment against the Baltimore owner. But when Rozelle declared that Rosenbloom's accusers withdrew their affidavits, Povich wondered what the commissioner meant by that. Both Maule and Povich speculated whether Rozelle was withholding information. However, Maule quickly dismissed his suspicion, concluding that his doubts were unfounded.

"On July 16, 1963, Rozelle made public his investigation of Rosenbloom. The commissioner claimed:

"'No proof whatever has been uncovered that Rosenbloom ever bet on a NFL game since becoming an owner . . . the charges were unfounded.'

"In an ironic turn of events, Rosenbloom's accusers had withdrawn their affidavits. According to Rozelle, McGarvey issued a new affidavit stating that he wagered on the football games and that to the best of his knowledge Rosenbloom 'never bet on a pro game.' As part of Rozelle's final report, the Baltimore owner 'freely admitted that he has bet substantial sums on activities other than professional football' but indicated 'that he has ceased such practices.' At the time of announcement, the media storm had long since subsided.

"It was unclear why Rosenbloom's accusers suddenly withdrew their affidavits. According to Harris, by the summer of 1963 Mike McLaney scheduled a meeting with Rozelle and supposedly handed the commissioner an envelope containing retractions of the previous charges. McLaney reportedly told Rozelle the 'Irish Mafia' was after him, the nickname given to the Kennedy political machine. Rosenbloom was a good friend of Joseph Kennedy and President John F. Kennedy.

"The validity of such charges is subject to debate, but Rosenbloom's connection with Louis Chesler, who had ties with organized crime, could have also pressured McLaney to withdraw his charges.

"Nevertheless, Rosenbloom was unhappy with the way Rozelle handled the investigation. According to Harris, Rozelle recalled that the Baltimore owner was 'upset about the delay and thought he was being left on the hook.'

"The *Baltimore Sun* reported Rozelle awaited the outcome of the private litigation against Rosenbloom. On June 28, the Baltimore owner was acquitted of all charges. Rosenbloom's son, Steve, explained: 'My father had helped Rozelle get his job but Rozelle had considered him guilty until proven innocent.'

"Rosenbloom's anger towards Rozelle was unfounded. The revelations of his gambling habits were the result of his business deals unrelated to the NFL. In many ways, Rozelle saved the Baltimore owner's reputation and imposed no fines or a suspension. In any event, Rozelle's verdict in the Rosenbloom investigation marked the start of a strained relationship between the two men that lasted for the next fifteen years.

* * * *

Lomax's conclusions:

On March 16, 1964, after serving eleven months of their indefinite suspensions, Rozelle reinstated Hornung and Karras. Both players' conduct during this period influenced the commissioner to lift their suspension. Rozelle met privately with both players prior to the announcement and found that they had a 'clear understanding of the seriousness' of what they did.

"For Hornung, the suspension marked the beginning of the end of his fabulous career in professional football. He did have one more productive season in1964, finishing fourth in the league in scoring. By 1966, Hornung lost his starting halfback position to Elijah Pitts and was out of the football the following year.

"Karras, on the other hand, had seven productive seasons with the Lions before he was released in 1971.

"In 1964, *Sports Illustrated* named Pete Rozelle "Sportsman of the Year." The sporting periodical broke from its tradition of naming an athlete, and Rozelle became the first executive to win the award. Rudeen argued, '[Rozelle] bucked the almost universal trend in professional sport by emerging as a strong commissioner—making vigorous decisions, not all of the them popular, and proving that he could act independently of the owners who hired him.' The commissioner asked the public to believe, with him, in professional football's integrity. Rudeen added, 'The public so believed; editorial voices, including most of those that had previously censured Rozelle, now spoke relieved praise.'

"The NFL's response to the gambling scandals served to standardize the league's policy on conduct detrimental to the league. The NFL's gambling policy can be summed up in three broad objectives: constant counseling of players and club officials to the importance of high standards of conduct; maintaining a strong intelligence system to discover and eliminate potential problems; and taking disciplinary action when rules or policy violations occur. But how effective was this policy? Was the NFL's gambling policy an integral part of the league's governance or a public relations campaign?

"Part of this answer lies in the way Rozelle handled the Rosenbloom investigation. To be sure, Carroll Rosenbloom was one of the NFL's most influential owners. His relationship with Bell lent him influence from the beginning, and his team's success enhanced it.

"Rosenbloom was at the forefront in getting the league to recognize the players' union, and he made an unsuccessful attempt to arrange a possible merger with the AFL. Although the Baltimore owner denied the charges regarding his betting habits, Rozelle contended he had no choice but to investigate. To do otherwise would have established a double standard.

"In fact, Rozelle established a double standard. According to his report, Rozelle found no evidence of players giving less than their best or trying to influence the outcome of a game. The players' association with 'known hoodlums,' leading to some betting, provided Rozelle the rationale to impose sanctions.

"On the other hand, Rozelle justified his actions to exonerate Rosenbloom when his accusers withdrew their affidavits and a court of law acquitted him of all charges. Yet no evidence was uncovered to suggest that Rosenbloom relinquished his relationship with Louis Chesler. Since Rozelle's status as commissioner was still in question, absolving Rosenbloom was understandable. Like the players, Rozelle was well aware of the power of the owners.

"Rozelle benefited from a cooperative press that led to the construction of a public relations campaign designed to protect the league's image. Several articles appeared in various periodicals highlighting the NFL's governance structure that dealt with gambling occurrences.

"The owners increased Rozelle's authority to impose sanctions that included a raised ceiling on fines and hiring James Hamilton, a former head of the Los Angeles Police Department's Intelligence Division, to counsel players and gather evidence of wrongdoing.

"More important, the overwhelming focus was investigating players, as opposed to owners. In this way, Rozelle and his press allies influenced public opinion into believing that the NFL was 'above suspicion' regarding gambling incidents.

"Much like his predecessor Bert Bell, Rozelle did not delude himself into thinking his public relations campaign would cleanse the sport of gambling activities. According to *Esquire* magazine, in 1965 college and professional football was projected to reap the richest gambling harvest of that time—over $13 billion. Gambling experts estimated that the total money bet on football was equal to all other sports combined and exceeded horse racing by nearly $2 billion.

"Like Bell, Rozelle sought to minimize the contacts of gamblers with players and owners as well as marginalize any rumors. Undoubtedly, his previous experience in public relations influenced the way he mediated the conflict.

"The NFL benefited from an informal ally to insure the sport remained above suspicion—the bookmakers themselves. As Sasuly argued convincingly, the league's security officers used the bookmakers as an early warning system. To profit from their bribes, fixers would have to bet heavily on what they hoped was a sure thing. The bigger bookmakers were constantly on the alert for very large bets from strangers. For example, a bettor who normally wagered $500 would cause the bookies to take notice if they suddenly bet $20,000.

"Bookies profit from random results, and if a game was fixed they face the threat of ruin from betting coups. Bettors buy information and pay for inside information, about injuries or the chance that an athlete has been reached. Bookies keep an eye on such information, too. What they really want to know is who is betting and how much.

"Although he handled the conflict somewhat indecisively, the gambling scandal was one of several ways Pete Rozelle further centralized power within the commissioner's office.

"It should be noted that the scandal occurred almost simultaneously with his efforts to obtain legal sanction for 'League Think' and his negotiation of a lucrative television contract with CBS. Combined with the external pressure from civil rights groups and the AFL's antitrust suit, Rozelle exhibited an ability to act independently of the owners who hired him. More important, Rozelle, like his predecessor Bert Bell, created the perception that the commissioner was the guardian of the game's integrity and image. A change in image more than the rules against gambling has been every bit as powerful and successful.

"Thus the way Rozelle handled the gambling scandal proved effective, and it secured his leadership role in the NFL.

"Professional football has not dealt with gambling scandals on the same magnitude as the 1946 championship game, or the Hornung, Karras, and Rosenbloom affairs in the 1960s. The league's public relations campaign has been very effective in keeping the sport above suspicion. Rumors still persist, however, over the years regarding the players' and owners' associations with gamblers. Because the commissioners have safeguarded the league's image and integrity, the NFL has remained above suspicion."

* * * *

Throughout the remainder of the off season, Babe did not hear from Rozelle or Hundley again. Slowly, as the days and weeks drifted by, the focus on, the furor over, Arthur's Farm began to fade. But like a blood stain on a shirt, it did not, nor would it ever, disappear entirely.

For Babe and Priscilla, life slowly began to settle once again into a calm, uneventful routine.

Things always worked out for the best.

Then one morning as he was driving into Boston, Babe turned on the radio.

And learned that he had been traded to the New York Jets.

CHAPTER 24

Perhaps it was because of the lingering, ominous shadow of Arthur's Farm. Perhaps his age. He was 39. Perhaps his salary. He was making $35,000-- peanuts compared to the gobs of money the owners in both leagues had been throwing about during the fierce draft-signing wars before the two leagues agreed to merge. But the Patriots' front office, long known for its reluctance to spend more than it had to-- and less if possible-- still had not appreciably changed its ways.

Years later, when he asked coach Mike Holovak why he had been traded, Holovak replied: "Babe, I had nothing to do with it."

Whatever the reason, he had been shipped to New York in exchange for Mike Taliaferro, the Jets' seldom-used, 26-year-old backup quarterback. In the 1963 NFL college draft Taliaferro had been the Giants' 10th round pick and the 138th player taken and in the AFL draft, the Jets' 20th round pick and the 219th player. During the 1967 season, Taliaferro had played in only three games, thrown only 20 passes and completed 11 for 96 yards with one touchdown and one interception.

Namath had completed 258 of 491 for 4,007 yards and 26 touchdowns and 28 interceptions.

At first, Babe had been dismayed. Five years. That's what The Bear had always said. Stay five years and move on because after more than five, you lose that edge, that fiery enthusiasm and you no longer encounter the demanding challenges that come with a new start.

Maybe that was so if you had had the good fortune to stay in a place five years. But Babe never had. Two years here, one year there, one year somewhere else—this was the first time, Boston the first place, where he had been a full-fledged starter, with his own team, for even one season, let alone six in a row.

And now here he was, not only pulling up stakes again, but this time, doing so knowing that he would remain a backup quarterback, never a starter, so long as the young, charismatic and talented Namath was healthy.

Whatever the benefits and/or advantages each side perceived in agreeing to the deal, the 1968 season would not be a sudden, or even gradual, first step back toward respectability for the Patriots. With Taliaferro and Penn State rookie Tom Sherman sharing quarterbacking duties, they would begin a protracted drought reminiscent of what had happened to the Oakland Raiders in 1961, 1962 and 1963 after Babe was traded to Boston. In 1968, the Patriots would finish 4-10; likewise in 1969; and 2-12 in 1970-- only 10 wins in 42 games.

As for the Jets, well, that was an entirely different story.

* * * *

Priscilla did not want to live in New York. Their comfortable home in Acton north and west of Boston was more to her liking and small-town upbringing. Babe and another Jets' newcomer, 29-year-old Bob Talamini, rented a room at the Sheraton near LaGuardia Airport for $10 a night. It didn't hurt that the manager was an avid Jets' fan. Each week, he drove back home to Acton. Talamini also was married commuted to and from home each week too. His was a somewhat longer trip, however.

His family was back in Houston.

In 1959, when Talamini completed his collegiate career at the University of Kentucky, he hadn't given much thought to playing pro football. Although he had won third-team All Southeastern

Conference honors as a two-way, 60-minute, offensive guard and middle linebacker, he had not been invited to participate in a single post-season all-star game. When the AFL held its first-ever draft, Talamini was selected in the 24th round by the Houston Oilers, third from last taken in the nearly 250-man draft.

The contract he received inviting him to try out stated that he would receive $7,000-- if he made the team. Nothing, if he didn't. In a bold move that must have surprised the Oilers' front office, Talamini said he would have to receive a bonus before he would sign.

They sent him $500.

He signed.

When he arrived at the Oilers' pre-season tryout camp, more than 300 players were competing for 33 places on the roster.

Talamini not only made the team, but became a starter as a rookie and beginning in 1962, was named to the All-AFL team six years in a row and appeared three times in the Pro Bowl. But after the 1967 season, when he requested, and was denied a pay raise, Talamini obtained his release and joined the Jets.

It didn't take Babe, Joe Namath, fullback Matt Snell, star receivers George Sauer and Don Maynard, and placekicker Jim Turner long to appreciate the presence of Tamalini, a bruising 6-foot 1, 250-pound guard. Just as he had in 1960 for Oilers' running back Billy Cannon, the 1959 Heisman Trophy winner, and quarterback George Blanda when the Oilers won the first –ever AFL championship and in 1961 when they did it again, Talamini would open up gaping holes for Snell to burst through and on pass plays, plug them up to give the Jets' receivers ample time to get open and Namath and Babe to throw to them.

Talamini was about to make an already good, experienced offensive line even better. And that could make a good running back, a good quarterback, a good receiver, a good placekicker—a good entire team—even better.

* * * *

Amid the sizzling, muggy heat of mid-summer, the Jets reported for pre-season training camp at Hofstra University, located in the Long Island village of Hempstead, 25 miles east of New York. Compared to his rookie days when the Packers had trained in a remote, rural Minnesota town on the campus of a tiny college whose name he could never remember, the Hofstra campus was like Times Square. No more being shut off from the rest of the world. After practice, no more riding a bus into a sleepy little place where there was were nothing to do when you got there. No more smuggling a six-pack of beer back to camp and getting caught trying to bury it and the coach confiscating it and taking it back to his room and drinking it himself.

Right away, it was easy to see that Head Coach Weeb Ewbank knew how to treat, how to communicate, with his players. He treated them like what they were: grown men, not college kids. Ewbank was no control freak like Paul Brown. No screamer, no ranter and raver like Vince Lombardi. No impatient, impulsive, hair-trigger retaliator like Lou Saban more likely to bench or trade a player for making a mistake than allow him the opportunity to redeem himself.

Weeb Ewbank trusted them.

And they trusted him.

* * * *

"Four seconds," Ewbank told Babe when pre-season drills began.

Four seconds? Four seconds before he had to pass or scramble or throw the ball away so it could not be intercepted?

Babe couldn't believe it.

All those years in Boston, he had never been able to count on more than 2.8 seconds —and all too often, not even that long.

* * * *

Ewbank told him something else. Told him more than once, both before and after the regular season began.

"Babe, I don't worry who's in there. Joe or you. It doesn't make any difference. Either way, we win."

Once, during the regular season when he told Babe that, Babe laughed and said:

"There's something wrong with this picture, Weeb."

"What do you mean, Babe?"

"Joe's got a $400,000, five-year contract and I'm being paid $44,000."

Ewbank smiled.

"Yeah, but he's Broadway Joe."

* * * *

But Babe knew his presence truly was reassuring to Ewbank. As a college senior, Namath had suffered a knee injury. If Namath went down, even for a game or part of one, the Jets needed someone experienced and durable who could fill in for him. Babe had plenty of experience and certainly had proved his durability. Following his severe shoulder injury in Cleveland in 1956 and after suffering a broken collar bone later on, some observers had considered him injury prone. But since then, even though, because of poor pass protection, he had been more prone to being prone than injured, he had not suffered another debilitating injury and had missed only a part of a few games over six seasons.

All of which made him feel glad about playing for the Jets.

* * * *

So did the shoes.

Free shoes.

In Boston, every player received one pair when they reported to training camp. After that, they had to buy their own.

With the Jets, he would receive several pair, all compliments of a promotion company.

All free.

* * * *.

Better pass protection, more time to throw, a coach who had every confidence in his players and said so, free shoes– more and more, it was beginning to look like being traded hadn't been so bad after all.

* * * *

Between two-a-day drills, Babe, Joe Namath, running back Billy Mathis, receiver Bill Baird and other teammates headed for a nearby student hangout called Bill's Meadowbrook. The place was always crowded; even more so when word circulated among Hofstra coeds that Joe Namath had arrived.

* * * *

Namath wasn't the only one to attract a crowd of admirers.

One day, as Babe was walking to the practice field with sportscaster Howard Cosell, they were surrounded by a mob of admiring autograph hounds.

"You're a bigger celebrity than Namath," Babe said.

Cosell turned and looked at him.

Arrogant, pompous, self-centered, overbearing, imperious – whatever else Cosell was, or was thought by many to be, no one ever accused him of being modest.

"Well, I certainly *hope* so," he sniffed.

* * * *

Although few knew it and even though Babe and Namath were both born and raised in Beaver County, Pa., both played college football for Bear Bryant and played against each other several times during the 1966 and 1967 seasons, they had never met until Babe arrived at the pre-season camp.

And even though they were totally different, Babe as quiet, as unassuming, as disposed to avoid the spotlight as Namath was gregarious, flamboyant and eager to bask in its glare, theirs was an easy transition from opponents to teammates.

Nights, they played cards and had a few beers in their room and talked.

Among other things, they talked about how Babe had enabled Joe to arrive well prepared for his first college practice at Alabama.

When Joe was a senior, Larry Bruno, Joe's coach at Beaver Falls High School, had come to Babe's house and asked for his help. Seeing as how Babe had played for Bear Bryant, would he be willing to explain the Bear's offensive system?

Babe had and as a result, Joe already knew the basics before he arrived.

What was not said was how Babe had already adapted – not reconciled, adapted-- to the idea of being a backup quarterback instead of starting, a goal he had wanted for so long and finally achieved, and sustained, for six seasons with the Patriots.

Despite his age – old for a professional athlete, even in a non-contact sport like baseball—he did not think of himself as over the hill; past his prime. Like Ewbank, he felt that should the occasion arise, either short term or long term, he was fully capable of doing everything that would have to be done to enable the Jets to remain not only highly competitive, but successful. There would be, he felt sure, no appreciable drop off. And while he never tried to put into words how he felt or draw a suitable analogy—and even if he had, would never have told anyone-- baseball fans back home in Westmoreland County , not far from Rochester, Pa., could have quickly provided an ideal comparison.

Joe Page.

Lefty Joe Page. The Fireman. The great flame-throwing relief pitcher who, between 1947 and 1950, had been a major force in helping the New York Yankees win three American League pennants and three World Series banners by strolling in from the bullpen when the stakes were highest, the pressure greatest and mowing down opposing batters like so many weeds.

When Joe Page was not needed, no problem. That meant the Yankees' fine starting pitchers, right-handers Vic Raschi and Allie Reynolds and southpaws Eddie Lopat and Tommy Byrne, were doing well. But if they weren't, it sure was a mighty comfort to his teammates and fretting fans to know Joe Page was out there warming up in the bullpen, ready and waiting for the call to come to the rescue.

* * * *

There was another reason Babe was well aware of his value to the Jets.

Not only was he the best field goal and extra-point holder on the team, he was regarded as the best in the AFL.

Goldfinger, some called him.

And why not? He had long ago lost count of how many times over the years that he had had a hand—literally—in successful field goal kicks and point-after conversions. No. That was not right. He had not *lost* count. He had never *kept* count. Statistics bored him, especially his own. The only number that mattered was the one on the scoreboard and that was a team, not an individual, accomplishment because football was a team game.

The Bear had taught him that.

But had he taken the time, or had even the slightest interest in checking the records, he might have been surprised to learn that during his seven seasons with the Patriots, when Gino Cappelletti had done all the kicking, and he had done all the holding , they had attempted 236 field goals and 255 extra points. One hundred and thirty-three successful field goals had produced 399 points plus another 248 on point-after kicks –647 points in all, or nearly 100 points every season.

So even if Babe never called a single play, never threw a single pass, he would play a key part in determining how successful the 1968 season would be.

Especially, perhaps, like Joe Page, when the game was on the line and the pressure the greatest.

He was, therefore, a vital member of a team within the team— a three-man team: snapper, holder and kicker. All three had to function with the seamless perfection of an automatic transmission. Two out of three would not get it done.

And so, that summer, once opponents, now teammates, the three of them began working together for the first time: John Schmitt, the center; Babe, the holder; and Jim Turner, the kicker.

* * * *

Babe also was a backup punter, someone Weeb Ewbank could turn to and depend upon, should he ever be needed. And so, Babe practiced kicking too, just in case he was.

One day, he sent a kick spiraling high and long.

And, wide.

The ball drifted, drifted, drifted like a blimp until it landed high up in the stands.

Babe asked for another ball.

"No," someone replied. "Let's get that one back."

And when his teammates began laughing, he finally caught on.

The one he had just booted had been filled with helium.

* * * *

Like Bob Talamini, Jim Turner, a quarterback and placekicker at Utah State, had not been a high draft choice. The Washington Redskins had selected him in the 19th round of the 1963 NFL draft, the 259th player taken. Then the Redskins had cut him and the following season, he had joined the Jets as a free agent.

Turner made 13 of 27 field goal attempts in 1964 and all 33 extra point kicks he attempted. By the end of the 1968 season, he had converted on 102 of 174 career field goal attempts and 177 of 181 extra point tries—97 percent, including an AFL single- season record 34 field goals.

During his first five seasons with the Jets, he contributed 483 points.

* * * *

John Schmitt, the- 25-year-old, 6-foot 4, 250-pound center, was about to begin his third season with the Jets, second as a starter. More than anyone else on the roster, he had felt right at home during the pre-season training camp workouts at Hofstra. He should have. Schmitt had played college football there.

Unlike Talamini and Turner, Schmitt had not been a late-round draft pick.

He had not been picked at all.

In 1964, his rookie season, and again in 1965, Schmitt had played in only two games. Just as his career had begun unsung, it remained tuneless, despite the fact that in 1966 he became the Jets' starting center and was so solid, so dependable, he continued to be their starting center in more than 100 games over the next eight seasons.

Schmitt was as skilled, as automatic, at delivering a quick, accurate snap as Babe was holding and Turner kicking. Individually, they never made headlines during the1968 season. But working together, they provided plenty of points.

Often, when the Jets needed them most.

* * * *

After training camp ended, the jets began practicing near Shea Stadium. Following a noon workout, Babe and Namath and some of their teammates had lunch at a restaurant across the street. Other times, they ate at the team cafeteria. Every time they did, Ewbank always stood up and asked the same question:

"How many of you guys won't be eating dinner here tonight?"

Babe and Joe and some of the others always held up their hand.

They knew it made Ewbank feel good because the more hands that went up, the less money management would have to spend that day. Ewbank was the Jets' general manager as well as head coach.

Invariably, the daily hold-up-your hands ritual reminded Larry Grantham, the team's madcap, perennial All-AFL outside linebacker, of those not-so-salad early days back in 1960 when he was a rookie and the team was known as the New York Titans.

"When payday came," Grantham, laughing at the absurdity of it all, liked to tell the rookies and newcomers traded to the Jets from other teams, "you had to rush to the bank. The first seven guys got their money. The rest had to wait to get theirs. Their checks all bounced."

But then following the 1962 season when attendance had plummeted and debts soared, Harry Wismer, the Titans' owner and former nationally known sports announcer, had sold the team to a syndicate headed by Sonny Werblin for $1 million. Werblin, who had made a name for himself along with a substantial amount of money as president of the Music Corporation of America, changed not only the team's name, but the design of its jerseys.

What he really needed though, Werblin believed, was to change its entire image. And in order to do that, he went looking for a charismatic star, someone who would make New York fans forget all about the Titans' dismal past and their NFL rivals, the New York Giants.

Someone who not only could play the part, but *look* the part. By signing Joe Namath to a five-year contract for a reported $427,000, Werblin had transformed the Jets from a floundering failure both on the field and at the ticket office to the talk of the town.

Joe Namath. Four hundred twenty-seven thousand dollars for a five-year contract. That was the story sports fans heard and that was the one they talked about.

What they didn't talk about because they never heard about it was the amount Bob Talamini and other linemen were being paid.

Despite having been named to the All-AFL teams six years in a row and playing in the Pro Bowl three times while playing for the Houston Oilers, Talamini's salary for the upcoming 1968 season would be $17,000.

* * * *

Three nights or so a week, Babe and other teammates drove over to Manhattan to a bar at 62nd and Lexington Avenue called Bachelors III.

It was a dark, narrow little place, but increasingly popular. The reason was Joe Namath. He was part owner. Joe was there frequently and even when he wasn't, there was always a chance he might come strolling in.

As a result, other New York celebrities began frequenting the place. Among those who joined Namath and Babe at their table were Cosell, celebrated sporting event artist LeRoy Neiman, singer Paul Anka and Dick Schaap, the popular sportswriter, broadcaster and author.

Babe met lots of other well known, not- so -well known and in many cases, unknown, people too, when he went to Bachelors III with his teammates. He said hello to and shook hands with so many so often, their names became a dizzying blur. They all had one thing in common though: they all wanted to stop by and meet, shake hands, talk with—and be seen—with Joe Namath.

Sometimes, some didn't so much want to talk to Joe and his teammates as they wanted Namath and his teammates to listen to them.

Foremost among them was Cosell, as always, as full of himself, someone once remarked, as a hard-boiled egg.

One night, after listening to Cosell longer than he cared to— it didn't take long--Gerry Philbin, the Jets' 6-foot 1, 245-pound defensive end, suddenly interrupted:

"Howard you're full of sh . ."

Cosell, after pausing long enough for dramatic effect, responded:

"Gerry Philbin. New York Jets' defensive end. Gerry Philbin, All-AFL honoree—how *dare* you verbally attempt to spar with the gifted one?"

They all laughed.

From his grinning reaction, Cosell had clearly chosen to believe they were laughing with him, not at him.

* * * *

A solid defense, an offensive line strengthened by the addition of Bob Talamini, Joe Namath, his two top receivers, George Sauer and Don Maynard, placekicker kicker Jim Turner—on paper, they seemed to be the strengths of the New York Jets as they began the 1968 regular season.

All did well, or reasonably well, in the Jets' season-opening 20-19 victory over the Kansas City Chiefs. Namath completed 17 of 29 for 302 yards and two touchdowns with one interception; Maynard caught eight passes for 203 yards and Sauer, five for 48 and Turner kicked two field goals, one from 32 yards; and the Jets added 101 yards rushing on 30 tries.

Defensively, however, although they limited the Chiefs to 118 yards rushing and 90 passing, the Jets had allowed a 17-3 halftime lead to melt to 17-13 going into the final quarter. Turner's clutch field goal increased the lead to 20-13 before the Chiefs kicked s pair to pull within one point. One was enough though to avoid starting the season with a loss.

* * * *

On Sept. 22, in Boston, the Jets beat the Patriots 47-31 as Namath threw for two touchdowns and 189 yards and Jim Turner kicked four field goals. However, they gained only 79 yards rushing and the defense, while holding the Patriots to only 55 yards rushing gave up 349 passing yards.

Mike Taliaferro, Babe's successor as the Patriots' quarterback, completed 17 of 30 for one touchdown and 276 yards against his former teammates but was intercepted four times.

Once again the Jets allowed a comfortable lead-- this time 44-17 early in the fourth quarter-- to shrink to respectability by giving up two touchdowns countered only by Turner's fourth field goal and sixth in two games.

* * * *

On Sept. 29, at Buffalo, Matt Snell rushed 12 times for 124 yards, Don Maynard caught three passes for 114 yards, George Sauer seven for 113 and Joe Namath threw four touchdown passes and the defense held the Bills to 197 net yards while the Jets piled up 427.

And lost, 37-35.

One big reason: Namath threw five interceptions, three of which were returned for touchdowns, one for 100 yards, another for 53 and the third for 45.

As he stood shaking his head, Weeb Ewbank turned to Babe and said:

"He got himself into this mess, now let him find his way out of it."

This time, it was the Jets who scored late to make the score closer than the game had been. Two of Namath's TD passes came too late with his team already trailing, 37-21.

Turner had no field goals.

* * * *

On Oct. 5, playing in Shea Stadium against the San Diego Chargers, Namath threw no touchdown passes; the defense gave up 347 net yards, 319 of them passing; the Jets managed only 82 yards rushing, were penalized 100 yards and Jim Turner kicked three field goals.

And the Jets won, 23-20.

* * * *

On Oct. 13, against the visiting Denver Broncos, Namath passed 41 times, and completed 20 for 341 yards. George Sauer caught nine of them for 191 yards and Don Maynard seven for 141 yards. The Jets also ran for 129 more to finish with a 460-222 advantage in net yardage. Turner kicked two field goals.

The Jets lost, 21-13.

Namath threw for no touchdowns and was intercepted five times.

* * * *

On Oct. 20, in a game in which they displayed little offense—145 yards passing and 97 rushing on 37 carries—and Houston even less (79 yards rushing and 73 net yards passing) the Jets squeaked past the Oilers 20-14.

After leading 13-0 in the final quarter, they gave up two touchdown passes to fall behind 14-13, then pulled it out on Matt Snell's two-yard plunge.

Once again, Namath threw no touchdown passes.

* * * *

The following week, at Shea Stadium, the Boston Patriots threw five interceptions and lost three fumbles as the Jets romped to their fifth win in seven games, 48-14.

After leading 10-0 at the half, the Jets doubled it to 20-0 in the third quarter. Early in the fourth, Babe scored on a two-yard run and the Jets extended their lead to 41-0.

Late in the game, with his team leading 48-14, Coach Weeb Ewbank sent in a play.

Throw long.

Go for another TD.

Babe called time out and trotted over to the sidelines.

"Weeb," he said, "that's my old coach (Mike Holovak) over there. I don't want to embarrass him any more than he already is."

Ewbank nodded.

"You're right, Babe."

Babe changed the play. The Jets made no attempt to score again.

* * * *

Half way through the regular season, the Jets had won five of seven, second-best in the league along with the Oakland Raiders and San Diego Chargers behind the Kansas City Chiefs (6-1). Although they had handed the Chiefs their only loss, the Jets had been beaten by two teams with losing records: the Buffalo Bills—the Bills' only win in eight games—and the Denver Broncos (3-4).

Twice, they had rushed for 170-plus yards; three times for fewer than 100.

Twice they had passed for 250-plus yards and once for 331, but in another game, for only 137.

Namath had thrown only eight touchdown passes, four of them in one game, and been intercepted 14 times—twice throwing five in one game.

He had not passed for a touchdown in four straight games—the entire month of October.

Defensively, the Jets had excelled against the run, five times holding their opponents to fewer than 100 yards. But pass defense had been erratic. Three times they had given up fewer than 100 yards but in two games, more than 300.

Their scoring defense also had faltered more the longer the game continued. The Jets had given up 23 points in the first quarter; 31 in the second' 33 in the third; and 69 in the fourth.

* * * *

On Nov. 3, at Shea Stadium, Jim Turner kicked six field goals, including two in the fourth quarter to give the Jets a 25-21 win over the Buffalo Bills (1-7-1).

Joe Namath completed 10 of 26 passes for 164 yards, but for the fifth straight game, failed to throw a scoring pass.

While Turner's performance was as noteworthy as it was game winning, it pointed out another continuing problem. The Jets were still having trouble scoring from within the 25 yard line. One of Turner's three-pointers against the Bills had come from the nine yard line and another from the 21. In previous games he had kicked one from the 11, two from the 12 and four within the 25.

* * * *

SHEA STADIUM
Nov. 10

Jim Turner kicked four goals and the defense held the Houston Oilers (4-6-0) to 166 total net yards and no points after a first-quarter touchdown to win their seventh game of the season.

Joe Namath completed seven of 20 passes for 185 yards but failed for the sixth game in a row to throw a touchdown pass.

* * * *

OAKLAND
Nov. 17

After leading 29-22 after three quarters, the Jets gave up 21 points in the fourth and lost to the Raiders, 43-32.

Joe Namath completed 19 of 37 passes for 381 yards and one touchdown—his first since Sept. 29--and Jim Turner kicked four field goals, but quarterback Daryle   Lamonica riddled the New York defense for four touchdown and 291 yards. The Raiders also rushed 31 times for 146 yards.

The Jets were penalized 13 times for more yardage (145) than they gained rushing (32 for 68).

* * * *

SAN DIEGO
Nov. 24

In his second straight bust -out game, Joe Namath completed 18 of 32 passes for 368 yards and two touchdowns   and the Jets piled up 510 total net yards of offense to smother the Chargers, 37-15.

Jim Turner kicked three more field goals and the defense held San Diego to 235 net yards and picked off four interceptions.

* * * *

Whatever happened to Babe Parilli?

Fans who read weekly Monday roundup stories about the previous day's AFL games but did not attend or watch them on television must have wondered. Through the first 10 weeks of the regular season, his name did not appear in a single one.

As a quarterback, he had played in only two games, thrown six passes, completed two for three net yards, and scrambled twice for four yards and one TD.

Those who paid attention to the details that mattered, however, knew that he, along with center John Schmitt, had been very much a part of the Jets' success.

Their accomplishments went unacknowledged because those of centers and kick holders never are. Who keeps statistics or wants to read about how many perfect snaps a center makes? How few, if any miscues? About how many consecutive times a holder positions the ball when and where it should be or handles an occasional errant snap and still manages to enable the kicker to convert?

And yet, all season long, Schmitt, Babe and Jim Turner had consistently been one of the Jets' most important, dependable offensive weapons. Their combined efforts had produced 28 field goals and a perfect 28 extra points – 112 or nearly 40 percent of the Jets' 289 points.

They had been the difference between winning and losing against the Chiefs (20-19), Chargers (23-20) and Bills (25-21).

On Dec. 1, Babe also completed 10 of 18 passes for 166 yards and three touchdowns as the Jets beat the Miami Dolphins, 35-17. All three came in the fourth quarter after the Dolphins had taken a 17-14 lead.

The following week, he completed seven of 15 passes for 80 yards and a touchdown as the Jets beat the Cincinnati Bengals, 27-14.

On Dec. 15, he threw 15 times and completed nine for 121 yards and another touchdown, giving him a three-game total of 26 completions in 48 tries for 367 yards and five touchdowns.

And so the Jets had completed the regular season 11-3.

Next stop: a rematch with Oakland Raiders, the last team to beat them, the only team to beat them, during the second half of the season.

* * * *

SHEA STADIUM
Dec. 29

Joe Namath's 14-yard touchdown pass to Don Maynard and Jim Turner's 33-yard field goal in the first quarter staked the Jets to a first-quarter 10-0 lead.

In the second, the Raiders' Daryle Lamonica hit Fred Bilit-nikoff with a 29-yard touchdown pass to cut the lead to 10-7 and Turner and George Blanda traded field goals to make the score 13-10, Jets, at the half.

In the third quarter, after Blanda kicked another field goal to tie the score, Namath threw a 20-yard touchdown pass to Pete Lammons to put the Jets back in front, 20-13.

In the fourth, Blanda kicked another field goal to make it 20-16 and then the Raiders scored on a five-yard run to go ahead 23-20.

Then Namath threw another touchdown pass, this one to May-nard from five yards out to give the Jets a 27-23 lead and win and their first AFL title.

Oakland gained only 50 yards rushing on 19 carries, but Lamonica completed 20 of 47 for 401 yards and one touchdown.

Namath completed 19 of 49 for 266 yards for three touchdowns to go with 144 yards rushing by Matt Snell and Emerson Boozer, giving the Jets 400 net yards of offense.

The Jets were on their way to the Super Bowl.

CHAPTER 25

For the American Football League as well as its nine member teams and more than 300 players, the impending matchup of the New York Jets and the NFL champion Baltimore Colts was far more than merely a bragging-rights championship football game. It was the latest obstacle in a long and costly struggle to achieve legitimacy and if not superiority, at least parity; to erase a long and universally held perception that it, and they, were nothing but a pale, brand-X imitation of the haughty, older, one-and-only kings of pro football.

Not only was Super Bowl III seen as a measure of the relative strength of the AFL's present and perhaps a glimpse of its future, but the validity of its past—including the accomplishments of its top performers during its nine seasons of existence. Yes, Boston Patriots' fullback Jim Nance had rushed for an AFL all-time high 1,426 yards in 1963 and George Blanda had thrown 36 touchdown passes in 1961 and Babe 31 to go along with 3,465 yards in 1964 and Joe Namath had passed for 4007 yards in 1967—but how credible was the competition?

Could they have done as well—or even anywhere near as well--in the NFL?

At the outset, beginning in 1959, the AFL's pursuit of the NFL seemed to have had all the ambitious absurdity of a mongrel chasing a Greyhound bus. In its first season, while NFL teams were consistently drawing crowds of more than 50,000, average AFL attendance ranged from 10,000 to 20,000. Low attendance resulted in immediate financial difficulties. Although none of its eight teams folded that first year—the only franchise to move was the Chargers from Los Angeles to San Diego—it had taken a $400,000 loan from Buffalo Bills owner Ralph Wilson to keep the Oakland Raiders afloat.

On Aug. 6, 1961, in a macho move apparently intended to prove that it was at least the *second*-best pro football league in North America, the AFL challenged the Canadian Football League to an exhibition game pitting the Buffalo Bills against the Hamilton Tiger-Cats. The two teams were chosen because of proximity—the two cities are only 65 miles apart. The Tiger-Cats were one of the CFL's better teams; the Bills, one of the AFL's less imposing. But so what? NFL teams had played CFL teams before and won handily every time.

It figured to be easy.

The Bills lost, 38-21.

While still on its feet, the league remained financially unsteady. The following year, even after winning the AFL title by beating the defending champion Houston Oilers, the Dallas Texans had been forced to relocate to Kansas City because they could not compete with the NFL Cowboys.

In 1963, tottering on the verge of financial disaster, Harry Wismer's New York Titans had been sold and renamed the New York Jets.

But for all its wobbly beginnings, the feisty AFL was already looking forward to the day when it could take on the NFL. After his team had won the 1963 championship by thrashing the Boston Patriots, 51-10, San Diego Chargers' coach Sid Gillman apparently believed that that day had had already come.

He proposed a game matching the two league champions.

NFL commissioner Pete Rozelle declined.

But beginning in 1964, in their bid to challenge the NFL on the field, the AFL took giant steps off the field that led to what would become known as Super Bowl I.

The first major breakthrough came on Jan. 24, 1964 with the signing of a $36 million contract with NBC which called for televising AFL games beginning with the 1965 season. That enabled suddenly affluent AFL teams to launch a fierce bidding war to sign the very best collegiate players. Although Gayle Sayers, the Kansas Jayhawks' sensational running back, signed with the Chicago Bears instead of with the Kansas City Chiefs in the 1964 draft and another high first-round prize, Illinois' two-time All-American center-linebacker Dick Butkus , chose the Bears over the Denver Broncos, the AFL made even bigger headlines.

Involving far bigger bucks.

On Jan. 2, 1965, the New York Jets signed University of Alabama quarterback Joe Namath to a reported five-year, $427,000 contract—by far the most ever paid to a college player.

A few months later, on May 6, Joe Robbie, a Minneapolis attorney, proposed establishing an AFL expansion team in Miami, Fla. On Aug. 16, the Miami Dolphins became the newest and ninth member of the AFL.

On April 7, 1966, when AFL commissioner Joe Foss resigned, his successor, Al Davis, head coach and general manager of the Oakland Raiders, launched another bold move. He launched a campaign to raid NFL rosters, most of all, quarterbacks. Within a few weeks, seven signed with AFL teams. The following month, several NFL owners and Tex Schramm, approached AFL owners to discuss merging the two leagues.

The merger was announced on June 8, 1966.

It stipulated that the two leagues would hold a common draft, the champions of the two leagues would play each year, a full merger into one league would go into effect by 1970, that Pete Rozelle would remain commissioner and that the NFL would received $18 million in indemnities over a 20-year period.

But now that the mutt had finally caught the Greyhound, becoming top dog on the field, as the Kansas City Chiefs and the Oakland Raiders would soon discover, would prove to be an entirely different matter.

On Jan. 15, 1967, in Super Bowl I, the Green Bay Packers, after leading 14-10 at the half, had beaten the Kansas City Chiefs, 35-10. On Jan. 14, 1968, the Packers, after leading 16-7 at the half, had pulled away from the Oakland Raiders, 33-14.

Afterwards, Packers' Coach Vince Lombardi was quoted as saying that he did not believe the AFL champions were as good as the better teams—teams, not team-- in the NFL.

Now it was the New York Jets versus the Baltimore Colts. In Super Bowl III.

The outcome this time didn't figure to be any different.

* * * *

Anyone looking for ample reason to believe that the Colts were almost certain to win didn't have to look very far.

First, there was their 15-1 record and 10-game winning streak.

Second, their resounding 34-0 plastering of the Cleveland Browns in the NFL championship game. The Browns had been the only team to beat the Colts (30-20) -- and that had occurred clear back on Oct. 20.

Then there was the long list of reasons the Colts had been so successful.

Offensively, they had scored 402 points, second only to the Dallas Cowboys (431) who had lost to the Browns in the playoffs, 31-20.

Although Johnny Unitas had been hurt most of the season, played only sparingly and completed just 11 of 32 passes for 139 yards for two touchdowns, former Michigan State star Earl Morrall, considered by some the greatest backup quarterback in NFL history, had been more than adequate, completing 182 of 317 for 2,909 yards and 26 touchdowns. The Colts also rushed for another 1,809 yards.

They had been forced to punt only 49 times to their opponents' 78.

Perhaps even more dominant, however, had been their defense, described by Vince Lombardi as one of the greatest he had ever seen.

They had given up only 104 points in the regular season, beating the '49ers 27-10; the Falcons, 28-20; the Steelers, 41-7; the Bears, 28-7; the '49ers again, 42-14; the Rams, 27-10; the Giants, 26-0; the Lions, 27-10; the Cardinals, 27-0; the Vikings, 21-9; Falcons, 44-0; the Packers, 16-3; and the Rams again, 28-24; and in the playoffs, the Vikings, 24-14 and Browns, 34-0.

Overall, they had held three teams scoreless; another, the two-time defending NFL and Super Bowl champion Packers, to a field goal; and five more to 10 or fewer points.

In their Oct. 20 loss to the Cleveland Browns, Leroy Kelly had rushed 30 times for 130 yards; in their Dec. 29 playoff rematch, 12 times for 28 yards.

Yes, there were many reasons to believe why the odds makers had declared the Colts –some sportswriters called them the greatest team in pro football history -- an 18-point favorite.

Meanwhile, there were plenty of questions about the Jets.

Beginning with Joe Namath.

Although he had had a couple of 350-plus yards games in the latter part of the season, he also had gone five games in a row in the middle of it without throwing a single TD pass. In the early going, on two occasions, he also had been intercepted five times.

The Jets' running attack had been inconsistent too, sometimes picking up fewer than 100 yards a game.

If the Jets were to have any chance, they had to do well both passing and running. But could they do either against the Colts' outstanding defense?

Even more suspect was the Jets' defense. In several games, after a strong first half, they had wilted in the second, particularly against the pass, and failed to protect a comfortable lead. A close review of the box scores suggested an answer of "not likely." Of the 280 points scored by the Jets' opponents in 15 games, 136 had come in the final quarter.

So, even if by some unlikely circumstance, the Jets went into the final quarter with a lead, could they hold it?

On the other hand, the Jets had given up only four touchdowns in the final quarter in their most recent five games and had stopped the Raiders three times deep in New York territory when a touchdown on any of the three possessions would have put the game out of reach.

Yes, there were lots of questions about the Jets. But the real question was: Did they have any answers?

* * * *

More than the score, more than the year in which it was played, more than anything, Super Bowl III was remembered for one reason.

A prediction.

A prediction that the underdog Jets would beat the vaunted Colts.

"I guarantee it," Jets' quarterback Joe Namath was quoted as saying three days before the game when he addressed the Miami Touchdown Club.

Namath later said he never meant to make a prediction and only said it in response to a heckler in the audience.

Some of his teammates laughed about it. Others dismissed it as nothing more than a commonly expressed, often wholly misunderstood southern colloquialism, more akin to saying "I think" or "I believe" than an arrogant Muhammad Ali-like "I am the greatest" boast.

But following the AFL championship game, Namath also reportedly had said that "at least" four AFL quarterbacks, Babe, the Chargers' John Hadl and Bob Griese of the Dolphins—and himself—were better than the Colts' Earl Morrall.

Regardless of the context in which Namath had guaranteed a New York win or why he said it, Jets' coach Weeb Ewbanks considered it an unfortunate blunder.

"All you're doing, saying things like that," Babe heard Ewbanks say, "is giving them even more motivation to beat you."

Privately, however, Namath, like Babe, truly did believe that the Jets could win.

Especially after they sat together, otherwise alone, in a darkened room and watched film.

* * * *

The team they were watching was not the Colts but the Oakland Raiders, the team they had just beaten in the AFL championship game.

The Jets had been lucky to win. They knew that.

Late in the fourth quarter, leading 23-20, the Raiders had driven inside the Jets' 15 yard line and from all appearances, were ready to score again. A 10-point deficit with the minutes ticking away would have been difficult to overcome But then had come that swing pass to the right that Daryle Lamonica had attempted and instead, thrown it behind his receiver making it a bouncing, loose-ball lateral which Jets' linebacker Bake Turner had recovered.

And after watching the entire game on film, Babe and Namath had come to the same conclusion.

"I think the Raiders are a better team than the Colts," Babe said.

"I was thinking the same thing," Namath replied.

The reasons were numerous. Rushing. Passing. Defense. Special teams. Overall talent. The Raiders had it all.

Watching film of the Colts also revealed something else. One big reason they Baltimore defense had been so effective was because other NFL teams did not handle the Colts' blitzing well. All too often, the Colts were able to get to the quarterback, not only inflicting physical wear and tear and costly loss of yardage, but even when they didn't, causing him to hurry his throws and disrupt the offense in general.

Babe and Namath knew they knew how to prevent that. It was called "Break and Read." Meaning, when the quarterback and his intended receiver sensed that a blitz was coming, they signaled to each other by making eye contact. Then, as soon as the defender charged in, the receiver broke to the spot that had just been abandoned and with his quick release, Namath would flip a short pass sure to gain at least a few yards and perhaps even more.

The biggest challenge—in more ways than one—would be stopping Bubba Smith, the Colts' 6-foot 7, 295 defensive end, widely if not universally regarded as the best pass rusher in the AFL.

Coach Weeb Ewbank felt he had an answer for that one too. He moved Dave Herman, at 6-foot 1 and 255 pounds, much smaller, but quicker and more experienced, to tackle to slow down Smith.

So, yes, the Jets were confident. Not cocky, but convinced, with what they considered to be good reasons, that having beaten the Chargers, they could topple the Colts too.

* * * *

Jan. 12, 1969

The temperature was 66 degrees. Humidity: 80 per cent. Wind: 12 miles per hour.

If the Colts' individual and collective pulse rate was pounding because of Namath's prediction, likewise for some of the Jets, although for entirely different reasons.

Winston Hill, for example. As a rookie drafted in the 11th round in 1963, the Colts had cut him. Now Hill, 6-4 and 270 pounds was a starting tackle for the Jets.

After drafting him in the seventh round of the 1958 draft, the Colts also had cut Johnny Sample. Now he was a starting defensive back for the Jets.

Now Don Maynard, a ninth round draft pick in 1957, was a future Hall of Fame receiver for the Jets.

All were eager to deliver a substantial dose of pent-up, red-hot payback to the league that had spurned them.

As the starters for both teams were being introduced, Babe stood along the sideline and gazed about the jam-packed stadium. He knew they were up there somewhere, although he had no idea where. In the press box, perhaps.

But he knew for sure where they weren't. They weren't down on the sidelines. Not this day. Not this year. Nor, as things would turn out, would they ever be again.

Never again would Paul Brown, the man who had shipped Babe back to Green Bay after his horrendous shoulder injury early in the 1956 season, lead a team back to a championship game.

Neither would Vince Lombardi, who had released Babe in 1959 and not been able to look him in the eye and say why.

A dozen seasons since he had been traded by the Browns and nearly a decade since Lombardi had let him go, here he was, Babe Parilli, playing in the Super Bowl.

He felt no animosity.

Only gratitude.

The Bear would have been proud.

* * * *

The Colts couldn't get to Joe Namath. The lightning blitzes that had rendered other NFL teams ineffective, that had punished as well as marginalized NFL quarterbacks, did not work against the Jets. Every time a defender roared in to slam the barn door shut, the horse was already gone. They sacked him only twice, for 11 yards.

Nor could they stop fullback Matt Snell. Propelled in large part by the blocking of center John Schmitt, and guard Bob Talamini, Snell would finish the day with 30 carries and 121 yards. Snell also would score the Jets' only touchdown of the game, a four-yard burst in the second quarter to give them a 7-0 halftime lead.

Going into the final quarter, the Colts had yet to score. Meanwhile, the precision team of center John Schmitt, Babe and kicker Jim Turner had converted three field goals, two in the third quarter and another in the fourth, to extend the Jets' lead to 16-0.

The Colts finally scored on a one-yard dive by Jim Hill but could come no closer.

The New York Jets, once the lowly, floundering, nearly bankrupt New York Titans, had won Super Bowl III.

* * * *

Leaving behind the joyous bedlam that had erupted on the field, Babe raced ahead of his teammates back to the locker room.

When he stepped inside, he was alone. Except for one person.

That person was sitting with the Super Bowl trophy in his arms.

It was NFL Commissioner Pete Rozelle.

"Congratulations, Babe," Rozelle said.

Babe looked at the man who had all but ordered him to retire the season before because of the controversial *Life* magazine article.

He did not reply.

Then the rest of the team stormed in and amid the deafening chaos he could hear Jim Turner shout:

"WELCOME TO THE AFL!"

Soon too came a horde of reporters and photographers, all surrounding Joe Namath and in the process, trying to outshout and elbow each other out of the way. Namath had been named the game's Most Valuable Player although he had not thrown a touchdown. Neither had he thrown a single pass in the final quarter.

Babe smiled as he stood back against a wall and watched.

His thoughts wandered back over the years to all the places he had played, all the teams he had played for, all he had been through, all he had done.

Mission accomplished.

He had never wanted to be the greatest quarterback in the world.

He just wanted to walk off the field a winner.

EPILOGUE

Babe played one more season, again serving as backup quarterback to Joe Namath and field goal and extra-point holder for Jim Turner. The Jets finished 10-4 during the regular season, but lost in the playoffs to Kansas City, 13-6. The Chiefs then proved that the AFL Jets' win over the NFL Colts in Super Bowl III was no fluke. They beat the Minnesota Vikings 23-7 in Super bowl IV.

After taking a year off to manage an apartment complex and help run a golf course, both of which he was part owner, he joined Head Coach Chuck Noll's staff as quarterback coach of the Pittsburgh Steelers.

After three seasons with the Steelers, who in 1972 won their first championship in 40 years, he became head coach of the New York Stars in the newly formed and short-lived World Football League. Midway through the season, the Stars became the Charlotte Hornets. He later became head coach of the WFL Chicago Winds.

He also returned to the Super Bowl in 1978 as quarterback coach for the Denver Broncos and for several seasons, coached arena football league teams.

Babe now lives in Denver and at the age of 81, plays golf daily and participates in celebrity fund-raising tournaments for charity across the country.

Compared to his playing days, they were mostly tame, those years of teaching and talking about football instead of doing it. But now and then, something happened that he had never heard, or done, of seen before.

Such as how Lou Riecke, former Olympic weightlifter and Steelers' strength coach, went about helping second-year quarterback Terry Bradshaw to relax before, and even more importantly, during a game.

The night before, Riecke hypnotized him.

Then Babe, slowly, softly offered advice sprinkled with words of encouragement like "relax" and "poise" and "confidence," although he was never sure Bradshaw would remember what he said because a little while later, even Babe couldn't remember exactly what he had said.

But after three games, it worked.

Or seemed to.

At least Babe and Riecke relaxed and felt poised and confident that it had.

* * * *

Then there was that play Babe called from the press box, hands down, or up, the most famous in the entire history of the sport.

The date was Dec. 23, 1972.

The place: Three Rivers Stadium.

With 1:17 left to play in an AFC Division playoff game, with Oakland, Raiders' quarterback Kenny Stabler had run for a 30-yard touchdown to give the Raiders a 7-6 lead.

With only 22 seconds remaining, after three straight incomplete passes, the Steelers faced a fourth and 10 at their own 40 yard line.

Sixty-six circle option.

That was the play Babe telephoned down from the press box.

He called it because he had noticed that Raider defensive back Willie Brown was playing well off Frank Lewis, the Steelers' fastest receiver. The object would be to pick up 14, 15 yards and get out of bounds to stop the clock.

But suddenly, Lewis was taken out of the game, replaced by rookie Barry Pearson, a possession receiver more than a speed burner.

As Bradshaw took the snap, Babe stood up and removed his head set and hurled it to the floor. Even if Pearson made the catch, there was no way Pearson was fast enough to get out of bounds fast enough.

Meanwhile, to make matters worse, Bradshaw could find no one open and was scrambling around, this way and that, as precious seconds ticked off the clock.

Then he spotted fullback Frenchy Fuqua momentarily open just inside the Raiders' 35 yard line. At about the same time the ball arrived, so did the Jack Tatum, the Raiders' All-Pro defensive back. The collision sent Fuqua sprawling and the ball, after bouncing off Fuqua, or maybe off Tatum, tumbled end over end several yards up field.

And just as it was about to hit the ground, here came Steelers' halfback Franco Harris. Harris, palms up, leaning forward like a man falling forward out of a chair, cradled the ball, kept his balance, eluded one defender, picked up a block, stiff-armed another Raider and ran to glory.

So certain was Steelers' owner Art Rooney, Sr. that with only seconds to play his team had no chance to win, he had already departed, missing what would forever thereafter be known as the "Immaculate Reception."

Up in the press box, Babe plopped down in his chair, shaking his head.

Things sure hadn't worked out exactly as he had expected.

But then, since his boyhood days back in Rochester, Pa., when had they ever?

When things looked the bleakest, they had worked out though.

Just like they always seemed to do.

ACKNOWLEDGMENTS

Thanks to Martha Edge, Babe's sister, for recounting child-hood memories of growing up in Rochester, Pa.: to Tony Neely and the University of Kentucky Athletics Department for providing vintage photographs and other assistance; to the Lexington Public Library for researching newspaper accounts of some of the games during the 1949, 1950 ad 1951 seasons; to Denver photographer Adam Mattivi who designed the cover; to my wife, Judy, and daughter-in-law, Timi Kae,, for proofreading; and most of all to Babe, for sharing his experiences, recollections and stories spanning a long ,colorful, eventful and productive life.

Dick Burdette
July 14, 2011
Wellington, Colorado